DIALOGUES IN THE MARGIN

From William Bates, *The Maclise Portrait-Gallery of "Illustrious Literary Characters" with Memoirs* (London: Chatto and Windus, 1891).

Wayne E. Hall

DIALOGUES IN THE MARGIN

A Study of the *Dublin University Magazine*

The Catholic University of America Press
Washington, D. C.

Published with the help of the Charles Phelps Taft Memorial Fund,
University of Cincinnati
Copyright © 1999
The Catholic University of America Press
All rights reserved
Printed in the United States of America

The paper used in this publication meets the minimum requirements of American National Standards for Information Science—Permanence of Paper for Printed Library materials, ANSI Z39.48-1984.
∞

*Library of Congress Cataloging-in-Publication Data*
Hall, Wayne E.
    Dialogues in the margin : a study of the Dublin University magazine / Wayne Hall.
    p  cm.
    Includes bibliographical references and index.
    1. Dublin university magazine. 2. Periodicals, Publishing of—Ireland—Dublin—History—19th century. 3. Literature publishing—Ireland—Dublin—History—19th century. 4. English literature—19th century—History and criticism. 5. English literature—Irish authors—History and criticism. 6. Dublin (Ireland)—Intellectual life—19th century. I. Title.
PN5150.D83H35   1999
052'.09417'09034—dc21
98-36818
ISBN 0-8132-0926-9 (alk. paper)

# CONTENTS

|   | Acknowledgments | vii |
|---|---|---|
|   | Introduction | 1 |
| 1. | Combinations and Challenges | 20 |
| 2. | The Step into Excellence | 52 |
| 3. | Principles of Morality and Religion | 85 |
| 4. | Geniality under Strain | 107 |
| 5. | A Native Periodical in a Time of Famine | 137 |
| 6. | Pragmatism, Optimism, Mediocrity | 179 |
| 7. | Doubling the Uncertainties of Authority | 194 |
| 8. | The Patterns Exhausted | 217 |
|   | Conclusion | 232 |
|   | Selected Bibliography | 241 |
|   | Index | 247 |

## ACKNOWLEDGMENTS

Even though this project has been cooking for an uncomfortably long time, that same time period now allows me the pleasure of acknowledging a great deal of generous support and encouragement along the way. My friend and colleague Tom LeClair guided my thinking in some fruitful directions very early in this project; and advice given by the late Hugh Staples during this formative stage also benefited the undertaking. Later on, I received some extraordinarily detailed readings and helpful suggestions from Terence Brown, Richard Fallis, Joseph McMinn, Deborah Hunter McWilliams, and Robert Welch.

I have also enjoyed a lot of support from my home institution. This book is getting published with the help of the Charles Phelps Taft Memorial Fund at the University of Cincinnati. That same Memorial Fund has also provided me with Grants-in-Aid of Research during the summers of 1984, 1988, and 1992. In addition, the University of Cincinnati awarded me Faculty Research Fellowships in the summers of 1982 and 1985.

An early version of chapter 2 originally appeared in volume 20 of the *Victorian Periodicals Review* (Summer 1987). The periodical *Eire-Ireland* also published early versions of chapters 1 (in vol. 22, Winter 1987) and chapter 7 (vol. 21, Summer 1986). More recently, some of the material in chapter 4 is scheduled to appear in *The Great Famine and the Irish Diaspora in America,* a volume of essays edited by Arthur Gribben and forthcoming from the University of Massachusetts Press. I am grateful to these two journals and to the Press for permission to reissue this material in the present volume.

Lastly, mostly, unceasingly, I am grateful to Heather Hall, my wife, partner, best friend, shrewdest critic. She has been a crucial part of this project since it started, and this book could not possibly have been written without her presence and her constant support. Like so much of the rest of my life, this book is dedicated to her.

DIALOGUES IN THE MARGIN

# INTRODUCTION

### I

The lead article in the first issue of the *Dublin University Magazine* is a fictional political dialogue by the Rev. Samuel O'Sullivan. The choice of form seems appropriate, evoking as it does the give and take of two minds picking their tentative way across disputed ground. As a dialogue, the article thus maps out an ambivalence characteristic of the magazine's creators, Irishmen looking toward England, nervously occupying the uncertain margins bordering both Catholic nationalism and British imperialism. O'Sullivan himself—a former Catholic who had undergone a conversion, become a Protestant minister, and enthusiastically immersed himself in the controversies of Irish religious debate—understood only too well the hazards of negotiating and defining such margins, and his writings frequently betray a suppressed and brittle tension, as in the title for his dialogue here: "The Present Crisis." Variations on this title would recur several more times in the *DUM*'s major political articles over the next few years. In July 1833, for instance, we meet "The Coming Crisis" and, in November 1835, learn that "The Present Is Not a Crisis."

From this distance, some 160 years later, such titles resemble the reports of a news anchorman harassed and bewildered by his first day on the job. Amid such chaos, however, and with an on-the-scene vision remarkable for its intelligence and steadiness, the *DUM* was drawing some useful distinctions within a cultural history regularly visited by crises. Throughout the 1820s, Catholics in Ireland had increasingly mobilized against the British connection and the Protestant presence. Passage of the Catholic Emancipation Act in 1829 had simply shifted political tensions and uncertainties over into the still greater upheaval surrounding the 1832 Reform Bill, with further crises sure to follow. Some Catholic nationalists had already begun demanding even bigger concessions, such as disestablishment of the Church of Ireland or even repeal of the Union between Great Britain and Ireland. In the same month that the *DUM* started publication, January 1833, the first reformed parliament began its own operations in Westminster. Who could confidently foresee the consequences of such change?

Had O'Sullivan consulted past models and lessons, he might have looked back to 1596, the year Edmund Spenser wrote *A View of the Present State of Ireland*. Working within the dialogue form himself, Spenser also sought to balance the many conflicting points of view that made England's governing of Ireland such a vexing matter. The issues for Spenser's dialogue resemble those for O'Sullivan's in remarkable ways, and the lesson seems clear enough: throughout Ireland's troublous history, not much changes. Within O'Sullivan's version of events for the 1830s, moreover, the crisis now threatens the very survival of the British empire. A staunch Tory and Unionist like O'Sullivan could have found only paralyzing lessons here, none of them conducive to launching a new magazine.

Yet his dialogue looks forward, not back, and more with confidence than dismay, an unlikely vision of the future in which the success of this new journalistic venture will actually contribute to the strength of the empire. In its next issue, the *DUM* defined itself with still more fervor in clarifying how such a process might work: the magazine would seek to "kindle, and fan into flame, the enthusiasm of virtue, the devotedness of honor, the stedfast firmness of integrity, and by these excellent lights, we would shew the populace the error and folly of their mad career" (Feb. 1833, 117).[1]

Published monthly from January 1833 to December 1877, the *DUM* attracted as its contributors—and in several cases its editors—nearly every major Irish writer from this period. In literature, the main figures are William Carleton, Samuel Ferguson, Charles Lever, Joseph Sheridan Le Fanu, and James Clarence Mangan, all of whom maintained significant connections with the magazine for much of its career. Other noted writers with substantial contributions include John Anster, William Archer Butler, Isaac Butt, John William Cole, Percy Fitzgerald, Thomas Caulfield Irwin, Patrick Kennedy, Denis Florence M'Carthy, Mortimer and Samuel O'Sullivan, and John Francis Waller. Besides these frequent contributors, many other writers appeared on only a handful of occasions in the magazine. Of these, British as well as Irish, noteworthy are William Allingham, Michael Banim, Stopford A. Brooke, Rhoda Broughton, Aubrey de Vere, Elizabeth Gaskell, Catherine Gore, Anna Maria Hall, William Rowan Hamilton, Felicia Hemans, Barbara Hemphill, James Hogg, T. H. Huxley, G. P. R. James, Samuel Lover, Harriet Martineau, William Hamilton Maxwell, Dinah Maria Mulock Craik, Standish James O'Grady, Caesar Otway, George Petrie, Anthony Trollope, Lady Jane Francesca Wilde, and, in his first published work, Oscar Wilde. The sheer volume of these lists, packing over three dozen names into this paragraph alone, suggests the scope and duration of the magazine.

In assessing the *DUM*'s literary or historical importance, however, such lists may mislead us, for the magazine was not simply a forum for many individual voices of note. Seamus Deane has argued that the *DUM* sought to become a Coleridgean "intellectual clerisy," one that would serve as "an integral part of the structures of the

---

1. Throughout this study, all citations from the *DUM*—as well as from similar nineteenth-century monthly magazines—are given in this fashion, parenthetically in the body of the text by month, year, and page number.

state, safeguarding the historical continuity and cultural complexity of the nation's heritage."[2] Surveying the results of this attempt, he concluded that the *DUM* had succeeded in giving "the Protestant intelligentsia a new focus and new heart."[3] Like Deane, W. J. Mc Cormack also regarded Coleridge as "one of the intellectual patrons" of the "Intellectual Revival" in Ireland and described the period from 1830 to 1850 as "best exemplified" by the *DUM*, "the supreme archive of Irish Victorian experience."[4] Elsewhere, Mc Cormack has stressed Coleridge's "notion of a 'clerisy,' an intellectual class devoted to aims at once religious and cultural . . . upon whom the future of the nation could safely depend. . . ."[5] On the *DUM* essay "Past and Present State of Literature in Ireland" (March 1837), Mc Cormack argues that its "greatest debt is undoubtedly to Coleridge" and especially to the second chapter of the *Biographia Literaria* for the belief that literature gradually expands its circle of civilization throughout a culture.[6] In an early issue of the *DUM*, John Anster asked, "Is there a master-spirit of the age which has not acknowledged intellectual obligations to Coleridge?" (July 1835, 10). If Wordsworth sought to write poetry in the actual language that people spoke, then Coleridge sought a language that was free from provincialism and that partook of universal and idealized thought, its source the poet's imagination rather than the ordinary life of society. The *DUM* valued Coleridge's conservative emphasis on traditional and enduring ideals, on the value of religion, culture, and education as necessary elements in a great literature, especially insofar as one might trace such a heritage throughout a nation's past.

2. Seamus Deane, *Celtic Revivals: Essays in Modern Irish Literature 1880–1980* (London: Faber and Faber, 1985), 98.

3. Seamus Deane, *A Short History of Irish Literature* (Notre Dame: University of Notre Dame Press, 1986), 99.

4. *The Field Day Anthology of Irish Writing*, ed. Seamus Deane (Derry: Field Day, 1991), 1:1173–76.

5. W. J. Mc Cormack, *From Burke to Beckett: Ascendancy, Tradition and Betrayal in Literary History* (Cork: Cork University Press, 1994), 44.

6. Mc Cormack, *Field Day*, 1:1200.

In following this overlapping trail of romanticism and intellectualism, both Deane and Mc Cormack have also traced it one step further back, into the writings of Edmund Burke, "a powerful influence in Irish political thinking throughout the nineteenth century."[7] Deane has recently described Burke's *Reflections on the Revolution in France* (1790) as a "foundational text," one that serves as "the first of Ireland's national narratives and the first political work in which the notion of a national, anti-modern narrative becomes a governing principle in its development."[8] In Burke's combination of romanticism, Anglicanism, and "anti-revolutionary adherence to a spiritual politics that has its roots in a specific national tradition,"[9] Deane identifies one central theme that we can further locate within the ideology of the *DUM*: its sense of nostalgic longing for a society that had been unified and enlightened by its humanistic ideals but that is now beleaguered by the forces of change. For the Irish writers seeking to launch this new literary-political venture, such forces threatened an intellectual tradition that had not yet even established itself. Their vision of a past that had not existed might not be allowed to exist in the future either.

Against the potentially paralyzing effects of such nostalgia, however, can be found a second theme in Burke, one emphasized by Mc Cormack as that of "fragmentary union," a delicate but enabling balance between isolation and community.[10] Within such groups as

---

7. Deane, *Field Day*, 1:809.

8. Seamus Deane, *Strange Country: Modernity and Nationhood in Irish Writing since 1790* (Oxford: Clarendon, 1997), 25.

9. On the role of nostalgia within this "spiritual politics," Deane adds that "from an Irish point of view, the renovation of tradition remained more closely attached to the notion that the renovation could only be desired, the more so because there was no state, no social or political apparatus to support it. It was a romanticism that needed the spectacle of ruin to stimulate it to an imaginative intensity that would be the more impressive precisely because it derived from a history that had been lost, displaced, a history that had no narrative but the narrative of nostalgia. Nostalgia was the dynamic that impelled the search for the future" (*Strange Country*, 2).

10. For a discussion of the concept of the "fragmentary union" as an influence on the aesthetics of nineteenth-century Anglo-Irish literature, see especially Mc Cormack, *From Burke to Beckett*, 30–33.

Burke termed "little platoons," one might still enjoy a measure of stability, moderation, and traditional values. Religion, Burke wrote, "is the basis of civil society, and the source of all good and of all comfort."[11] In this general sentiment—in his faith in education and his belief in the importance of its religious basis and in his support for the establishment of the church within society and for that church's right to hold property—he prefigures much that would occupy the *DUM* throughout its career. Like Burke, the *DUM* would emphasize the spirit of nobility and of religion as strands within society that sustained civilization, a product of tradition, intelligence, and continuity against the shapeless tide of democratic change.

The very first article in the *DUM*, Samuel O'Sullivan's dialogue "The Present Crisis," praised Burke as "a hero in celestial panoply" (Jan. 1833, 5). Later that same year, Samuel Ferguson's "A Dialogue Between the Head and Heart of an Irish Protestant" closed by invoking those heroic figures from the past who might now inspire the new magazine: Luther, Calvin, Burke with his "virtuous energies" (Nov. 1833, 593). Similarly significant in defining the *DUM*'s ideology is the later manifesto, "Past and Present State of Literature in Ireland," which chronicled the "splendid results" and "master spirits" within Irish letters: Sheridan, Grattan, Curran, Goldsmith. In first place here, however, "the comprehensive in views—the profound and searching in reason—the consummate in elocution—the high-souled and chivalric in feeling," stands Burke (March 1837, 372). Twenty years after it began, the *DUM* still spoke of the *Reflections* with reverence, a work of "prophetic wisdom and comprehensive science," "the great masterpiece of British constitutional politics" (March 1853, 388).

II

In *The Anglo-Irish Tradition* (1976), J. C. Beckett wrote, "In origin and outlook the *Dublin University Magazine* was a typical expression

---

11. Edmund Burke, *Reflections on the Revolution in France, and On the Proceedings in*

of the Anglo-Irish spirit as it had developed since the union."[12] Later inquiries, while they continue to examine the *DUM* against the social history of "the Anglo-Irish spirit," do not share Beckett's assumptions, barely ten years earlier, behind such a phrase as "typical expression." With the 1985 publication of Deane's *Celtic Revivals*, with David Lloyd's *Nationalism and Minor Literature* and John Hutchinson's *The Dynamics of Cultural Nationalism* in 1987, or the David Cairns-Shaun Richards work *Writing Ireland* in 1988, we begin to encounter a fundamental critique of long-accepted cultural bywords. The most detailed and painstaking of such analyses, however, are Mc Cormack's. His 1994 study *From Burke to Beckett: Ascendancy, Tradition and Betrayal in Literary History* is a revision and expansion—via *Dissolute Characters* in 1993—of a 1985 study *Ascendancy and Tradition in Anglo-Irish Literary History from 1789 to 1939*. The full titles indicate just how uncertain all of this terrain has become. By the time of Mc Cormack's 1994 work, the treacherous term "Anglo-Irish" has vanished, while the seeming precision of the earlier dates has now been replaced by authors linked as much by the alliteration of their last names as by anything less random. As for the earlier concepts of ascendancy and tradition, they are now relegated to the subtitle along with betrayal, a concept that further destabilizes the other two. If we wish to understand the notion of "Protestant Ascendancy," Mc Cormack argues, we must follow it through its devious process of ascending: from its bourgeois origins and pejorative connotations for Edmund Burke, it would eventually assume the mantle of heroic Irish aristocracy in the work of W. B. Yeats. Mc Cormack points to an 1868 political speech by William Ewart Gladstone as a key event in the development of the concept of the Ascendancy. Prior to Gladstone's "lengthy and orotund . . . invocation of Protestant Ascendancy" there, the term "had little idiomatic ac-

---

*Certain Societies in London Relative to That Event,* ed. Conor Cruise O'Brien (Harmondworth: Penguin, 1969), 186.

12. J. C. Beckett, *The Anglo-Irish Tradition* (Ithaca: Cornell University Press, 1976), 135.

ceptance in the vocabulary of political debate, and certainly it did not name any readily identified social group or 'class.'"[13] "Perhaps the most seductive of all Yeats's historical fictions," Deane concurs, "is his gift of dignity and coherence to the Irish Protestant Ascendancy tradition."[14]

Such analyses remind us of the prominence of fiction-making within the processes by which "Protestant Ascendancy" comes to dominate so much of our current sense of Ireland's cultural heritage. By the end of Yeats's career, in "Under Ben Bulben," he could confidently include "hard-riding country gentlemen" and "lords and ladies gay" as an integral part of "the indomitable Irishry." The poem directs its readers to "scorn" the "unremembering hearts and heads" and instead to "cast your mind" to "well made" and "heroic" fictions, ones in which aesthetically and ethically more powerful transformations may occur, the general term "Irishry," for instance, gracefully sweeping aside the base-born prejudices that might separate social classes. As easily in the nineteenth century as in the twentieth, Irish Protestants could see around them the effects of those prejudices and separations. What wonder, then, that some took up literary-political fictions as weapons against hostile facts, or that observers then—as now—have difficulty distinguishing the fiction from the fact?

In assembling our definitions of the identity or spirit or history or tradition of Irish culture at any point within the nineteenth century, then, we have first to draw the lines that will distinguish between a number of different cultural entities, some of them overlapping: rural Catholics, middle-class Catholics, Ulster Protestants (some rural, some industrial, some middle class), Anglo-Irish (some landed gentry, some Dublin professional classes, some middle class), and English (as a colonizing presence of some historical standing).

---

13. W. J. Mc Cormack, *Dissolute Characters: Irish Literary History through Balzac, Sheridan Le Fanu, Yeats and Bowen* (Manchester: Manchester University Press, 1993), 186.

14. Deane, *Celtic Revivals*, 28.

All of these groups, including the English, at one point or other sought to establish their authority at least in part with reference to some unique or indigenous "Irish" culture. David Lloyd's 1993 study *Anomalous States* is only one of the more recent examinations of colonial relationships and post-colonial world views to remind us that such attempts face insuperable difficulties.

Even apart from the usual problems attendant upon recovering a lost point of origin, those who would reclaim an "essentially Irish" culture had further to sift through layers of colonial experience. The English had thoroughly disseminated their influence and domination throughout Ireland by the end of the seventeenth century. Over the next hundred years, elements of native Gaelic culture continued to weaken, disappearing completely by the 1850s, after which there was no longer any uniquely "Irish" cultural experience to which a reclamation project could directly refer. Cultural nationalists thus faced two conceptual limitations: the culture surrounding them had already been largely shaped and defined by England, and England had also largely shaped and defined the ways in which they themselves viewed that culture.

By the nineteenth century, then, the concept of "Ireland" itself—never mind "Protestant Ascendancy"—already contained a heavy component of fictionalizing, not necessarily deliberate, but still constructed out of immediate ideological necessities. Lloyd writes:

> the nationalism of a colonized people requires that its history be seen as a series of unnatural ruptures and discontinuities imposed by an alien power while its reconstruction must necessarily pass by way of deliberate artifice. Almost by definition, this anti-colonial nationalism lacks the basis for its representative claims and is forced to invent them. In this respect, nationalism can be said to require an aesthetic politics quite as much as a political aesthetics.[15]

The concept of "Ireland" thus proved useful as artifice, for both

---

15. David Lloyd, *Anomalous States: Irish Writing and the Post-Colonial Moment* (Dublin: Lilliput, 1993), 89.

political and aesthetic purposes; but whether as history or literature, it also needs to be interrogated, destabilized, problematized. Just as we still may refer to the writing of Somerville and Ross, Yeats or Lady Gregory, Moore or Joyce, Synge or O'Casey, as "Anglo-Irish," we can, of course, continue to speak of their cultural experience as being "specifically Irish"; but we need to keep in mind that its colonial legacy is only one of many features that keep Ireland from being particularly specific.

### III

Beyond these theoretical difficulties to investigating the *DUM* lie logistical ones, such as its practice, typical of nineteenth-century British periodicals, of publishing the bulk of its contributions anonymously. For decades, commentators on nineteenth-century Irish literature or history have routinely mentioned the *DUM*'s significance, and bibliographic questions have been largely resolved for the major literary contributors. Yet the magazine's policy of anonymity has so far helped to confine these studies to isolated writers. Even with the appearance of volume IV of *The Wellesley Index to Victorian Periodicals* (1987), many attribution problems still remain, even for a figure as instrumental in the development of the magazine as Samuel O'Sullivan.[16] Partly for these reasons, the only readily acces-

---

16. See Wayne E. Hall, "Attribution Problems: the *Wellesley Index* vs. the *Dublin University Magazine*," *Long Room* 36 (1991): 29–34, for a discussion of problems with and limitations on the *Index*'s attributions of anonymous contributions. Of the 246 entries ascribed by the *Index* to Samuel O'Sullivan, for instance, 188, or 76 percent, are attributed to him on the basis of internal, stylistic evidence alone. Complicating such attributions is the fact, as the *Index* notes, that the writing styles of Mortimer and Samuel O'Sullivan and Isaac Butt are quite similar. The Archives of the *Wellesley Index*, housed at the Margaret Clapp Library at Wellesley College, include the contributors files for these three writers. As "working" notes and materials, these files further indicate, even more than their published version, that many of the attributions for Butt and the O'Sullivans rely heavily upon the subjective impressions and judgments of the *Index* researchers. I am indebted to Ms. Wilma R. Slaight, Archivist at Wellesley College, for making copies of this material available to me.

sible systematic discussion of the magazine's entire career is the introductory essay in the *Wellesley Index*.[17]

In my own approach to the *DUM*, my study will relate many ideological positions to the magazine as a whole ("According to the *DUM* . . ."), even as I elsewhere may refer to a specific author ("According to Samuel O'Sullivan . . ."). Such an approach has the advantage of flexibility within the additional shifts between chronological and thematic guidelines. In general, I will trace the history of the magazine in chronological order, the chapter divisions corresponding to the various editorships. Within this approach, however, I also follow various themes backward and/or forward in time, focusing on politics or history for one section of a chapter, literature for another.

As a chronicle model, this approach suggests certain assumptions, ones characteristic of older and more confident forms of literary history: as we advance through time, one event leads logically and inevitably into the next, moving through a series of cause-and-effect patterns so as to find its proper place within the natural order of things. Such a model, moreover, conveys to its reader the sense that "you are there," experiencing this re-creation of history as it happened, as it must have been perceived by its original inhabitants.

17. *The Wellesley Index to Victorian Periodicals 1824–1900*, ed. Walter E. Houghton (Toronto: University of Toronto Press, 1987), 4:193–210. The introduction for the *Wellesley Index* section on the *DUM* is written by Jean H. Slingerland, from notes compiled by Walter Houghton before his death in 1983. For an influential early survey of the *DUM*, see Michael Sadleir, "*Dublin University Magazine*, Its History, Contents and Bibliography," *Bibliographical Society of Ireland Publications* 5, no. 4 (1938): 59–85, as well as "Dublin University Magazine," the lead article in the *Irish Book Lover* 10 (April–May 1919): 75–79. While short and sketchy, this article also provides a great deal of the information that turns up in Sadleir's essay and in the *Wellesley Index* introduction. Other valuable overviews, surveying the *DUM* up until 1852 in both cases, include John P. McBride, "The *Dublin University Magazine*: Cultural Nationality and Tory Ideology in an Irish Literary and Political Journal, 1833–1852," 2 vols. (Ph.D. diss., Trinity College, Dublin, 1987), and Joe Spence, "Nationality and Irish Toryism: The Case of the *Dublin University Magazine*, 1833–52," *Journal of Newspaper and Periodical History* 4, no. 3 (Autumn 1988): 2–17.

The overall progression of events gradually accumulates its own truth-value, gathering further weight and momentum as it advances. In a similar manner, the writers and editors for the *DUM* sought to create just such a historical progression. The longer the magazine lasted within the journalistic marketplace, the more articles and issues and years it could string together, the more legitimacy and authority it would accumulate. A forty-five-year run becomes a considerable historical fact.

Newer forms of literary history have, of course, exposed the fictions underlying this chronicle model, the problematic relationship by which the chronicler often imposes compelling patterns that he himself has invented and then brought to and imposed upon the subject matter. The mass of material under consideration here—ninety volumes of the *DUM*, each one in excess of seven-hundred pages—gives a researcher room to prove theses of all kinds, whether explicit or implicit, carefully thought out or glibly assumed. The chronicle model thus seems to need some kind of balance between social forms and literary ones—again, not unlike the balance sought by the *DUM* itself. At the same time in the field of Irish studies, much more work on this magazine remains to be done.

For these very reasons, however, for these same methodological difficulties, the *DUM* serves as a well-placed vantage point from which to survey modern Irish literature and history. It is hardly a stable point. If reading one Irish volume of some six-hundred-plus pages—James Joyce's *Ulysses*—is a destabilizing experience, then how does one "survey" these ninety volumes written over a much longer time and through the collaborative efforts of well over five-hundred writers? Still, telling markers seem to emerge to help chart the boundaries—Samuel Ferguson's oft-cited work, for instance, "A Dialogue between the Head and Heart of an Irish Protestant," in the *DUM* for November 1833.[18] In his use of the phrase "Protestant

---

18. Ferguson's essay is reprinted in *Field Day*, 1:1177–85.

ascendancy" here, Ferguson helped to advance its status within political debate. It "promised to make us another England" (589), Ferguson claimed, later describing it as "indeed a noble scheme and worthy a great politician" (592). Yeats's fictions and metaphors might ultimately add the necessary layer of style to consolidate our idea of "the Ascendancy." First, however, had to come some extensive cultural reclamation projects, among which the *DUM* occupies a prominent place.

In its influence on the development of Irish cultural history, then, the *DUM* can be seen to possess a kind of corporate identity, complex, ambiguous, contradictory, and subject to frequent change, to be sure, but nonetheless one whose character we can describe and analyze. Moreover, the dual nature of the magazine, its attention to both England and Ireland, helps us to understand the sometimes guilty and reluctant, sometimes celebratory and passionate, union of the different cultural traditions and values.

One of my operating theses is that the *DUM* expressed a complex brand of Irish national identity that defined itself partly in cultural and partly in political terms, and that helped create a position for Protestant ascendancy in some ways self-contradictory and self-defeating, in other ways surprisingly consistent and resilient. In considering this expression of national identity, we may recognize elements of a romantic, imaginative, and idealized Ireland in the *DUM*, even as we also encounter elements of a realistic, cosmopolitan, worldly Ireland. The first of these looked inward, at Ireland's particular cultural traditions, its geography or history or literature; the second looked outward, renouncing separatism as hopelessly provincial, seeking to maintain instead a role for a continued British influence. Whereas the romantic vision tended to define Ireland in terms of the internal, the authentic, and the essential, the cosmopolitan worked more in terms of the external, the performative, and the conventional.

This hybrid blend of cultural and political values harbored an uneasy dualism not unlike that of other brands of Irish nationalism. As a general conception, nationalism might be either ethnic and exclusive (the nation as a coherent, unique entity distinguishes itself from the rest of the world community, thus fragmenting people), or social and inclusive (the nation's sense of identity cuts across boundaries such as class, race, religion, economics, or politics, thus uniting people). A secure national identity and coherent national history may bring these conflicting impulses into balance. For a nation such as Ireland, however, shaped over centuries by a powerful colonizing presence, fragmented by class or religion or history, no security or balance could be achieved by just sitting back to wait for a nationalist consciousness to evolve. Civilization in nineteenth-century Ireland seemed too fragile to wait, too much in need of programs and guarantees, visions and contracts. From the point of view of the *DUM,* the Irish renounced or denied their British heritage at great risk, for in the making and sustaining of civilization in Ireland, such a heritage was essential.

In drawing up such programs or insisting on such guarantees, in seeking its own balance between excluding and including, between culture and politics, the *DUM* developed one main pattern that recurs over and over in its pages: the magazine's political commentary stakes out the ideological ground with varying degrees of rigidity and exclusivity, while its literary contributions expand the magazine's total scope to embrace a much wider and more generous vision of "Irishness." In an overview of the magazine on the occasion of its twenty-first birthday, the *DUM* itself noted: "From the commencement we advocated Conservatism in politics, and Protestantism in religion. . . . As for literature, we avow ourselves to have ever been . . . thorough latitudinarians" (Jan. 1853, 3). It is, of course, a humanistic commonplace to find in literature the broad, universal spirit that gets quickly disregarded in political debate. For the *DUM,* however, the literature draws much of its energy and strength from politics. The evangelistic zeal that, at one level, produced diatribes against papist repealers also expressed itself through fiction of impressive power. Whether we choose from the magazine a political article or a short story, we are likely to encounter the same essentially idealistic principles.

Within the terms and tensions of the *DUM*'s journalistic dialogue, then, we can see the political and the literary values jostling against each other, both influencing and influenced. If the magazine serves as a detailed and thorough record of conservative political thought in the nineteenth century, it also shows us that Irish political events have drawn much of their shape from the literature, even as that literature was being shaped in turn by politics. It is, of course, yet another commonplace to say of Irish literature that we can only fully understand it when we locate it against the "background" of Irish politics or within some historical context. In the *DUM*, however, politics and literature occupy and define the foreground simultaneously, and the magazine offers us the rare opportunity to study the two forces as they act together so closely over such a long period of time.

In its sense of its own mission and purpose, the *DUM* sought to give voice to its version of the world view of conservative and Protestant Ireland, in turn to shape that world view still further, and ultimately to impose it on the country as a whole. As a contributor to the expanding role of print in the formation of nineteenth-century culture, such a magazine could not only reach a substantial and influential portion of society but also conceivably center the thinking of many people around its own desired concept of "Irishness." At the end of its first full year of operation, the *DUM* described its ideal function: it hoped to serve as a "medium of communication" by which "Irishmen who have risen to importance in the councils of the kingdom or in the world of literature, and who wish to direct or steady public opinion in either of these branches," might further their ends (Insert for Dec. 1833, 5). More generally, the journal "aspired to be the monthly advocate and representative of the Protestantism, the intelligence, and the respectability of Ireland" (Dec. 1835, 710).

To consider the *DUM* in these terms is not to reduce it to the level of mercenary propaganda or upper-class snobbery and complacency. Protestant ascendancy consisted of many different, complex, and frequently conflicting points of view, none of which allowed for any comfortable and settled ideological agenda. In his own studies of the uncertainties underlying Irish cultural identity, Oliver MacDonagh sees the Act of Union in 1800 as a central event, "a failure of nerve on the part of many members of the Protestant ascendancy,"[19] a political "act of ambiguity, not to say self-contradiction."[20] On the one hand, Ireland was henceforth to enjoy equal status with Great Britain, a partner within the world's strongest empire, a beneficiary of British cultural and technological progress. On the other hand, Ireland was a separate nation, a colony held in check by an occupying bureaucracy and army, a provincial backwater that kept requiring separate legislation to address needs and demands that the British found generally curious and occasionally outrageous.

Relatively specific groups such as the Protestant intelligentsia of Trinity College might have even more layers of ambiguity to sort out. Their city, once a flourishing European capital, had seen much of its grandeur depart for London after Ireland's Parliament House closed its doors. An early essay in the *DUM* would contrast the "lifeless streets and dull marts" of Dublin with "the glare, glitter, and magnificent ostentation of the central city of the civilized world" (March 1837, 372). The same circumstances, however, seemed to favor the advances in fortune of those professional men—barristers, ministers, physicians, journalists—who might help to connect the two nations in various ways, and who might also once have studied at Trinity. In a broader sense, one that affected the cultural status of

---

19. Oliver MacDonagh, *The Nineteenth Century Novel and Irish Social History: Some Aspects* (Dublin: National University of Ireland, 1971), 5.

20. Oliver MacDonagh, *States of Mind: A Study of Anglo-Irish Conflict 1780–1980* (London: George Allen and Unwin, 1983), 52.

all Irish Protestants rather than the specific professional careers of a few members, Protestant ascendancy had begun the century by abdicating power, by turning itself into a cultural anachronism that had no clear function or responsibility apart from helping to man the British garrison. For the rest of the century, however, many Protestants kept insisting on their own status as a legitimate authority, both spiritual and material, over a populace that largely refused to accept the garrison's presence. A magazine that sought to balance these conflicting claims and give coherent voice to these ambiguous positions was setting itself a formidable agenda.

Models, such as *Blackwood's* and *Fraser's* magazines, were available, and the *DUM* set out consciously to imitate them, producing a page layout, for instance, virtually indistinguishable in appearance. Just as consciously, however, its creators calculated the odds and tempered their initial hopefulness with some sober misgivings about the life expectancy of such enterprises: "We know that there is a prejudice against Irish periodicals which it will require much caution on our part to overcome" (Jan. 1833, 88). Whereas Caesar Otway's *Christian Examiner* had been running successfully since 1825, no other comparable Irish periodical in recent experience had lasted much beyond a single year.[21] Yet the very atmosphere of crisis that seemed to link the fortunes of press and parliament engendered a reckless and idealistic zeal that carried the *DUM* through those first uncertain months and on into a career that became more devoted, steadfast, and excellent than its founders had any reason to hope for. In a remarkably short time, the *DUM* proved, to itself and the world, that "an Irish periodical can both exist and flourish . . ." (Dec. 1835, 709). And flourish it did: during the 1840s, at the peak of its circulation, the journal appeared at the rate of over 4,000 copies a month. Looking back over the first two decades of its existence, the *DUM* could proudly announce: "Ireland has now her own literature,

---

21. For a discussion of magazine publishing during this period, see Barbara Hayley, "Irish Periodicals from the Union to the *Nation*," *Anglo-Irish Studies* II, ed. P. J. Drudy (Atlantic Highlands: Humanities, 1976), 83–108.

her own vehicle of thought, her own exponent of feeling. Whatever may happen, of one thing we feel assured, that she will never again lapse into silence" (Jan. 1853, 8). Later events, while they would baffle the political and religious hopes of the journal, never ceased justifying this claim for Ireland's literary voices.

IV

Perhaps the most enduring piece from the *DUM*'s first year, and one that in many ways echoes O'Sullivan's opening article, was Samuel Ferguson's "A Dialogue between the Head and Heart of an Irish Protestant." Ferguson had published several poems and short stories in the early months of 1833. But his November 1833 "Dialogue," like O'Sullivan's, goes far beyond these literary works in its complex exploration of the ambivalences, tensions, doubts, fears, and misgivings underlying Protestant ascendancy. Parliament in 1833 had passed one of the strongest coercion bills ever directed against Ireland, a political event that Ferguson's "Dialogue" seeks to understand. His "Head," counseling reason and moderation, puts the best possible light on a bad situation, while "Heart" rages against the indignities visited by the Whig government upon Irish Protestantism.

The "Dialogue" recognizes that many Irish Protestants are simultaneously dependent upon and alienated from England, isolated within Ireland at the same time that they deeply love and identify with this country that no longer feels quite like home. In a passionate sweep through the social and political complexities facing such Protestants, "Heart" defines their marginal position in Ireland:

> Deserted by the Tories, insulted by the Whigs, threatened by the Radicals, hated by the Papists, and envied by the Dissenters, plundered in our country-seats, robbed in our town houses, driven abroad by violence, called back by humanity, and, after all, told that we are neither English nor Irish, fish nor flesh, but a peddling colony, a forlorn advanced guard that must conform to every mutinous movement of the pretorian rabble—all this, too, while we are the acknowledged possessors of nine tenths of the property of a great country, and wielders of the preponderating influence be-

tween two parties; on whose relative position depend the greatest interests in the empire. (591)

Despite his frustration, however, "Heart" cannot escape or deny one overriding emotion—that he loves both Ireland and its people.

Ferguson proposes to himself that he act upon his love for his "Popish countrymen" by seeking to convert them to the saving grace of Protestantism. And indeed, this faith in religious education continued to rally the magazine's spirits for years to come. As "Head" notes, "We must fight our battle now with a handful of types and a composing-stick, pages like this our field, and the reading public our arbiter of war" (592). If but a single magazine could boldly speak the truth, surely a nation would listen and learn, surely its people would recognize this truth as perhaps the last chance for them to avert their downward slide into anarchy and desolation. But even as Ferguson's "Heart" hoped that such things could be, his "Head" settled itself grimly to face the future. The *DUM* would come to impress the world with Ireland's literary quality, and its political stance would lend the magazine the clarifying sense of mission and identity needed to help it survive for nearly half a century. Making up barely ten percent of the population, Irish Protestants would still play a remarkably influential role in Ireland's future, in part because the *DUM* served as a voice that made itself heard. And for all that, Protestant ascendancy would still ultimately fail to secure for itself a lasting place and function within Ireland. Like participants in a dialogue, however brilliant and well-informed they might be, its spokesmen were speaking directly only to each other, while the mass of Ireland's people moved on to other gatherings.

I

## COMBINATIONS AND CHALLENGES

I

Throughout its entire career, the *Dublin University Magazine* defined itself in its subtitle as "A Literary and Political Journal." Indeed, even during the several decades leading up to 1833, literature and politics had already been pressing toward the birth of just such a magazine as the *DUM*. While these two areas of interest seem thoroughly intertwined, not just on the title page of the *DUM*, but during any period in modern Irish history, we can also consider them as separate programs: the literature for representing Irish experience, the politics for acting upon it.

In part, the *DUM* emerged out of an Irish national consciousness that had begun to take concrete shape toward the end of the eighteenth century. In England during the 1760s, a general romantic interest in the primitive and antique had popularized Macpherson's "Ossian" poems. In the 1770s, and on a more scholarly level, Johann Gottfried von Herder had identified language as a key factor underlying national character and a nation's sense of its own cultural origins. Within this Enlightenment attention to locality and native place, the Royal Irish Academy, founded in 1785, began formulating its own systematic investigations into the Celtic languages and Irish past. Yet the line between popular interest and antiquarian scholarship was hard to draw and frustratingly prone to controversy. The historiographer Rev. Edward Ledwich, for instance, in *Antiquities of Ireland* (1790), cast doubts not only on the authenticity of many native Irish texts but even on the existence of St. Patrick himself. Later scholars would find it easier to correct Ledwich's errors than to keep political assumptions from coloring their own investigations.

The publication of Charlotte Brooke's *Reliques of Irish Poetry* (1789), a collection of poems in both the original Irish and translation, established a starting point for a more specifically literary revival that would continue throughout the nineteenth century to build its advances upon verse translations. The decade just before the *DUM* was launched thus saw the publication of Thomas Stott's *The Songs of Deardra* (1825), James Martin's historical poem *Ireland's Dirge* (1827), and James Hardiman's *Irish Minstrelsy* (1831), a volume primarily remembered now as the loser of a one-sided skirmish conducted by Samuel Ferguson within the pages of the *DUM*. For Irish writers working wholly in English, 1800 marks a convenient starting point. In that year, Charlotte Brooke's friend Maria Edgeworth published *Castle Rackrent,* the first regional novel in English. Edgeworth's depictions of her landed-gentry class were joined a few years later by the novels of Lady Morgan, and the two writers continued well into the 1820s to define not only a relationship of Ireland's people to its land and historical past but also an Irish literary genre that was comparable in stature to the novel in England.

Between 1824 and 1830, John and Michael Banim, Gerald Griffin, and William Carleton significantly expanded the range of Irish fiction, beyond the Anglo-Irish confines of the Big House and into the life of the middle classes and the peasantry. Carleton's *Traits and Stories of the Irish Peasantry* portrayed Irish rural experience with a rich and informative detail, even as it blurred distinctions between fiction and fact. Seamus Deane has summarized this period and its literary conventions as follows:

From the 1820s, Ireland produced a sub-genre of memoirs, sketches, tales, legends, all of which were devoted to the recording of the hitherto occluded life of the Irish peasantry and many of which did so in an antiquarian spirit, setting down what they feared would soon be lost forever. These were sometimes indistinguishable from Irish fiction, both in purpose and quality. Among many examples, one could select Gerald Griffin's *Tales of the Munster Festivals* (1827), *Tales of the O'Hara Family* in the same year by the Banim brothers, Crofton Croker's *Fairy Legends and Traditions of the South of Ireland*, Eyre Evans Crowe's *Today in Ireland*, both of 1825, Cesar Otway's *Sketches in Ireland* (1827), Mrs A. M. Hall's *Sketches in Ireland* (1829)....[1]

The combination of fact and fiction here helped to create a mythology about the peasantry that lasted deep into the next century. In James Joyce's *A Portrait of the Artist as a Young Man*, a novel that blends autobiography and irony in confusing ways, we learn from Stephen Dedalus's journal about two other fictional characters, John Alphonsus Mulrennan and an old man living in a mountain cabin in the west of Ireland. Stephen imagines struggling with this man, who has himself already imagined "terrible queer creatures at the latter end of the world." While such blends of Irish fact and fiction continue to perplex us, Deane's overview demonstrates that readers in the early nineteenth century hardly had an easier time of it.

II

One reason for the sharp increase in antiquarian and authorial effort early in the nineteenth century was the demand in England, arising out of the Act of Union in 1800, for more information about Ireland, whether in the form of regional tales and sketches, scholarly research, or parliamentary studies. Like the reports from other colonial outposts, such material allowed English observers to judge for themselves whether their various possessions were peopled by rational and enlightened beings or by barbarous and exotic savages. For Irish writers looking in their turn to exploit the English market,

---

1. Seamus Deane, *A Short History of Irish Literature* (Notre Dame: University of Notre Dame Press, 1986), 94–95.

this posed a question that had to be answered again and again throughout the century: should one seek to inform one's readers and thus to shape their opinions in more consciously didactic ways, or instead, just tell them what they wanted to hear? As a more systematic and far-reaching project of translation, the Ordnance Survey began in 1824 to remap and rename the Irish landscape, quickly expanding beyond its topographical agenda and entering into concerns of archeological, historical, and linguistic matters. Involving such Irish cultural figures as James Clarence Mangan, George Petrie, John O'Donovan, Eugene O'Curry, Samuel Ferguson, and W. F. Wakeman, the Survey continued operating throughout the 1830s and played a significant role in the collecting and editing of many early Irish manuscripts.

Among the more current Irish social issues to concern British onlookers were the ongoing state of poverty afflicting much of the country and, of greater sensationalist appeal, the recurring acts of rural violence, much of it sectarian in nature. Historians now differ about the actual extent of violence in pre-Famine Ireland,[2] but at the time, the prevailing view from England, useful in maintaining political support for continued domination, was of an Irish countryside constantly seething with faction fights, election riots, and midnight raids upon isolated Protestants. While some of the violence arose out of resentment against authority that was perceived as illegitimate because British, economic upheavals played the more significant role. Joel Mokyr's study *Why Ireland Starved* (1983) concludes:

> During 1750–1814, tillage products were more profitable and land was converted from pasturage to arable. At the end of the Napoleonic Wars this trend was reversed. . . . the movements toward and then away from tillage

2. Samuel Clark, *Social Origins of the Irish Land War* (Princeton: Princeton University Press, 1979), 66, claims that "Pre-famine Ireland was a remarkably violent country"; but K. Theodore Hoppen, *Elections, Politics, and Society in Ireland 1832–1885* (Oxford: Clarendon, 1984), 342, argues that "in reality, the violence of pre-Famine Ireland was both less constant and less universal than has often been supposed."

were a primary—though not the sole—cause of violence and lawlessness. . . .[3]

The high demand for Irish agricultural goods during the Napoleonic Wars slackened and gave way to an inflationary period lasting for nearly two decades after the end of the Wars. Many of the farm families used spinning and weaving to supplement their income from agriculture. British industrial production was now expanding rapidly, however, and to make matters worse, in 1824 the tariffs that had shielded Irish industry from British competition were lifted, seriously hurting cottage textile producers.

In a climate of unstable economic conditions and mistrust of civil authority, the status of Irish Protestants as a privileged minority made them a frequent target for social unrest. Desmond Bowen has described the anxiety and fear among "most Protestants, most of the time" that Catholic violence would be unleashed upon them.[4] Although the first two decades of the century offered Catholics and Protestants a period of relative harmony and tolerance, people still recalled the Rebellion of 1798 and experienced every day the class and social differences separating the two religious groups, a gulf economically systematized through the tithes paid by Catholics for support of the Church of Ireland. Also known as the Anglican, the Established, or the Irish Church, it was most galling to the tithe-paying Catholics because of its nature as a Protestant church.

By 1820, the evangelical wing of the Church of Ireland had aggressively expanded its proselytizing work among Catholics. The Religious Tract and Book Society distributed pamphlets, and missionaries preached at local gatherings, handed out bibles translated into Irish, and offered religious education to the poor. Such evangel-

---

3. Joel Mokyr, *Why Ireland Starved: A Quantitative and Analytical History of the Irish Economy, 1800–1850* (London: George Allen and Unwin, 1983), 144–45.

4. Desmond Bowen, *The Protestant Crusade in Ireland, 1800–70: A Study of Protestant–Catholic Relations between the Act of Union and Disestablishment* (Dublin: Gill and Macmillan, 1978), 132. The full title of Bowen's book gives the parameters for this excellent and detailed study of the Church of Ireland.

ical activity was part of a general reform movement within the Church of Ireland that managed to eliminate much of the earlier inefficiency, scandal, neglect, and abuse of privilege. In the face of mounting criticism, the Church had begun a period of reform that, from 1800 to 1829, resulted in more than 600 churches being either repaired or constructed, "equalling the effort of the Church during the previous 270 years."[5] The evangelical fervor of some within the Church, such as the Archbishop of Tuam, Power le Poer Trench, was directed ultimately toward winning souls; since many converts also tended to enjoy increased economic and social advantages, however, such spiritual efforts reminded some critics of less exalted pursuits, British imperialism, for instance.

This same period saw a sharp increase in millennialist sentiment among many Catholics in the countryside, particularly inspired by pamphlet versions of the prophecies of Bishop Charles Walmesley. Under the pen name of "Signor Pastorini," Walmesley had published *The General History of the Christian Church* in 1790, a work that foretold the Second Coming. Some thought it would herald the end of world Protestantism. The harvest failure of 1821 further encouraged millennialist speculations and the anti-Protestant agitation that reached its most intense form in the rural terrorism of Catholic Rockite groups.

In October 1822, then, a sermon by William Magee, Protestant Archbishop of Dublin, sounded to many in Ireland like a religious call to arms. Magee's sermon proved to be the beginning of a New or Second Reformation within Ireland, one that would heighten both religiosity and sectarian conflict at least until Disestablishment of the Church of Ireland in 1869. Launched as a revitalized Christian and missionary movement, the Second Reformation predictably resulted in further alienation of Protestants from Catholics. Since these missionary efforts were partially inspired by political motives

---

5. Edward Brynn, *The Church of Ireland in the Age of Catholic Emancipation* (New York: Garland, 1982), 402.

and by a concern for temporal power and status, evangelicalism contributed to a broader Protestant impulse toward exclusion and introversion and toward increasing hostility against Catholics. For their part, the Catholic clergy also soon came to be fully involved in the political arena, largely through the methods of Daniel O'Connell.

### III

Daniel O'Connell's political greatness derived from his ability to identify, early in the process, not only the issues that would later prove central to a developing Irish nationalism but also the methods that would best foster that development. Even before the Act of Union went into effect, he had pronounced it a worse arrangement than the earlier penal codes. An early supporter of emancipation, as well, by 1812 O'Connell had become a virtual leader of this movement. Sentiment for emancipation had existed in Ireland since the previous century. But it took O'Connell's Catholic Association, founded in 1823, for a political organization to become capable of gathering together many scattered grievances and issues into a mass movement. Of O'Connell's far-reaching methods, Fergus O'Ferrall claims, "The Catholic Association foreshadowed in almost every single feature modern democratic political parties...."[6] A major turning point in Irish politics, the point at which it became unmistakably clear that popular movements and clerical influence could have a decisive effect, came in 1826. In the general election that year, victories by candidates supported by the Catholic Association showed that democratic political strategies could succeed within a framework of constitutional action. General elections increasingly addressed national rather than purely local issues because of the potential benefits that legislated reforms could offer to the whole of Catholic Ireland.

---

6. Fergus O'Ferrall, *Catholic Emancipation: Daniel O'Connell and the Birth of Irish Democracy, 1820–30* (Dublin: Gill and Macmillan, 1985), 272. I rely heavily on O'Ferrall's detailed study for my sense of political developments in Ireland for the period 1820–1830.

In June 1828, O'Connell stood for a by-election in Clare, the first election since the 1690s in which a Catholic was a candidate. Of his victory here, O'Ferrall notes: "The election was the decisive event shaping nineteenth-century popular politics and in the evolution of political democracy in Ireland."[7] The Catholic masses could now count on some measure of independent power, especially with many of their clergy now fully involved in helping to shape and direct that power. In parliamentary terms, O'Connell had created the framework for a more unified and nationalist Irish political party that would increasingly push for separation from England. The resurgence of agrarian violence in the 1820s had been channeled into a form of pressure that England could no longer address simply with new coercion laws.

O'Connell's background and training as a lawyer inclined him to avoid violence and instead to work as much as possible within a constitutional and parliamentary framework. Oliver MacDonagh's biographical study points to an early political speech, in 1813, as defining "the philosophy of political action which was to govern O'Connell's entire agitatory career," a key feature of which was "a specific repudiation of the revolutionary tradition."[8] Within the troubled context of his own time, however, O'Connell's critics typically failed to understand his abhorrence for mass social violence. He thus always had the implicit threat of rural agitation as an incentive for England to grant concessions. In 1830, then, when O'Connell founded the Society for the Repeal of the Union, separation indeed seemed dangerously near, especially once O'Connell's movement began winning elections for Irish parliamentary members committed to the issue of repeal. In such an atmosphere, the British feared that agitation could erupt on a massive scale anywhere in Ireland, especially during elections in the late 1820s and early 1830s. Even the

---

7. Ibid., 188.
8. Oliver MacDonagh, *The Hereditary Bondsman: Daniel O'Connell, 1775–1829* (New York: St. Martin's, 1988), 115.

military and police seemed unreliable, since these units contained so many Irish recruits.

By the end of the 1820s, the threat of mass disorder arose in England itself as industrial workers protested against their distressed conditions. In Europe, too, political violence and revolution remained an ongoing possibility, one that might well spill over into England. Pressure for emancipation had mounted throughout the 1820s until some of its opponents, such as Wellington and Peel, shifted their position because of the expedient hope that such a major concession would pacify Ireland where armed force had failed. If Catholics were given a bigger stake in the Union and some responsibility for the continued operation of the constitution—or so the argument ran—perhaps they would then begin helping to foster harmonious relations with Great Britain.

## IV

The Emancipation Act in 1829 opened most political and civil rights to Catholics, allowing them to hold seats in the British Parliament and to serve in many higher offices of the state and the legal system. Such gains came about, however, only through an Irish Parliamentary Elections Act that simultaneously reduced the numbers of county voters, from 216,000 down to 37,000.[9] These enormous cuts resulted from a negotiated arrangement whereby emancipation would be conceded, but only when linked to the disenfranchisement of the forty-shilling freeholders and to the substitution of a ten-pound suffrage. This legislative package was generally designed to head off democracy for the masses in Ireland and to create instead an electorate of the propertied and educated classes.

This same intention was part of a broader political strategy in England, during the years 1830–1832, to separate the middle from the working classes and thereby to defuse the radical potential of this

---

9. These figures are cited in Roy Foster, *Modern Ireland, 1600–1972* (New York: Viking, 1988), 302; see also Hoppen, *Elections*, 1, for similar figures.

combination. Like the Emancipation Act, then, the Reform Act of 1832 assigned the franchise along economic lines, to persons of property and financial responsibility. The middle classes might thus come to identify their own values and life style, not with those too poor even to have a vote, but with the reliable and stable elements of the upper classes. This strategy did in fact succeed for a time in sustaining the political power of the landed class. Even while economic foundations were changing within the society as a whole, government authority remained largely in traditional hands. Indirectly, however, the new patterns and alliances would eventually create major changes, and conservative Tory arguments against the Reform Act would be revealed as an accurate prediction of its overall effects and consequences. As representation of the middle classes grew, power gradually shifted away from the aristocracy. Capital would come to be the basis for political power in Great Britain, even when it did not exist in the long-standing form of a powerful landed estate.

In a similar manner, the indirect effects of such legislation in Ireland were more significant than the direct ones. J. C. Beckett's study *The Anglo-Irish Tradition* claims that Emancipation in 1829 and the Reform Act of 1832 "undermined, and almost destroyed, the basis on which the ascendancy of the Anglo-Irish had rested since the seventeenth century."[10] Fergus O'Ferrall comments that "Catholic Emancipation inaugurated the liberal democratic era."[11] Positions and influence in government, at both the local and national level, remained dominated by Protestants for decades to follow. At the same time, it was now clear that a broad-based popular movement could agitate effectively for change and that occasional threats or acts of violence might well benefit such a movement. Within an unstable countryside, Irish tenants continued to press for further reforms,

---

10. J. C. Beckett, *The Anglo-Irish Tradition* (Ithaca: Cornell University Press, 1976), 89.

11. Fergus O'Ferrall, *Catholic Emancipation*, 273.

heightening tensions through the violence of the Tithe Campaign. Begun in the winter of 1830–1831 and continuing throughout the rest of the decade, the Tithe Campaign sought to end the tithes paid by Catholics to the Church of Ireland.

Through the movement for emancipation, the Catholic clergy had become a strong political force, "their old passivity and timidity in the face of British power," Oliver MacDonagh claims, now "generally replaced by confidence and even, in many cases, truculence."[12] The issue of tithes thus readily engaged this same political energy, and James Doyle, Roman Catholic Bishop of Kildare and Leighlin, voiced open support for the campaign as early as 1831. MacDonagh comments, "despite the apparent dominance of repeal as the issue of the 1830s, the most significant development of the decade was probably the junction of Catholic politics and traditional agrarian resistance in the form of the anti-tithe campaign."[13] Just as the threat of widespread social disorder had played a role in winning emancipation, it now helped to break the tithe system by the end of the 1830s. For some in Ireland, however, British concessions on tithes meant, not just the success of another major campaign, but also the prelude to even bigger prizes.

The increase in Catholic expectations at the social, economic, and political levels also led to reforms in education. In 1831, Lord Stanley, the Chief Secretary to Ireland, announced Whig proposals for a National Board of Education to create and run a system of nondenominational elementary schools in Ireland. The evangelical wing of Protestantism strongly objected to this system, since it would end direct funding for Protestant education. Given Irish Protestantism's emphasis upon education, the National Board remained for decades an ongoing irritation to the Protestants in Ire-

---

12. Oliver MacDonagh, "The Economy and Society, 1830–45," in *A New History of Ireland, V: Ireland Under the Union, I (1801–70)*, ed. W. E. Vaughan (Oxford: Clarendon, 1989), 238.
13. Oliver MacDonagh, *States of Mind: A Study of Anglo-Irish Conflict 1780–1980* (London: George Allen and Unwin, 1983), 43.

land. Even as many Protestants feared Catholicism as a political force whose superior numbers could lead to a redistribution of wealth and power and also to separation from England, they also saw it as a moral or ideological force. From such a sectarian standpoint, Catholics were enslaved to another foreign power in Rome, to an authoritarian center of rule, and to a superstitious form of religion. Education was thus of particular importance in helping to preserve individual freedom and conscience on religious matters and to induce enlightened Catholics to convert to the Established Church.

Another concession to Catholic forces, the Irish Church Temporalities Act in 1833, further eroded the status of Protestantism in Ireland, in part by raising the specter of disestablishment. Even the Church itself could no longer ignore the fact that it was over-staffed and over-endowed, and that some reform was necessary to eliminate abuses of power. The Church addressed these problems by simultaneously opposing legislative reform and beginning its own process of internal reform. In the first case, it resisted government movements to intervene in the control of Church property and revenues, branding these incursions as the first step towards disestablishment. In the second case, and as a way to head off further parliamentary intervention, it began a genuinely productive and effective period of self-improvement, reducing its administrative structure but at the same time creating a much more efficient organization.

For the most part, though, the Church of Ireland resisted the whole spirit of reform that had begun to reshape Irish and British society. D. H. Akenson finds that "Catholic emancipation set in motion a trend towards rigid conservatism in the Church of Ireland at the very time the United Kingdom as a whole was experiencing a trend towards greater flexibility and liberalism."[14] Throughout the series of retrenchments and encroachments, the Church repeatedly

---

14. Donald Harmon Akenson, *The Church of Ireland: Ecclesiastical Reform and Revolution, 1800–1885* (New Haven: Yale University Press, 1971), 145.

fell back upon the issue of property rights to defend itself. As a general ideological issue, property assumed the aura of an almost sanctified right; if it were disregarded or destroyed in the case of the Church, this would have profound implications for the spiritual and economic state of the whole nation. The Church thus sought to identify its own interests with those of other landed elements in the country, emphasizing, for instance, the similarity between rents and tithes. The tithe united Church and state: the state insured the economic well-being of the Church, while the Church gave spiritual authority to the concept of private property. From a different direction, the Church could argue that removal of tithes would simply result in an increase of rents. In either case, it was a strong, although ultimately unsuccessful, defense against the government's right to interfere with Church property.

Edward Brynn's study, *The Church of Ireland in the Age of Catholic Emancipation* (1982), has identified some of the internal contradictions and inconsistencies that limited the Church's overall defense insofar as it depended upon the principle of property:

> In time such obsession with property rights further weakened its claim to be the nation's spiritual counselor and prompted even more dramatic demands by parliamentary radicals for ecclesiastical reform. Around such Benthamite catchwords as "utility" and the "greatest happiness for the greatest number" gathered the Church's foes. In consequence the Irish Establishment became the first great historical institution to be measured by evidence of its usefulness to the nation.[15]

In a similar vein, Desmond Bowen writes, "[t]he gulf between what the Church of Ireland professed to be and what it was, was so great that the whole communion existed in a state of institutional anxiety."[16] Despite the problems inherent in its own position, however, the Church continued to define and defend itself through this very relationship between spiritual and material wealth. It clung to

---

15. Brynn, *Church of Ireland*, 5.
16. Bowen, *Protestant Crusade*, 47.

the principle of tithes even after the economic events of the 1830s had made it clear that commutation of tithes would ultimately work to the financial advantage of the Protestant clergy, besides removing a source of popular agitation against them. And it continued to interpret material prosperity as evidence of spiritual well-being. Civilization, the Church claimed, was the manifestation of Christianity in a society; furthermore, and even more emphatically, the Church insisted upon Protestantism as the only true manifestation of Christianity. Despite its status as an isolated, outdated, and easily dispensable minority, the Church of Ireland clung tenaciously, and with surprising success, to its power and privileges. It avoided disestablishment until 1869, and even then, after losing its place as the official religion of the state, it remained a major intellectual training ground for many of Ireland's cultural leaders through the end of the nineteenth century.

v

By the late 1820s, however, with the British Whigs apparently all too willing to grant further concessions to Irish radicalism, it was clear that the Church alone could not succeed in maintaining Ireland's status quo. Oliver MacDonagh has stressed the "dominant theme of Irish politics" for the 1820s and 1830s as "the sectarian contest for the diminution or retention of the protestant ascendancy, material and symbolic alike."[17] British hopes of controlling this theme by pacifying Irish Catholicism were quickly proving delusive, with the additional effect of making British political leadership seem vacillating, weak, and ineffectual, ready ultimately to betray and abandon Irish Protestantism. The House of Lords could slow, but hardly halt, the growing legislative power of the Commons. For those in Ireland who identified with Protestant ascendancy, then, and who feared their loss of exclusivity and the imminent collapse

---

17. Oliver MacDonagh, "Ireland and the Union, 1801–70," in *A New History of Ireland, V*, ed. Vaughan, lv.

of Irish society into barbarism and chaos, some kind of political response of their own also came to seem essential. In 1828, local organizations began to form, called Brunswick Clubs, to give more focused direction to Tory politics. In 1831, Exeter Hall, a convention center for evangelical causes, opened in London. The 1832 Reform Act further heightened this increased sectarian politicizing and mobilizing. Politics had become synonymous with religion in Ireland, and the relative harmony between Catholics and Protestants during the first two decades of the century had given way to permanent divisions.

In order for the various sides and issues to take shape, some means of publishing the agendas and providing the forums were necessary. The political and religious controversies thus helped to spawn a large number of Irish periodicals during this period, over 150 being launched during the first half of the century, according to Barbara Hayley's count.[18] A number of penny magazines with huge circulations sought to meet the demand for both information and cheap literature. In 1825, the Rev. Caesar Otway and Dr. J. H. Singer started the *Christian Examiner and Church of Ireland Magazine,* one of the few significant periodicals within a typically short-lived business. The *Examiner* published many travel pieces on Ireland and its sights, as well as some of William Carleton's early tales.

A group of young Trinity College Tories, firmly allied to the conservative politics of Protestant ascendancy, determined to create their own forum, albeit one that was more substantial than the typical penny journal. The *Dublin University Magazine* was thus launched, in January 1833, in part to counter the new political doctrines exemplified by the 1832 Reform Bill, as well as the feelings of despair and ruin that such doctrines were now causing in Tory circles. In calling for the "resuscitation of the Church of Ireland," the first issue warned against social change, expedient compromises

---

18. Barbara Hayley, "Irish Periodicals from the Union to the *Nation,*" in *Anglo-Irish Studies* II, ed. P. J. Drudy (Atlantic Highlands: Humanities, 1976), 83.

and concessions, the "yawning chasm" of democracy, and that "audacious demagogue" Daniel O'Connell (Jan. 1833, 9, 90, and 10). The journal would build its authority upon a combination "at once elegant and solid, ornamental and yet chaste" (Jan. 1833, 89), in which political commentary alternated with artistic and cultural pieces. In the years that followed, articles opposing Catholicism, the Tithe Campaign, agrarian conspiracies, Home Rule agitation, and disestablishment of the Church of Ireland ran alongside scholarly essays, travelogues, reviews, short stories, poetry, and serialized novels.

The magazine reflected several times over the next few years upon its own genesis and continued existence. In part, this self-consciousness arose from delighted surprise at the *DUM*'s own success. Looking back at the end of the first year of operation, the inaugural editor Charles Stuart Stanford admitted that "we hoped rather than really expected" to have lasted so long (Insert for Dec. 1833, 2). Similar ventures in the past had always failed, the *DUM* suggested, because of a "general belief" in "some inexplicable fatality connected with every thing Irish" (Dec. 1835, 709). In the "Postscript to Our Hundredth Number," the *DUM* elaborated on this prejudice: "Our magazine was Irish; and nothing Irish had possessed sufficient vitality to exist twelve months. Published in Dublin, actually written for the most part by authors resident in Ireland, and seeking, as the principal basis of support, an Irish circulation!—against such an accumulation of unfortunate circumstances, what could avail?" (April 1841, 528). While the *DUM* had posed such bluff rhetorical questions from the outset, the early answers would have lacked the later confidence. Seeking to disprove general beliefs in Irish fatality, the initial founders still more than half believed in it themselves.

The magazine sprang up as a spontaneous impulse within an informal Trinity College gathering known as "The Porch." In its most detailed account of its founding, a September 1840 retrospective, the *DUM* regretted that the inevitable Irish "stumbling-block" of politics had prevented some of these college intellectuals from throwing their support behind the magazine (267). Assessing the origins of the *DUM* in a 1988 article, Joe Spence suggests that this splinter group shifted its energies into the creation of a less controversialist journal, the *Dublin University Review,* launched in the same month as the *DUM* but fated to fold before year's end. Upon the demise of the *Review,* then, these "seceders" may have "transferred their allegiances back to the *DUM*."[19] While Spence's article remains speculative on many points, it does remind us of the dangers of overgeneralizing about the "Protestant" founders of the *DUM*. The "Big House" of Irish Protestantism enclosed many differing and shifting political interests and agendas, not just Whigs and Tories, but also varieties of conservatives within the Tory party, within Dublin and within Trinity College, even within a Trinity student organization as narrowly constructed as "The Porch."

Despite encountering political differences even before their journal could make its public appearance, the majority from "The Porch" still determined to hold out "stoutly for the good old Conservative cause." The magazine had two goals from the start, "one being to further the cause of Protestantism throughout the empire, by affording it a new organ in connection with literature . . . , and the other to prove by experiment the possibility of a literary Periodical *living* in this country." For models, both in physical appearance and editorial policies, the founders could look toward *Blackwood's* and *Fraser's,* "having these two formidable personages their allies in politics, it is true, but their rivals in literature" (Sept. 1840, 267). Having in several cases already written for *Blackwood's* and similar magazines, members of "The Porch" could bring considerable journalistic experience to their Irish project.

In a letter to his mother, Isaac Butt reported that he had given fifteen pounds to the new venture.[20] The others involved—John An-

---

19. Joe Spence, "Nationality and Irish Toryism: The Case of the *Dublin University Magazine,* 1833–52," *Journal of Newspaper and Periodical History* 4, no. 3 (Autumn 1988): 2.

20. Terence de Vere White, *The Road of Excess* (Dublin: Browne and Nolan, 1946), 8.

ster, William Archer Butler, Samuel Ferguson, Samuel O'Sullivan, Caesar Otway, and Charles Stuart Stanford—may also have contributed ten to fifteen pounds each. After several months of operation, the group was joined by John Francis Waller, the one figure most closely associated with the magazine for its entire career. But by then, the enterprise was well under way.

Besides their conservative political sympathies, members of the group were further united—like most of their early contributors—by past or present affiliations with Trinity College, Dublin (or, Dublin University). Regarding Trinity from his militantly nationalist end of the Irish political spectrum, Young Irelander Sir Charles Gavan Duffy described it as "a fortress of Protestant ascendancy, the amphitheatre [sic] where young athletes were trained to defend the Established Church, the land code, and the exclusive magistracy and municipalities. . . ."[21] While Catholics had been eligible to attend the college since 1794, they could not receive fellowship assistance, and they remained a small minority. Trinity thus served as the intellectual center of energy for the Church of Ireland, even as it brought together students whose backgrounds represented the whole range of Irish Protestantism.

Trinity's clubby atmosphere of social privilege, its network of connections for professional careers in law, government, or the ministry, gave to the DUM's founders a high degree of journalistic unity. Until Charles Lever assumed editorial control in 1842, the DUM's identity took its shape from in-house, interest-group, or corporate dynamics rather than from a single, well-established literary figure. It is thus not surprising that, for its first editor, the group selected Charles Stuart Stanford, the person now perhaps least known from the original circle of founders and the one whose association with the magazine lasted for the shortest period of time. Even though he reacted "in amaze" when told of his new post (Sept. 1840, 267), he

---

21. Sir Charles Gavan Duffy, *Thomas Davis: The Memoirs of an Irish Patriot, 1840–1846* (London: Kegan Paul, 1890), 7.

had already developed the role of literary mentor for "The Porch," as well as the self-effacing personality that the project seemed to demand.

Born in 1805, Stanford entered Trinity perhaps as early as 1820, becoming noted as "a very good classical scholar" who also possessed "considerable poetic talent, together with a refined taste."[22] Under what would become the standard editorial pseudonym of "Anthony Poplar," so chosen because of Stanford's tall, slim frame, he edited the *DUM* until August 1834, soon afterwards taking up a curacy in a remote parish in County Tyrone. Although he later became involved in various religious–political controversies, he never again published in the *DUM* once he had relinquished its editorship.

The strongest literary reputation from among the group of founders belonged to John Anster. His widely acclaimed translation of the first part of Goethe's *Faust* had appeared in *Blackwood's* in June 1820, following the 1819 publication of a major collection of his poems and translations from the German. But it was the Protestant converts, brothers Mortimer and Samuel O'Sullivan, who set the ideological tone of the *DUM* in its early stages. One of Protestant Ireland's foremost religious spokesmen during this period and, according to Desmond Brown, "the most intelligent and interesting of them,"[23] Mortimer had begun his public career with *Captain Rock Detected* (1824), a response to poet Thomas Moore's *Memoirs of Captain Rock* (1824). When Moore published another defense of Catholicism, *Travels of an Irish Gentleman in Search of a Religion* (1833), O'Sullivan countered again, and this response, *A Guide to an Irish Gentleman in His Search for a Religion* (1833), was described by the *DUM* as "one of the ablest defences of the Church of England that has appeared since the days of Jewell" (Sept. 1833, 303). "Tommy" Moore's book, by contrast, received a vicious attack in a *DUM* review by

---

22. This descriptive language is from a letter about Stanford from Joseph Napier, ex-chancellor of Dublin University, cited in Stanford's obituary in the *DUM* (Nov. 1873, 617).
23. Bowen, *Protestant Crusade*, 117.

Robert J. McGhee (July and Aug. 1833). Another influential Protestant controversialist from the 1830s, McGhee would later publish *Romanism As It Rules in Ireland* (1840), a work co-authored by Mortimer O'Sullivan.

Rounding out this tight circle, then, was Mortimer's brother Samuel. In its obituary on Samuel in 1851, the *DUM* claimed that its pages had been "almost unintermittingly enriched by his essays" ever since its beginnings. The obituary went on to express deep gratitude for O'Sullivan's contributions and proudly to include an extract from the obituary in the Dublin *Daily Express:* the *DUM* "may be almost described as created by Dr. O'Sullivan.... In the first number of that work he stated the principles on which it would be conducted, and honestly and independently has it since supported those principles" (Oct. 1851, 506–7). Although Mortimer's career kept him more involved with public activities over the next several years, with Samuel playing the greater role in the operations of the *DUM*, both brothers were heavily represented in the magazine.

VI

The role of the O'Sullivans as ideological godfathers ensured that any discussion of politics in the *DUM* would quickly turn to strategies for advancing specifically Protestant interests. *Blackwood's* and *Fraser's* had already established an anti-Catholic editorial tone, but in this area, at least, the *DUM* would outdo both of them. "The Conservative cause is the cause of religion ...," the magazine asserted (Feb. 1833, 117), and with another article in the same issue, entitled "Church and State," argued for a continued constitutional relationship between the two. A later piece, "The Good Old Cause," went on to link the happiness of a nation to its reliance on the principles of "true religion" (Sept. 1833, 241). On the other side of religious truth stood "that monstrous and incestuous offspring of infidelity and superstition" (April 1833, 400), "the most finished and most abominable superstition on this earth—POPERY!" (July 1833, 111). Despite the hope that "Popery seems to have reached the lowest point of moral deterioration . . ." and thus must soon crumble because of its own corruption (March 1833, 255), determined political action was still urgently needed. Proselytizing among Catholics, for instance, would show many of them the obvious errors and abuses of their faith.

Irish Protestants could also benefit from education. The landed gentry should learn from England's ill treatment of the Irish Church and clergy that their own salvation lay only in united strength. An apocalyptic article "On the Emigration of Protestants" warned against the consequences of this loss of population from within the "English garrison" in Ireland (May 1833, 472); one answer here was for landowners to rent out holdings to responsible tenants only— that is, to Protestants (March 1833, 263–64). And even though the Churches of Ireland and of England were so closely connected that "the death of the one will be soon followed by the death of the other" (Jan. 1833, 9), all Protestants needed to realize that England had chosen to ignore this possible fate and thus could not be depended on any further to protect the right and proper interests in Ireland. In establishing the Irish Church Temporalities Act in 1833, for instance, England's political leaders had once more given in to "political expediency" in seeking to conciliate Irish Catholics (April 1833, 400).

Much of the *DUM*'s quarrel with England originated in the 1832 Reform Bill. This "so called, reformation of the house of commons was the most insane and reckless project that ever disgraced the councils of profligate political empirics" (Feb. 1833, 211). The reformed parliament "will henceforth resemble dogs with kettles tied to their tails" (Jan. 1833, 7), partly because the Tory party is "now all but utterly demolished" in the wake of Reform and thus cannot operate as an effective opposition (Feb. 1833, 112). When expanded into more specific and less spectacular prose, such arguments proved eventually to be an accurate assessment of the future results of reform: the bill would legitimize public pressure as a political force, benefit the middle classes and industrial interests, and aid the supporters of democracy. While Whig advocates of reform continued to deny that such unwanted effects would ever come to pass, the farsighted conservatives of the *DUM* knew better and expanded their attacks wherever possible. The British Whigs, through their unholy alliance with Daniel O'Connell, their ineffective concessions to the Irish peasantry, and their attempted reforms of the Church of Ireland hierarchy, had done nothing but further encourage political activism and violence. In short, the present government consisted of an "outrageously impudent set of quacks" (Oct. 1833, 465).

The criticisms frequently went beyond name-calling and prophecies of doom into suggestions for specific policies that might mitigate the crisis. Besides improvements in education, the *DUM* advocated better transportation and public works systems, more support for the Protestant clergy and for the tithe collectors, coercion laws that were not as severe (and thus not as divisive and impossible to enforce) as in the past, and legal controls over the kinds of parliamentary maneuvers that O'Connell used so profitably. Lengthy articles, similar in style to eighteenth-century political pamphlets, marshaled factual data and authoritative sources to analyze Irish political ills. Yet each article also contained biting passages in which the social and political problems were approached as if they were military obstacles in a holy war. The lead article for April 1834, on the "State and Prospects of the Country," warned of the long struggle ahead: "Our people must journey through the wilderness, and we ourselves do not expect even to get a sight of the promised land" (373–74).

## VII

The *DUM* balanced such political-religious analyses with cultural items much lighter in tone and purpose, articles like "The Bores of my Acquaintance" or "A Trip to the Falls of Tequendama," or poems like "Here in this lonely Cave" (by "Bizarre"). The frequent book reviews typically included lengthy extracts from the work under consideration, just as the political articles frequently cited from public or parliamentary speeches. Travel pieces covered the west of

Ireland as well as many international locations. William Archer Butler, who would later become Professor of Moral Philosophy at Trinity, wrote a piece applying metaphysics to scripture (Feb. 1833), and Mountifort Longfield, then Trinity's first Whately Professor of Political Economy and "one of the outstanding analytical economists of the 19th century,"[24] contributed a book review. There were verse translations by James Wills, Michael J. Barry, and others. Approaching politics from the chatty side, William Johnston (as "Terence O'Ruark") and Harry Rowley (writing "Familiar Epistles from London") both contributed intermittent pieces, in the style of a breezy travelogue, giving on-the-scene accounts of parliamentary events. Most issues ended with a section on university business, one of which announced a lecture series at Trinity College by a Berlin professor named Zander, who followed in the very next issue with an article on German art and literature. In January 1834, James Clarence Mangan published translations from the German verse of Schiller, beginning a relationship with the *DUM* that would see far more of Mangan's translating.

While the *DUM* followed the common nineteenth-century practice of anonymity for most of its contributors, there were exceptions, such as Felicia Hemans, whose reputation as poet and translator was already well established in the 1820s, or the Scottish poet Robert Gilfillan. Other writers were identified indirectly through previous work, such as William Carleton ("The Author of 'Traits and Stories of the Irish Peasantry'") or the Reverend William Hamilton Maxwell ("the author of 'Wild Sports of the West'"). And the most regular contributors adopted fanciful pseudonyms. Digby Pilot Starkey published frequent poems and some facetious prose

---

24. S. Rashid, "Political Economy in the *Dublin University Magazine*, 1833–40," *Long Room* 14–15 (Autumn 1976-Spring/Summer 1977): 16. Rashid's article discusses and praises the quality of the *DUM*'s essays on political economy during the years 1833–1840, arguing that the *DUM* showed an intelligent and informed approach to political economy, one that avoided the biases of sectarianism and that considered various sides of an issue.

works as "Advena," and John Francis Waller used the name "Iota" to identify his poetry and a short story about star-crossed lovers. This last theme appeared frequently in the *DUM*'s literary pieces from this period, as in short stories by Maxwell ("The Unknown," Sept. 1833) or by Isaac Butt ("Village Annals," Feb. and March 1833). It is revealing to look to *Blackwood's,* however, for perhaps the most explicitly political rendering of this theme in Samuel O'Sullivan's short story "Castle Elmere" (March 1834, 353). A potential love relationship between a Protestant girl and a Catholic boy falls prey to the animosities and treachery of Catholic agitators. In their emphasis on misunderstanding, suspicion, meddling outsiders, and historical enmities, these stories of star-crossed lovers served to reinforce the *DUM*'s political sense of the Protestant gentry and the native Irish having been ideally meant for each other but somehow, tragically, now prevented from realizing their perfect union.

Two short stories, "Barny O'Reirdon the Navigator" and "Little Fairly," were of particular interest to the *DUM* as evidenced by the inclusion of Samuel Lover's name as author as well as his etchings to illustrate the works. By the late 1820s, Lover had established his reputation as one of Dublin's best painters of miniatures. In his story "Barny O'Reirdon," which began running in the *DUM*'s first issue and concluded in the second, Barny is a local hero in a small town on the west coast of Ireland who maintains his status by sheer bluff and bluster. He decides to sail his small fishing boat to Fingal but is too proud and vain to admit that he has no idea of the whereabouts of this Irish port. So he mistakenly follows an English ship bound for Bengal and ends up hopelessly lost in the mid-Atlantic. Barny survives, but only through the intercession of the friendly English sea captain, who takes pity on him and who is also amused by his naivete and charming verbal eccentricities. The story opens with a comment on the Irishman's "unwillingness to be outdone," and Lover attributes this national characteristic, not to vanity, but to "a deep-seated spirit of emulation" (Jan. 1833, 17). This formula certainly flatters Barny more than the rest of the story does, and for all the humor of his adventure, the political moral seems discouragingly inescapable: the Irish would indeed do well to emulate the English, but until they have learned from their betters, they must be guided by England's benevolent wisdom. The English, after all, ranging knowledgeably between Fingal and Bengal and fully aware of the difference, still control the empire.

Lover's story "Little Fairly," appearing in April, also describes a hero who relies on verbal cleverness, although he is otherwise generally more competent than Barny. The *DUM* had already given Lover the "greatest praise" for his portrayals of Irish character, since he did not resort to "coarse vulgarity or worn-out provincialisms" (Jan. 1833, 33). In this same review, William Carleton's *Traits and Stories of the Irish Peasantry—Second Series* received similar praise: his accurate and sympathetic depictions of country life offered valuable lessons, not only to British legislators about the Irish, but also to Irish landlords about their own peasantry. Carleton's first story in the *DUM*, "The Dead Boxer," then appeared in December 1833, inaugurating a long and often stormy relationship between author and magazine. The story itself begins promisingly enough with a more complex and realistic treatment of the star-crossed-lovers theme than *DUM* readers were accustomed to getting. In the second half, however, the plot and cast of characters become hopelessly tangled because of the fact, crucial to the story's resolution, that nearly everyone is unwittingly related to everyone else. As all of the long-lost relatives finally celebrate their reunion, they realize that the bitter factionalism and rivalries that had created so many conflicts in their community were based on little more than mistaken identities. Despite the aesthetic shortcomings of the story, Carleton's advocacy of peasant pacifism would still have been attractive, as themes go, to those readers, both Catholic and Protestant, English and Irish, who worried throughout the 1830s about Whiteboyism, the Tithe War, and other forms of inexplicable violence within the Irish countryside.

Carleton offered his short story "The Resurrections of Barney

Bradley" for "John Bull's perusal" so "that it may serve to correct his views of Irish life and character" (Feb. 1834, 193). For the most part, though, the political messages within Lover's and Carleton's stories remain fairly subtle and unobtrusive. In the *DUM*'s first serialized novel, by contrast, *Love and Loyalty: A Leaf from the "Old Almanack,"*[25] we are repeatedly admonished to overlook none of the lessons of history: "to Ireland, in the nineteenth century, it was reserved for the popish priesthood to re-enact in a degree, the horrors of 1641, and use all but fiendish agency to further the purposes of their bigoted hatred and secure the promotion of their temporal ambition" (Feb. 1833, 155). The novel is set mostly in England at the time of Charles I, whose problems result from such errors as his "favouring of popery and innovations upon the Established Church" and his concessions to "the power of the republican faction" (Feb. 1833, 146 and 147). The Irish hero, O'Brien De Lacy, is a loyal, enlightened Protestant who fully understands the evils of materialism, the social and personal benefits of master-slave relationships, and the importance of the Protestant cause: "Orange! proud and glorious colour of courage and of truth" (April 1833, 368). The novel ends happily, before the beheading of Charles I, but therein lies the warning: English readers must recognize the present threat to the monarchy, and Irish readers must recognize the possibility that a modern Cromwell might once again ride forth to deal with Catholic insurrection.

### VIII

Amid the reputations of several more notable *DUM* writers at the time, no one could have recognized that the most significant literary contributions to appear during Stanford's editorial tenure would come from Samuel Ferguson. Then in his early twenties and the author of but a handful of pieces in *Blackwood's,* Ferguson was begin-

---

25. February through June 1833, 5 installments. Much to my frustration, I have not been able to discover the name of this novel's author. He identifies himself in the *DUM* only as "C" and adds the information that he spent his boyhood in a small town in the South of Ireland. He also writes badly.

ning a long poetic career that would establish him as a major voice in the development of modern Irish literature. "The Fairy Thorn" ranks as his most famous poem in the DUM from this period, an account laden with terror and tragedy of a young woman stolen by fairies (March 1834). Ferguson's most important entry, however, was a four-part essay critiquing James Hardiman's work *Irish Minstrelsy* (1831). The series began in April 1834, with the remainder appearing later that same year, in August, October, and November, under Isaac Butt's editorship. Peter Denman suggests that Ferguson hoped to publish the first installment in *Blackwood's*—hence the time lag separating it from the others, as well as its greater sense of physical distance from Ireland.[26] With the first part in place, though, Ferguson clearly came to envision the remaining three installments as elements toward a unified whole. His opening sentence for part I addresses the "fair hills of holy Ireland," the very words that form the final line of the poem that closes part IV. The image expands, in both essay and poem, to cast Ireland as the woman for whose beauty, love, and wealth various battles are waged. In his essay, Ferguson mounted his own assault in his claim to be more worthy of recovering the ancient Irish past than Hardiman and his team of translators.

Ferguson developed three primary objections to Hardiman's work: the translations were poorly done, the prose commentary was inaccurate or misleading, and the underlying ideology of the whole endeavor was narrowly prejudiced. To account for the first problem, Ferguson noted Hardiman's "laudable desire of making the English reader acquainted with the style and sentiment of our native poetry . . ." (Oct. 1834, 453). Nonetheless, the attempt of the translators to elevate and refine their material had destroyed the uniquely Irish nature of the originals and only produced versions that were "spurious, puerile, unclassical—lamentably bad" (Oct.

---

26. Peter Denman, *Samuel Ferguson: The Literary Achievement* (Savage, Md.: Barnes and Noble, 1990), 20–22.

1834, 453). Hardiman's commentary also seemed to Ferguson an unscholarly betrayal of his sources. The love song of a Catholic priest for his beautiful young parishioner Roiseen Dubh, for instance, was presented as an absurd political allegory because of Hardiman's nationalist bias and his prudish defense of priestly chastity. Ferguson, for his part, instead advised the narrator "to pitch his vows to the Pope, the Pope to purgatory, marry his black rose-bud, and take a curacy from the next Protestant rector" (Aug. 1834, 159). In the face of such high passion, political motives seemed stuffy indeed.

Obscured within such verbal heat, however, was Ferguson's own wish to dampen a different kind of ardor latent in Hardiman's love song. A dozen years later, James Clarence Mangan would produce, in "Dark Rosaleen," the most famous English version of this poem, one that fanned its potential as nationalist political message to a fever pitch. Later commentators have tended not to see in this any vindication of Hardiman, however, in part because Mangan had only a slight knowledge of Gaelic, in part too because Ferguson's vision of romantic Ireland was aesthetically more attractive than Hardiman's.

Ferguson did not dispute Hardiman's general right to give *Irish Minstrelsy* a political agenda, but he did object to its nationalist Catholic nature. For his own part, Ferguson proposed to address the political concerns of "the Protestant wealth and intelligence of the country" (April 1834, 457). In so doing, he relied on the same strategy that he had employed in "A Dialogue Between the Head and Heart of an Irish Protestant": professed sympathy for the position and point of view of Ireland's Catholics. Part I of Ferguson's essay thus approached his subject with an emphasis on the positive: "Mr. Hardiman's collection is truly a boon to the Irish reader" (April 1834, 456). Already by part II, though, Hardiman was described as being "politically malignant and religiously fanatical" (Aug. 1834, 153), not unlike other enemies of Protestant Ireland who had indulged in nothing but cowardly policies of "reproach and agitation" over the past twenty-five years (April 1834, 457). Ferguson preferred opponents from the ancient past, warriors who fought in the open, at midday, heroic representatives of native Ireland at its best. Ferguson's ideal Catholic reader would thus put down his copy of the *DUM* and shamefacedly cancel plans for the next midnight raid on the Protestant rectory. As Ferguson recognized, though, no Catholic readership was available to the *DUM* to be swayed by his unfavorable comparison of modern revolutionaries with those of the ancient and conveniently dead past. Instead, he sought to involve his Protestant audience in his proposed cultural-recovery project by showing a necessary connection between study of the past and prosperity in the future: Protestant "wealth has hitherto been insecure, because [Protestant] intelligence has not embraced a thorough knowledge of the genius and disposition of their Catholic fellow-citizens" (April 1834, 457). In challenging Hardiman for possession of this national tradition, in part through the claim to offer a more accurate representation of that past, Ferguson sought to establish that Protestants loved and identified with Ireland as much as anyone did. Through their study, through their recovery of old "Irish" texts and their production of new ones, Protestants would thus also accumulate cultural authority with which to legitimize their political position, eventually to graduate out of their ascendancy role as alien usurpers and to earn a rightful place in Ireland's future.

There is much to admire in this vision, and much that will reappear in Matthew Arnold's work *On The Study of Celtic Literature* more than thirty years later. Against the "pathos" and "desire," the "natural piety," and the "patriarchal loyalty" that Ferguson perceived in the native Irish character, he offered Protestant Ireland's tradition of "enlightenment," "free inquiry," and "representative government." Inspired by poetry and the very atmosphere of Ireland, enemies would set aside generations of war and famine to unite in a common bond. "What material for an almost perfect society does the national genius not present?" (Oct. 1834, 467), Ferguson asked, and part IV of his essay begins with a rich description of just such a society. Couples sit by a clean hearth, a milkmaid sings, the linen trade revives, and Ireland enjoys its "legitimate prosperity."

Ferguson here envisions, not just a rich cultural past and a prosperous material future, but also a powerful continuity between the two. A century later, Eamon de Valera would successfully shape his political and economic strategies around a similarly arcadian idyll, while writers and literary critics have continued to mine this style and sentiment to the present day. Robert O'Driscoll defined the ideal limits of this literary market with his 1976 appraisal:

> Ferguson's analysis of the qualities of Irish poetry in 1834 and his assessment of the character of the people who produced this poetry was the first time an enlightened member of the ascendant nation with original literary sensitivities had investigated imaginatively the cultural heritage of his Catholic countrymen.... Indeed, so significant were Ferguson's translations from the Irish that we can point with conviction to 1834 as marking the beginning of the movement that produced a distinctive Irish literature in English.[27]

More recent commentators, by contrast, such as David Cairns and Shaun Richards, have stressed Ferguson's political agenda, his plan "to enter into the study of the Irish past in order to set the rules of its discourse. Once this was accomplished, the identification of the Anglo-Irish and the masses could be underpinned by culture and this would enable the successful proselytization of the Irish and

---

27. Robert O'Driscoll, *An Ascendancy of the Heart: Ferguson and the Beginnings of Modern Irish Literature in English* (Dublin: Dolman, 1976), 77–78. For a similar but more recent assessment of Ferguson's role in the development of the *DUM*, see also John P. McBride, "The *Dublin University Magazine*: Cultural Nationality and Tory Ideology in an Irish Literary and Political Journal, 1833–1852," 2 vols. (Ph.D. diss., Trinity College, Dublin, 1987). McBride claims that Ferguson's contributions to the magazine "most clearly exemplify the *DUM*'s capacity to transcend tribal platitude, to replace it with genuine investigation into what being Irish signified and sincere speculation on what being Irish could signify. Ferguson exhibits the encounter between the magazine's political and cultural aspirations at its most fruitful" (1:360).

their winning from Popery."[28] Between such views, where might the legitimate prosperity of the Hardiman essay lie?

Whether we regard Ferguson's essay as ideal prophecy or cynical souperism, we still cannot fail to note its emphasis, not on harmony and mutual compatibility between the two religions, but on the spiritual triumph of Protestantism over Catholicism. Consider O'Driscoll's sequence of modifiers to describe Ferguson's essay: *first, enlightened, ascendant, original literary, imaginatively.* The implied logic contains assumptions that seem to render Hardiman irrelevant on an increasing number of counts. Nor did Ferguson himself have much room for Hardiman within his ideal vision of the future. Part I of his essay had begun with a rhetorical question: who dares to keep Protestants apart from the Catholics of Ireland? Not until part IV would he answer this: "Mr. Hardiman has interposed himself between us and our countrymen at large . . ." (Nov. 1834, 516). Two pages further on, the vision has sunk much lower to accommodate an extended description of Hardiman grotesquely choking on his own words.

Ferguson had no Catholic readers to offend by this tasteless flight of fancy. They would, in any case, have been well prepared for it by a proposal in part III of his essay: scriptural education. What this had to do with investigating Ireland's ancient heritage Ferguson did not explain, although his agenda for the modern age was clear: "to check the progress of Popish domination" (Oct. 1834, 450). In the earlier piece "A Dialogue between the Head and Heart of an Irish Protestant," too, Ferguson's "Head" had looked forward longingly to "the conversion of the Irish Romanists" (Nov. 1833, 589). Yet we disregard his achievement if we dismiss his essay on Hardiman for urging Protestants to proselytize, since it also contains Ferguson's aesthetic criteria as well as his own verse translations. This latter combination would help reveal a genuine cultural resource for Ire-

---

28. David Cairns and Shaun Richards, *Writing Ireland: Colonialism, Nationalism, and Culture* (Manchester: Manchester University Press, 1988), 31.

land, one in serious danger of dying out as Gaelic came increasingly to seem the language of poverty, backwardness, and famine. Ferguson rendered Gaelic verses into English with a poetic skill markedly superior to Hardiman's. Even though Ferguson's translations did not appear in book form, as *Lays of the Western Gael*, until 1864,[29] they still felt even then like a fresh new voice in Irish literature. And by then his career had sorted out the interwoven claims of politics and literature: he had dedicated his work primarily to words, not causes, and for future writers like W. B. Yeats, his words had a great deal to say.

29. Although the title page of *Lays of the Western Gael* shows the date 1865, the volume actually appeared in late 1864.

2

## THE STEP INTO EXCELLENCE

I

Taking stock of the *Dublin University Magazine* in December 1833, after its first year of operation, inaugural editor Charles Stuart Stanford had good reason to congratulate the magazine: "We have already, as we think, done wonders . . ." (Insert for Dec. 1833, 7). After only six monthly issues, James M'Glashan, operating through the firm of the *DUM*'s publisher William Curry, had picked up the financial burden previously carried by the original group of founders; favorable reviews had appeared in both the national and the foreign press; and an international readership was steadily expanding. As Stanford noted, "there are now few of the libraries at home or abroad where we are not to be found . . ." (4). Stanford attributed much of this growth to those who appreciated the magazine for its conservative political analyses. But since it billed itself as a literary as well as a political magazine, and since the literary contributions too often showed "too manifest a rusticity in the garb" (4), the *DUM* could so far still only dream of one day rivaling *Blackwood's* and *Fraser's*, not just in physical appearance, but also in overall quality.

In but a few more years, though, the magazine could well claim that it offered its readers an excellent choice of both literature and politics. In addressing the relentless series of crises that kept battering Irish Protestantism, the *DUM* continued to serve as both political witness and forum. At the same time, and with equal complexity and intellectual sophistication, the literary strengths of the *DUM* soon established it as a magazine known and respected throughout Europe. Samuel Ferguson published his four-part essay on Hardiman and a long series called the *Hibernian Nights' Entertainments*. James Clarence Mangan contributed regular poems, translations, and essays. William Carleton and Charles Lever serialized their first novels here and would continue their affiliation with the *DUM* for years to come, as would Joseph Sheridan Le Fanu after beginning his literary career with a series of short stories in the magazine.

One factor contributing to these literary achievements was the new editor, Isaac Butt, who took over from Stanford in August 1834 and who stayed on until November 1838. A brilliant undergraduate at Trinity College and one of the original founders of the *DUM*, Butt was still only twenty years old when he assumed the editorship, little more than a literary and political amateur. Nonetheless, during Butt's four-year term the magazine improved in striking ways. While its first year had prospered more than anyone expected, the future still looked tentative at best. Under Butt's editorship, the *DUM* took those last few necessary steps into the established journalistic marketplace, where it held its own for the next forty years.

II

An August 1834 editorial in Butt's inaugural issue of the *DUM* touched on most of the ideological themes that would concern the magazine for the rest of his tenure as editor: the crucial role of the Established Church in Ireland, the treachery and error of Catholicism, the folly of the liberal Whig government in Westminster, the need for religious education, and, in startling ways, the possibility of the repeal of the Union.[1] While Daniel O'Connell had introduced

---

1. Authorship of this editorial is uncertain. *The Wellesley Index to Victorian Periodicals 1824–1900*, ed. Walter E. Houghton (Toronto: University of Toronto Press, 1987), 4: 221, attributes it to Samuel O'Sullivan on the basis of internal evidence, whereas

the question of repeal into the House of Commons earlier that same year, it was a prospect that the *DUM* had so far refused to countenance. The editorial in Butt's inaugural issue, however, entitled "The Irish Church Commission, and the Coronation Oath," begins with "a truth" from which other propositions and conclusions will be derived: "Great Britain is a Protestant State" (Aug. 1834, 121). Not surprisingly, one of the conclusions, further demanded by "all the maxims of political wisdom, and all the sanctions of religious duty," is that the government should "employ every means which the spirit of Christianity will recognise, to destroy and exterminate Popery in Ireland" (128). For Catholicism, the *DUM* warned, is "the worst tyranny, civil or religious, that ever trampled upon the slaves of superstition . . ." (124).

Some readers missed the fine distinctions drawn here; the London *Sun,* for instance, which reviewed this August issue and came to the conclusion that the *DUM* desired simply to do away with all Irish Catholics. Not so, retorted the magazine indignantly (Oct. 1834, 468); it had carefully defined the problem, not as Catholics, but as Catholicism. Within the *DUM*'s view, the Catholic people themselves had originally and deservedly lost their property in Ireland and afterwards suffered under the discriminatory penal code because of their hostility towards the British constitution and the principles of civil liberty; but the motivation for this treason had come from their allegiance to Rome and to a priest-ridden dogma that continued to enslave their consciences. A later article repeated the *DUM*'s insistence that Protestants should not abandon the Catholics of Ireland to their "debasing superstition." The people still possessed noble virtues amid "all their crimes and follies" and despite "the thraldom of Rome" (July 1836, 7).

Subsequent monthly issues brought greater precision to the discussion as well as more violence to the rhetoric. The priesthood, as

---

Terence de Vere White's biography of Isaac Butt, *Road of Excess,* 11–12, attributes it to Butt.

"the colossal curse of Ireland," was deemed directly or indirectly responsible for "all the crimes, and the misery, and the heartburnings, and animosities, and bloodshed, and treasons that darken the face of the land . . ." (Sept. 1834, 312). The *DUM* then cast suspicious eyes on the secrecy of the confessional, where priests routinely questioned women about their sexual behavior and thus violated the virtue of Irish womanhood (Aug. 1835, 140). Laws of logic, politics, religion, and even common decency clearly demanded the extermination of Irish Catholicism.

Unfortunately, the *DUM* felt, this solution to so many of England's and Ireland's problems was blocked by the British Whigs. The magazine lashed them for their "folly and presumption," their "magic spells" and "necromancy." One specific target was a government commission recently formed by Parliament for the purpose of conducting a religious census in Ireland. Some parishes contained but few members of the Established Church, and these smaller benefices might be abolished following the results of the census. The surplus income from the suppressed benefices would then apply toward the education of the whole population, with no regard for religion. Along with so many other political events considered by the magazine in its early years, this one quickly assumed crisis proportions: "The new commission puts the Irish Church upon her trial . . ." (Aug. 1834, 124). Weakness or inaction on the part of Protestants would only encourage those who sought to diminish the power of the Church of Ireland, hence the need to head off this government proposal to divert Protestant revenues into priestly pockets. The thinking behind such a plan, the *DUM* charged, confused the "religious wants" of the Protestant community with the "ignorance or the superstitions" of the Catholics (Aug. 1834, 220). "A Plain Thinker" accounted for the folly of the current government by describing the Whigs as political atheists. The Tories, by contrast, properly "acknowledge that nations as well as individuals are bound by the sanctions of religion . . ." (Feb. 1835, 125).

While the apocalyptic tone of such discussions moderated only slightly over the next few months, the *DUM* did expand its repertoire of explanations beyond the limits of religion and "magic spells" to include the material processes of history as well. On the issue of Catholic Emancipation, for instance, "the first great wound given to Protestantism in Ireland" (Jan. 1837, 124), the *DUM* complained, in its earlier and more strident phase, that the new Catholic M.P.s had "introduced Popish barbarism, falsehood, and treason into our English legislature" (Nov. 1835, 521). From their new platform in Westminster, they could violate their constitutional oaths with impunity, by encouraging violence in the Irish countryside, because the Whigs allowed political expediencies to overrule religious truths. Three years later, by contrast, and with considerably more insight into the significance of emancipation to broader patterns of Irish history, the *DUM* noted that "it gave vigour and courage to the friends of revolution by giving an example of a great public change effected by a system of agitation which was little short of treason" (July 1838, 113). The realization that agitation brought results would indeed profoundly change the whole nature of nineteenth-century politics in Ireland.

### III

A common pattern to the *DUM*'s political commentary from this time showed a periodic alternation between bleak pessimism and guarded confidence. In 1835, one article could hearken back to the lead editorial in the *DUM*'s inaugural issue, Samuel O'Sullivan's political dialogue "The Present Crisis," but now with a hopeful title: "The Present Is Not a Crisis" (Nov. 1835, 505). Not half a year later, the *DUM* felt compelled to note that "the present is the most awful crisis in the history of England" (April 1836, 436). Such instability, within both the political and the editorial landscape, could easily have caused the magazine to collapse. Writers like Butt and O'Sullivan could still recall the ideological disagreements that had prevented some of their own Trinity College friends from joining the venture at the outset. Moreover, at the back of their minds lingered that half belief in Irish fatality and failure. One article, seeking to account for the miscarriage of the Reformation in Ireland, suggested: "There seems to be a spirit walking through the length and breadth of the land that delights in marring every thing . . ." (May 1835, 594). A follow-up piece complained ominously that "everything has been crushed to the earth by that dark doom that enshrouds all that seems calculated to emancipate our island from her darkness, her sorrows, and her crimes" (July 1835, 50). Conscious of its own ambition and potential as an emancipator, the *DUM* was just as keenly aware of the odds against such a magazine realizing its lofty ideals. Besides all of the external threats—from journalistic competitors and a fickle readership, from British Whigs and Irish agitators—the magazine also warned against internal enemies: the "apathy," the "disunion," or perhaps even the "cowardice" of Protestants themselves (Aug. 1834, 135). The magazine could stoutly claim, "To our political principles we have been steady . . ." (Dec. 1835, 709). At the same time, and representing a shrinking minority that already occupied but a vague margin of Irish society, the *DUM* had plenty of good reasons for abandoning the whole business.

While it might waver between pessimism and confidence, however, the *DUM* never showed cowardice or apathy. The magazine rejected the passive, defensive policies it had perceived within the Tory party and instead pursued a conservative line, active, energetic, fearlessly on the offensive. The boldness of such intellectual assaults derived in part from a strong faith in education, an ideal that the *DUM* had stressed since its inception and one that English policy makers had also embraced. In the early 1830s, for instance, the Committee of Public Instruction in Bengal confidently assumed that an English educational system would soon convert the local Indian population, not just to an "English" culture, but also to the Christian religion. As the *DUM* saw it, a political magazine could play an informative role for all of Great Britain and Ireland simply by occupying a prominent niche within the journalistic marketplace. More specifically and ambitiously, though, the magazine called for major increases in religious education: "We advocate a system of *Proselytism* on a large and extended scale, supported by the public and patronised by the government . . ." (Sept. 1834, 312). Such proposals, common in Ireland since well before the start of William Magee's "Second Reformation," developed further throughout the evangelical movement that included such *DUM* figures as Mortimer and Samuel O'Sullivan and Caesar Otway. While proselytizing did little more than add fuel to Catholic agitation over tithes, emancipation, and repeal, claims for the efficacy of religious instruction persisted in Protestant Ireland as late as the 1859 evangelical revival. In the mid-1830s, therefore, it was still easy to hope that such instruction might one day lead Catholics as well as Bengalis out of error, both political and religious, and into the unifying, harmonizing Protestant Church.

Until such time as these civilizing conversions could take place, however, the *DUM* suggested that the country might realize other benefits of education within the more accessible confines of the voting booth. An expanded franchise had everywhere revealed the "cloven foot of democracy" (March 1838, 353), the magazine insisted, and it saw Irish Catholics in particular as having flagrantly abused the voting privileges granted them under the Relief Act of 1793. Voting qualifications thus needed closer scrutiny so as to strike from the rolls those too poor or ignorant to deserve a vote. The *DUM* argued that a more extensive registration of Protestants, as well as more protection of Catholic voters against priestly intimidation, would produce a responsible electorate that would support good government in Ireland. The magazine's calls for drives to register the "right" voters and for various degrees of franchise reform illustrate a common conservative premise for this period, one that also led to proselytizing: the truth, in the hands of good, well-informed people, will work. The abstract terms of the premise retain their humanistic innocence up to the point at which they get translated into Ireland's concrete religious and political experience.

A closely related concern was the "infidel" National Education system. Founded in 1831, it had eliminated the previously existing grants to Protestant schools and replaced them with a state system of elementary education, separate from any denominational religious instruction. The *DUM* opposed the national system throughout Butt's tenure. In 1835 it termed the National Education Board an "offspring of crafty priests and silly ministers," an "expensive and ostentatious nuisance" (Dec. 1835, 696), devoting major articles to the subject in February and July 1837 and February 1838. The Whig government only compounded the outrages of such a system by proposing a tax on the Church of Ireland in order to fund the program it had so foolishly originated. By 1838, the *DUM* still felt that "the educational system which is patronised by the government is one of the greatest of the curses which Whig misrule has ever inflicted upon unfortunate Ireland" (Feb. 1838, 195–96). Throughout these charges, or the demands for franchise reform of the electorate, or the repeated calls for greater scrutiny, more inquiry, further investigations, there runs a firm faith in the power of truth and the benefits of education. The problem with the British government, insisted the magazine, was its ignorance of Ireland's real situation, its repeated attempts to impose British solutions onto Irish problems. Once all the facts became known, Whigs and Irish Catholics alike would surely embrace a more conservative position with the zeal of converts.

Like most of the political issues that would confront the *DUM*'s new editor, education was also mentioned within the editorial that inaugurated Butt's term. The most startling item in that editorial, however, because unprecedented in the pages of the *DUM,* was the hint that Irish Protestants, under some circumstances, might justifiably support repeal of the Union with Great Britain. The *DUM* relied on the process of logic to prove its point: the Act of Union in 1800 established Protestantism as the state religion of Great Britain and Ireland; if the British Parliament later suppressed Protestant benefices in Ireland, then under the terms of the Act, the Union would be repealed. "We know well," the *DUM* continued, in language even more threatening, the manly determination—the moral confidence—the undaunted bravery of the Orangemen of Ireland; and we know also, that it needs but a little more of faithless oppression, of unprincipled ingratitude, on the part of the British government, to cause all that determination, all that confidence, and all that bravery, to be employed against British connexion as energetically, aye, and as successfully, as it ever was in its behalf. When the moral energy of the Protestant is united with the physical force of the Roman Catholic population, the combination will be irresistible. (Aug. 1834, 133)

The *DUM* little knew how accurately it was forecasting the political combination that Butt himself, on behalf of what would then be called Home Rule and not repeal, would later help to foster.

IV

Butt's first issue as editor was not entirely taken up with political causes. There were poems by regulars such as James Clarence Mangan and William Blacker ("Fitz Stewart"), a facetious piece called "Twenty-Two Illustrations of 'Humbug,'" a travel piece on Spain, a review of a military history by W. F. P. Napier, and a further installment of the *DUM*'s first significant serialized novel, written by Henry David Inglis and entitled *Scenes from the Life of Edward Lascelles, Gent*. Inglis, mostly known for his popular travel books on Europe, had begun his novel in March 1834, and it continued, with several long gaps between issues, until July 1837 (15 installments), the same year in which it saw book publication.

*Lascelles* is a "nautical novel," a genre popular in the 1830s in part because of British naval involvement in the Napoleonic Wars. It recounts six years in the life of its narrator and central character, the Yorkshireman Edward Lascelles, who goes to sea as an officer while still a boy of thirteen. Lascelles's status as a gentleman gains him not only his position as ship's officer but also the immediate and automatic respect of the whole crew. Within the utopian framework of shipboard life, away from the complexities and abstractions of land-based social structures, the officers and crew can rely on all the best traditions of their shared British backgrounds and so conduct business efficiently, contentedly, and with perfect justice. This sometimes means tracking down a vicious slave ship, at other times excusing a sailor from a deserved flogging because the captain's superior wisdom and mercy can bend the iron laws of the sea.

Within the novel's loosely episodic structure, the recurring theme of justice always serves to anchor the disparate sea-going adventures. As the novel progresses, it becomes increasingly less of an adventure story and more the kind of travel book that Inglis frequently wrote. Greater attention to different civilizations, however, means greater complexity and a growing fear that the universe may finally be governed, not by justice, but by chance. No longer can the benevolent comradeship of life at sea protect promising young men from sudden and violent death, for instance. When Lascelles leaves behind the pettiness, squalor, and incompetence of lesser ships, though, and transfers to the flagship of the fleet, he discovers that such values as justice do, in fact, continue to survive in life, sustained by the British aristocracy:

> the Flag-ship was officered by *gentlemen;* and where this is the case, there is little fear but everything will go on pleasantly and well. This vessel, indeed, may be said to have been a perfect ark of aristocracy; she numbered, among her officers, young men of the first families in England. (Oct. 1835, 426)

The aristocratic system began Lascelles's career by placing him above older and more experienced men; late in the novel, his reaffirmation of this system not only establishes an aesthetic unity to his whole narrative, it also mirrors the nature of the system as a closed, self-perpetuating circle.

Just as flagships were hard to come by, however, unity and harmony within such circles were hard to maintain, with differences of opinion emerging, for instance, even among the *DUM*'s own contributing writers. In a review of Inglis's book *Journey Through Ireland in 1834,* the *DUM* detected a "Whig bias" underlying his observations about the state of the Irish nation (Jan. 1835, 1). Another author closely associated with the founding stages of the *DUM,* Samuel

Lover, was roughed up more thoroughly in a review of his 1837 novel *Rory O'More, a National Romance:* "He has miserably failed" (Jan. 1838, 71). The romance had also worn thin in the relationship between the magazine and its namesake university, the *DUM* getting quite blunt on this point after only two years of operation: "We desire that there should be nothing in our pages to distinguish us as a University Magazine. The truth is, that if we had our name to choose, our present denomination is not the one we would adopt." While the magazine no longer felt free to give up the name under which its already considerable prestige had been won, it did want to emphasize that it was in no way "the organ of the heads of the University—of them we are perfectly independent" (Dec. 1835, 710). Besides objecting to some of the University officials who were Whigs, the *DUM* also disliked the recent tutoring system. Such local complaints typically got aired in the miscellaneous column that Isaac Butt wrote, still under the pseudonym of "Anthony Poplar," at the close of many of the issues from his editorship.

One of the *DUM*'s most prolific contributors during this period continued to be Samuel Ferguson. He had published about one poem per issue from mid-1833 to mid-1834; now, under Butt's editorship, Ferguson's main contributions became prose works such as the remainder of the Hardiman essay, travel pieces promoting Ireland, or *Hibernian Nights' Entertainments,* a loosely framed series of tales that ran almost monthly from December 1834 to May 1836 (fifteen installments).[2] Supposedly narrated by an Irish *shanachie,* or storyteller, in 1592, these historical romances, often drawn from Irish mythology, recount experiences of heroic failure, treachery, and ruin. W. J. Mc Cormack unravels several narrative layers within these tales, layers that derive their ironic resonance from Ferguson's role as a voice for Protestant ascendancy. Like the Arabian Nights' tales, like the *DUM* itself, the *Hibernian* tales seek "a postponement,

---

2. About the *Hibernian Nights' Entertainments,* Peter Denman, *Samuel Ferguson,* 34, claims (incorrectly) that it was the "first serial fiction to be published" in the *DUM*.

perhaps even a transvaluation, of extinction."³ Peter Denman relates the tales to similar patterns of ambivalence and wavering within Protestant Ireland: "All of the pieces in *Hibernian Nights' Entertainments* are, in one way or another, fictions of crossover, in which the loyalties of a character are, through misunderstanding or persuasion, transferred at least in part to the opposing side."⁴ Ferguson's collection did not appear in book form until 1887; nonetheless, like his Hardiman essay, these tales forecast with remarkable accuracy the themes that would dominate so much of the consciousness of later Irish writers such as W. B. Yeats.

Ferguson followed the *Entertainments* with a series of four essays expanding the *DUM*'s attention to travel writing that would look increasingly toward Ireland for its scenery of choice (July, Sept., and Dec. 1836, and Jan. 1837). A closing passage in the final installment, "The Capabilities of Ireland," summarizes the flavor of the whole series:

> In fine, whether we consider our country as a scene in which the tourist may converse with nature under her most agreeable forms; or as a theatre in which the philosophic traveller may study society under its most interesting and characteristic aspects; or as a field of commercial adventure, in which the practical and the moneyed man may look for a fair reward for industry, and a compensating return for capital, in the prosecution of meritorious labours and benevolent speculations, we see on every hand good cause for hope, and honest pride, and self-congratulation. (Jan. 1837, 57)

Denman argues that these four essays had a "far-reaching effect on Ferguson's poetic career," insofar as they drew him to the favorable attention of Charles Gavan Duffy, whose 1845 anthology *The Ballad Poetry of Ireland* would come to include a number of Ferguson's poems, several of them originally published in the *DUM*.⁵ Even within the *DUM*'s own range of offerings, however, the series made a com-

---

3. Seamus Deane, ed., *The Field Day Anthology of Irish Writing*, vol. 1 (Derry: Field Day, 1991), 1185.
4. Denman, *Samuel Ferguson*, 43.
5. Ibid., 33.

pelling case for why the magazine might build its travel writing in large part around Ireland. The unlikely blend here of romantic idealism and utilitarian practicality also illustrates an impulse that would continue to characterize both the *DUM* as a whole and Ferguson in particular. While his prose here inevitably reminds us of chamber-of-commerce brochures, its boundless optimism and inclusive sweep point to those qualities that would go on to establish him as one of Ireland's main advocates in the nineteenth century.

v

W. B. Yeats's poem "To Ireland in the Coming Times" numbers Ferguson as one of his nineteenth-century forerunners but also includes another of Butt's most prolific contributors, the poet James Clarence Mangan. Better known for his later and more nationalistic work, which the *DUM* would not see fit to print, Mangan already showed, through his technical experiments in the 1830s, the stylistic sophistication that would later catch Yeats's ear. Many of Mangan's innovations developed out of English renderings from German poets such as Goethe and Schiller. His *Anthologia Germanica,* a series of essays and accompanying translations of German poets, began in January 1835 with a piece on Schiller, perhaps Mangan's favorite German writer. The series ran through twenty-three installments, until 1846, and became the only book-length volume Mangan published during his lifetime. A similar series, *Stray Leaflets from the German Oak,* added another ten installments over the same period (Aug. 1836–Nov. 1847). Along with John Anster, Mangan helped make German literature a regular feature in the *DUM* from its outset, a cultural interest that continued to flourish in the magazine until Mangan's death in 1849.[6]

Other poets who were well represented in the *DUM* during Butt's editorship include Digby Pilot Starkey (still writing under the pen

---

6. See Patrick O'Neill, *Ireland and Germany: A Study in Literary Relations* (New York: Peter Lang, 1985), 96–117, for a discussion of the *DUM*'s coverage of German literature during its career.

name "Advena"); Felicia Hemans (until her death in 1835); the Scotch poet Robert Gilfillan; the later editor of the *DUM* John Francis Waller ("Iota"), who contributed poems as well as verse translations from Italian; and James Wills ("J.U.U."). Besides a number of poems, Wills also contributed essays and a short story (June 1836) about an Irish family tragedy. His literary career had gotten off to a controversial start when he allowed the Irish Gothic novelist Charles Robert Maturin to publish Wills's poem *The Universe* (1821) under Maturin's name. While this rescued Maturin's precarious finances, he then refused ever to acknowledge Wills as the author. Even more embarrassing to Wills's career was his own attack on a book by Henry O'Brien, a review published in the *DUM* (April 1834) and supposedly so upsetting to O'Brien that he killed himself. Whether because of or in spite of such credentials, Wills also served as the acting editor of the *DUM* during Butt's tenure, for "two or three months in the early part of 1836."[7] As a writer, Wills ranged widely in his interests, from literature to metaphysics to Irish folklore and history. In January 1836, the *DUM* unveiled the "Gallery of Illustrious Irishmen," a long-standing series of biographical sketches from the past. Wills contributed two early items to this series and later issued his own biographical work, the highly regarded *Lives of Illustrious and Distinguished Irishmen*, a multi-volume study published in Dublin between 1839 and 1847.

From the other writers in Butt's stable, the Irish novelist Barbara Hemphill made her first appearance in print with a short story, "The Royal Confession" (Sept. 1838), and another short story was contributed by Anna Maria Hall (Nov. 1838). In the review "Chinese Historical Dramas and Romances," the *DUM* claimed for itself the distinction of being the "first periodical to bring the popular literature of China before the British nation" (Nov. 1834, 555). William Archer Butler was a frequent contributor—his works included re-

7. Letter from Isaac Butt, cited in *University Magazine* (June 1879, 710). The *DUM* for October 1875, 404, however, claims that Wills served as the magazine's acting editor for up to twelve months "during the absence of the editor from Dublin."

views and essays on American poetry, poetic imagination, Oliver Goldsmith, natural theology, and romantic vision, besides his own poems and a political prophecy—set in 1898—warning of the dangers should disestablishment of the Church of Ireland ever become a reality. The "Ettrick Shepherd" James Hogg contributed a short story in November 1834, and William Hamilton Maxwell continued his "Rambling Recollections," a series of autobiographical/fictional sketches begun in April 1834 and lasting until November 1835 (five installments). John Anster published in book form in 1835 an acclaimed translation of the first part of Goethe's *Faust*, much of which had appeared in 1820 in *Blackwood's;* for the *DUM,* he now wrote reviews of the poetry of Goethe, Wordsworth, and Coleridge.

On the nonliterary side, William Johnston continued his on-the-London-parliamentary-scene commentary, and the Scottish naturalist John Scouler wrote reviews of such subjects as science and natural theology. A twelve-part series, *By-Ways of Irish History,* probably written by Mortimer and Samuel O'Sullivan, ran from August 1837 until March 1839.[8] The series was needed, according to the *DUM,* since other histories of Ireland were misleading because of their British bias (Aug. 1837, 205). Also including prose writers such as Charles Lever, William Carleton, George Brittaine, and Joseph Sheridan Le Fanu, this stable of writers helped establish the *DUM* as a genuine rival to *Blackwood's* and *Fraser's.*

VI

In the second year of Butt's editorship, however, and not at all buoyed by the excellence of its rising literary fortunes, the *DUM* pitched its perennial tone of crisis to even more pessimistic levels. The immediate occasion arose out of Sir Robert Peel's resignation as Prime Minister. Peel had taken office in December 1834, but on a

---

8. The *Wellesley Index,* 4:233, attributes this series to the O'Sullivans on the basis of strong internal evidence.

Tory base so shaky that he had to step down in April 1835, when the Whigs took over behind Lord Melbourne. Even so, their own losses in the 1835 general election forced the Whigs into an alliance, the "Lichfield House Compact," with Daniel O'Connell, Peel's old political enemy and the *DUM*'s all-purpose monthly scapegoat. "The Protestants of Ireland have been sold," raged the magazine: "they have been sold by the Whigs for the support of Mr. O'Connell" (May 1835, 604). The "Whigling Deformers" were "paltry" and "pernicious," the Melbourne-O'Connell alliance "monstrous," a "degrading tyranny." The "foul slanderer" O'Connell continued to receive his usual savaging in the magazine's political commentary, in December 1835 even meriting a lengthy and vicious political satire entitled "The Jew and the Beggarman." Peel, by contrast, "the first statesman of his own day" (Feb. 1837, 141), rose higher and higher in the *DUM*'s estimation, even though the Lichfield Compact was holding distressingly fast and would continue to do so until 1841.

During the mid-1830s, various reform measures continued to shake the power of the Church of Ireland, and various organizations sprang up in an attempt to control the losses. In 1836 alone, the Irish Protestant Association, the Church Missionary Society, the Society for the Relief of Distressed Protestants, and the Irish Metropolitan Conservative Society were founded. This latter group, an offshoot of the earlier Protestant Conservative Society of Ireland, is a particularly revealing map of the political, religious, and class anxieties that swirled around and converged within the *DUM*. Main figures connected to the Society included Samuel O'Sullivan, the economist and *DUM* contributor Mountifort Longfield, and Butt himself. W. J. Mc Cormack describes the Society as "essentially an urban organization" and estimates the membership at "about one thousand, the bulk of whom lived in Dublin and were connected with the professions or with commerce."[9] In April 1836, the same month that

---

9. W. J. Mc Cormack, *From Burke to Beckett: Ascendancy, Tradition and Betrayal in Literary History* (Cork: Cork University Press, 1994), 144.

saw the founding of the Society, the *DUM* described such new Protestant organizations as "the only hope of rallying the friends of religion and of order, against the advocates of unmitigated democracy in the one country, and of democracy demonized by the spirit of popery in the other. The final battle is now to be fought" (436), all the more perilous because even England now posed more of a threat than a bulwark.

On the political front, and despite support from Peel and many of the Tories, the Church of Ireland soon came to rely far more on the House of Lords than on the Commons for its survival. Fearing the worst itself, the *DUM* nonetheless shifted its editorial position on Church reform. The magazine initially had refused to countenance any proposals to regulate and redistribute Church revenues, since previous concessions had invariably just led to new demands. With the Whigs back in power, though, the *DUM* began softening its intransigence on the grounds that the Whigs had put the Irish Protestant clergy into a desperate position and that something thus had to be done to prevent the complete destruction of the Church (March 1835, 241; May 1835, 493). Trouble for the clergy had been building throughout the last half of the 1820s, when worsening economic conditions led the peasantry to resent even more tithes paid for the support of the Protestant establishment. Here, too, the *DUM* welcomed reform, seeing the substitution of composition-rent, to be collected by the landlords, as preferable to direct tithes, collected by the clergy, for the magazine felt that these measures would strengthen the position of the Protestant clergy (Jan. 1835, 79). The Tithe War, begun in 1831, was ended by the Rent-Charge Act in August 1838, which introduced the kind of financial arrangement that the *DUM* had advocated. In that landlords now absorbed many of the costs of tithes previously borne by the tenants, the Church of Ireland gained through these measures, and the issue of tithes was effectively and permanently settled.

As Desmond Bowen points out, however, one pernicious effect of the Rent-Charge Act was to increase further the isolation of the

Protestant clergy from the Catholic masses.[10] While the *DUM* recognized this possible consequence, it also saw the Tithe War putting heavy economic pressure on the clergy, especially those in the more isolated rural communities. On a different issue, however, a proposed Poor Law Bill for Ireland, the magazine was able to argue for a close connection between Protestant and Catholic. In July 1837, with that Bill under consideration in Westminster, the *DUM* reviewed Isaac Butt's pamphlet discussing the proposal and agreed with Butt in seeing this legislative response as unsuited to Irish problems. Not only did it place an unfair burden on Irish landlords, but it also institutionalized the administration of charity. Relief should instead be controlled at the local level, the *DUM* insisted, where parish vestries could apportion funds more knowledgeably and fairly. Moreover, this system would also allow the Protestant clergy a chance to offer the people spiritual as well as material relief, since "the physical sufferings of the people can only be efficaciously and permanently relieved, by raising them from their state of moral degradation" (July 1837, 77), that is, from Catholicism. While the death of William IV in June 1837 delayed Irish legislation, by 1838 Parliament had passed a Poor Law for Ireland, one that neither addressed Irish poverty in a sufficiently comprehensive way nor followed the principles advocated by the *DUM*.

## VII

A powerful combination of Catholic political, agrarian, and religious forces would continue to influence Westminster throughout the 1830s; but it also drove conservative Ireland, including the Established Church, into an increasingly reactionary position in response to the incursions. Still, the conservative position never lost its ability to adjust quickly to changes, to reunite, and to reorganize for more effective resistance to further change. The strategy kept proving its resilience, coherence, and durability throughout the century.

---

10. Bowen, *Protestant Crusade*, 176.

Perhaps the most radical example of this strategy within the *DUM* centered around the issue of repeal of the Union. Throughout 1833, despite criticism of various Whig policies, nothing in the magazine seriously advocated any kind of separation from England. In June 1834, the *DUM* praised "Britain's glory" as all but immortal and pronounced repeal "a question which could only have originated with the wicked or the brainless . . ." (June 1834, 713). By the time Butt assumed the editorship, however, this view no longer applied, and the *DUM* restated its sentiments a year later: if the property of the Established Church is ever confiscated, "no Irishman owes the imperial parliament any further obedience—the compact of the Union is violated—and the Union is, to all intents and purposes, *repealed*" (Aug. 1835, 134). Later articles sought to establish that England's unjust and unwise policies had kept Ireland from ever enjoying proper government and that persistent misgovernment would lead to either repeal or civil war. By mid-1836, the "days of British greatness" seemed numbered, and should this prove to be the case, then "in the convulsion that may rend the empire asunder, the Irish nation may rise upon the ruins, and maintain a proud position of civil and religious independence" (July 1836, 7). Sentiments like these, central to Butt's early conservatism, had already by the 1830s pointed the way for him toward the nationalist Home Rule platform he would later occupy with much greater popular visibility, albeit to the scorn and dismay of the magazine that he had so ably edited at the outset of his career.

To justify its frequent tone of apocalyptic immediacy, the *DUM* developed a lengthy but fairly simple domino theory, whose first stage hinged upon the outcome of Irish elections: "The destinies of mankind hang upon the contest, and the Protestants of Ireland who guard the Thermopylae by which British greatness is assailed, hold the keys of the Protestantism of the world" (Sept. 1837, 252). Protestants in Ireland function as "an incorruptible fortress in a hostile land, . . . a stable barrier against the first outbreak of revolt" (Jan. 1837, 122). Protestant apathy would result in election defeats and, shortly thereafter, the end of Irish Protestantism, which would cause English Protestantism also to fall. Its crucial religious foundation shattered, the whole British Empire would go next, since England now stagnated under the reign of an eighteen-year-old queen named Victoria, who almost certainly could not tell a good conservative adviser from a bad liberal one. Next would fall Western civilization, which rested upon the Empire, followed by world Protestantism, and after that, there really was nothing left to speak of. Much depended, therefore, on the civilizing presence of Ireland's small Protestant minority, a barrier against the outbreak of revolution.

The most visible members of this barrier were the resident Protestant rectors scattered throughout Ireland, men like Joseph Sheridan Le Fanu's father. Dean Le Fanu had previously been chaplain of the Royal Hibernian School in Phoenix Park, a position then taken over by Samuel O'Sullivan. After 1835, the *DUM* began devoting increasing space to regular accounts of violence against these isolated representatives of the Church of Ireland. The *DUM* also pinned many of its hopes on the Protestant middle classes in general, for "their attachment to the constitution" defined "the real strength of Conservative principles" (Sept. 1837, 243). Pushing the issues into more definite focus, the magazine suggested: "If political salvation is to be hoped for, it is in that class it will be found" (Nov. 1837, 532). At the same time, the *DUM* had a realistic sense of just what could be expected from the future. In an October 1838 essay called "Cassandra in Ireland," the magazine looked sixty years up the road and foresaw, accurately, that Irish Protestantism would not succeed in avoiding the fatal step of disestablishment.

After giving up his editorship of the magazine in 1838, the year in which he was called to the bar, Butt embarked on what would become a much more auspicious career in law and politics. In the 1860s he ably defended several accused Fenian prisoners, established the concept of Home Rule as a political constant in Ireland, and finally built upon these nationalist credentials to head the Home Rule party in the early 1870s. The seeming inconsistencies between his early *DUM* conservatism and the nationalism of his later years suggest that he underwent some kind of political conversion. The four years of Butt's editorship reveal, however, not only his ability to help gather together some of the best Irish writers of the time, but also, from the pages of the *DUM,* an early exposure to many of the features of Home Rule politics.

### VIII

Perhaps the most popular Irish writer from the nineteenth century, if not its most accomplished, was Charles Lever, whose first novel appeared in the *DUM* as *The Confessions of Harry Lorrequer.* The magazine would ultimately publish a huge amount of his work, much of it while he was editor from 1842 to 1845. Lever began his fruitful association with the *DUM* because of his good friend, William Hamilton Maxwell, whose own work was then enjoying considerable success. Maxwell serialized various travel sketches in the *DUM,* such as his *Rambling Recollections,* but his most famous works were *Wild Sports of the West* (1832) and *Stories of Waterloo* (1834). The first of these, based on Maxwell's experiences as an underworked Protestant rector in a parish that boasted superb hunting opportunities, became a prototype for that style of Irish country-life sketches invariably described—at the time and ever since—as "rollicking."[11] And in *Stories of Waterloo,* as the *DUM* later noted, he "first suggested what may be called the military novel" (Aug. 1841, 222). For Lever, then, already charmed by Maxwell's waggish personality, the general formulas for *The Confessions of Harry Lorrequer* were readily available.

In *Harry Lorrequer,* as in Maxwell's *Stories of Waterloo,* the title character is a British army officer stationed for much of the time in the Irish countryside. Lever began the work, not as a novel, but as

---

11. Also within this vein but even more famous than Lever's work now is the late-nineteenth and early-twentieth series by Somerville and Ross, their "Irish R.M." tales.

an irregular series of sketches that would provide him a framework for a few items from his extensive collection of anecdotal adventures. The immediate popularity of the series astounded both author and publisher, however, and the increase in magazine sales occasioned a faster and more extensive output than Lever had ever imagined. New installments of *Harry Lorrequer* kept appearing from February 1837 until February 1840, nineteen in all, becoming increasingly more extravagant as they went on and even extending beyond *Lorrequer*'s publication in book form in 1839. Although Lever claimed that "in sketching Harry Lorrequer I was in a great measure depicting myself...,"[12] his creation resembles an idealized self-portrait much more than a realistic one. Nonetheless, the fantasy quickly gathered substance, allowing its creator to begin entertaining thoughts of abandoning his career in medicine to become a professional man of letters.

Set in the early nineteenth century, the novel follows Lorrequer through a series of adventures connected in much the same offhandedly episodic manner as Inglis's *Scenes from the Life of Edward Lascelles*. While several of the same minor characters show up in a variety of places, and while one early but major love affair finally gets resolved late in the novel, the most powerful unifying device is the theme of deception. Lorrequer, for instance, enjoys performing as an amateur Shakespearean actor on occasion. More commonly, though, the role changes originate in a drinking bout among the officers, who then decide to play a practical joke on some friend, or who perhaps help the same friend fool some rich young woman into marriage. Guided by such impromptu charades, the characterization often leans towards thinly drawn types: the snobbish aristocrat who gets his comeuppance; the frolicsome officers whom Lorrequer can always trust in a pinch, as long as the liquor is free and plentiful; the Irishman abroad who drinks and fights too readily,

---

12. Lionel Stevenson, *Dr. Quicksilver: The Life of Charles Lever* (London: Chapman and Hall, 1939), 70.

even by Lorrequer's standards, but who has a heart of shamrock-plated gold; and the interchangeable women, valuable if they have money, still worth an evening's flirtation if they have nothing more than good looks and a short memory.

In a typical episode midway through the novel, Lorrequer's officer friend Curzon has arranged to elope with a wealthy young woman whose father disapproves of the marriage. To preserve at least some dignity, she insists on an older man accompanying her as she elopes, to act as chaperone, and Curzon asks Lorrequer to disguise himself so as to take on this role. The usual drinking party the night before, however, leaves Lorrequer so groggy the next morning, when he sets off to meet the woman, that he mistakenly boards a carriage intended for the regimental doctor. Also confused in the darkness, Dr. Fitzgerald then takes Lorrequer's coach, which plunges him into disaster. Some pranksters have told his wife that he has a mistress, so she follows Fitzgerald on the fateful morning when his unwitting carriage driver sets out for the scene of the elopement. There, Fitzgerald assumes the young woman to be the daughter of his patient, while his wife, with greater certainty, believes the worst. The elopement ends with the young woman fleeing in guilt-stricken terror back to her father's house, and the Fitzgerald marriage just barely survives the outing. Lorrequer, meanwhile, realizes what is happening in time to invent plausible medical opinions for Fitzgerald's new patient and then to return, unscathed, with a great story for the next night's drinking bout.

The layers of deception keep multiplying in complexity and seriousness throughout the novel. Characters knowingly take on false roles only to fall unexpectedly into different ones, which they must then interpret and adapt to. Other double-agents step forth upon the Irish political stage, where the potential violence of a secret agrarian society gets defused by the ever-present informer. Within the frequent narrative shifts, minor characters also tell long stories but with the same style and themes that Lorrequer uses. No one has any set identity, and in Lorrequer's case, in fact, success often depends upon his avoiding recognition as himself. Throughout the novel, he not only dodges all responsibility for his madcap adventures, he even attains those material goals so valued by his officer class when he finally marries into wealth and a high-ranking government post.

While *The Confessions of Harry Lorrequer* meant easy success for both narrator and author, it only briefly diminished Lever's financial worries, a concern that would hurry his work into print for the rest of his career. Just as embarrassing was the charge that artistic haste kept leading Lever into stage-Irish stereotypes, especially when the critic was fellow novelist and *DUM* contributor William Carleton. Lever's feud with Carleton began early, following the publication of Lever's first contribution to the *DUM*, a May 1836 short story entitled "The Black Mask." Carleton claimed already to have read the story and accused the author of literary fraud. Lever had, in fact, given the story to a friend several years earlier on the understanding that the friend would place it for him in some British journal. When it did finally appear in England in 1833, so much time had elapsed that Lever had lost track of it. Carleton's mistaken cry of plagiarism died down but not the hard feelings between the two writers. In 1843, while Lever was editor of the *DUM*, Carleton put his talent to work for a new and highly nationalist journal, the *Nation*, from which he attacked Lever for pandering to the more profitable British marketplace.

IX

Within the next few years, by 1850, Carleton would come to cut his own deals on the London market; even so, he was clearly a better writer than Lever. Butt printed his short story "Lha Dhu; or, the Dark Day," in October 1834, having previously described it to Carleton as "almost the most exquisitely beautiful and touching tale that I have ever read."¹³ In an idyllic Irish village named Ballydhas, pas-

---

13. Isaac Butt to William Carleton, Sept. 24, 1834, *The Life of William Carleton: Being His Autobiography and Letters; and an Account of His Life and Writings, from the Point

toral harmony breaks down over a proposed marriage between a well-to-do man and a poor woman when the groom's brother flies into a rage and strikes him. Complications from the wound kill the groom shortly thereafter, but although the lovers end tragically, they do remain true to their ideals and also help demonstrate the story's moral: "learn to restrain your passions and temper within proper limits" (Oct. 1834, 441). Carleton used the same moral two years later, in his much longer tale "Jane Sinclair; or, The Fawn of Springvale," and again, a pair of star-crossed lovers occasions the central conflict. Jane Sinclair's violent passion for a beautiful young man leads her to dissemble about her feelings before her clergyman father. Although she soon confesses her love, her brief and harmless act of dishonesty keeps on haunting her, as do her growing suspicions of the young man's faithlessness. Several emotional breakdowns later, she soon falls ill and dies, but not before exhorting others—"our fair young readers," in particular—to lead a life of humility and duty towards parents, to shun vanity and ambition, and to keep emotions from overrunning one's reason and religious sense.

In 1837, the DUM ran a three-part series by Carleton entitled "The Autobiography of the Rev. Blackthorn M'Flail, Late P.P. of Ballymacwhackem, Written by His Cousin, the Rev. Phedlim M'Fun, Roman Catholic Rector of Ballymacscaltheen" (Jan., April, and Oct. 1837). The title promises anti-Catholic farce, and the series obliges by portraying a priest who drinks too much and is politically unscrupulous. In an 1838 sketch, "Rickard the Rake," Carleton combined literature and politics in an imaginative portrayal of an agitator who serves as a typical "impersonation of the Ribbon System" (March 1838, 383). Like both "Jane Sinclair" and "Lha Dhu," and like nearly every novel and short story to appear in the DUM during this period, these sketches have peasant violence in the background and

---

*at which the Autobiography Breaks Off,* David O'Donoghue (London: Downey, 1896), 2:29. The title of Carleton's story as it first appeared in the DUM, "Sha Dhu," was a misprint.

so find some didactic way of condemning emotional behavior. The narrator of M'Flail's "Autobiography," for instance, criticizes not only his own people but even his fellow priests and religion: "Mirth and murder are more nearly related with us than they are in any other country under the sun" (April 1837, 491).

A less common feature of "Jane Sinclair" and "Lha Dhu," though, and also unlike Carleton's earlier contributions to Caesar Otway's *Christian Examiner,* is the complete absence of any religious rancor despite the presence of religious themes. The narrator of "Jane Sinclair" decries Calvinism's "frightful and merciless dogma" by which Jane fears herself cast away from God (Dec. 1836, 702). And in "Lha Dhu," all three of Ireland's religions harmoniously coexist in the village. Carleton's Ballydhas contrasts sharply, for instance, with the village setting of George Brittaine's novel *The Orphans of Dunasker* (Nov. 1837–May 1838, 6 installments). In *Dunasker,* Catholic superstition and a rabble-rousing priest consistently thwart any Protestant attempts at progress or prosperity. Brittaine's sprawling plot line, advanced primarily by desultory gossip among the villagers, finally gains some focus because of conflict between rising Catholic anarchy and a local Orange order that affords Protestants "the only human means of protection from impending destruction" (March 1838, 286).

Such anti-Catholic propaganda characterized, and limited, many of the *DUM*'s literary contributions. To this extent, the imaginative works were simply reflecting the direct propaganda of the political material. Sir Charles Gavan Duffy later suggested Samuel O'Sullivan's influence here, complaining that much of the magazine's excellence was "smothered in masses of furious bigotry" and a "monotony of hysterics" from O'Sullivan.[14] At the same time, the *DUM* was capable of a much broader and more complex view of Irish experience. While "Jane Sinclair" may depict human emotion with no

---

14. Duffy, *Thomas Davis,* 55.

more style than a mediocre middle-class romance, it does avoid political and religious demagoguery. And even the zealous convert O'Sullivan, in a *Blackwood's* sketch from this period (Sept.–Oct. 1829), could on occasion sympathize with the point of view of the Catholic peasantry and also recognize abuses and neglect within the Church of Ireland.

Running through four installments, from September through December 1836, "Jane Sinclair" ended up as Carleton's longest story to date in the *DUM*. Like so much of his serialized work from this period, though, whether in the *DUM* or the *Christian Examiner,* it remained too short to give his sprawling talent the space it needed. Regarded in isolation, Carleton's short stories frequently lean too heavily toward a particular theme, narrative technique, or character type. A reader who takes them up individually will thus often find some lack of balance, a heavy-handed message, perhaps, or maudlin lovers, grotesque violence, or relentless dialect.Even as long a story as "The Poor Scholar" does not develop its full power until placed alongside all of *Traits and Stories of the Irish Peasantry* (1833). Within the framework of that whole collection, the various parts balance out their excesses since they then are allowed to follow the pattern announced by Carleton's title. If we would understand the Irish peasantry, we must see it as the sum total of its different traits and many stories.[15] It is a measure of Carleton's greatness that he could capture so much of that complexity within the limits of a short tale.

By early 1837, though, Carleton was anxious to try a much longer individual work.[16] The result was his first novel, *Fardorougha the Miser; or, the Convicts of Lisnamona,* a work that abandoned the tepid emotions of "Jane Sinclair" and returned to Carleton's most power-

---

15. For an analysis of the "carefully planned and patterned artistic performance" that shapes Carleton's *Traits and Stories of the Irish Peasantry,* see Julian Moynahan, *Anglo-Irish: The Literary Imagination in a Hyphenated Culture* (Princeton: Princeton University Press, 1995), 64–66.

16. Robert Lee Wolff, *William Carleton, Irish Peasant Novelist: A Preface to His Fiction* (New York: Garland, 1980), 73.

ful literary subject, the Irish peasantry. Serialized from February 1837 to February 1838 (7 installments), it began running in the same issue of the *DUM* as Lever's *Harry Lorrequer*. In sharp contrast to Lever's randomly strung individual episodes, however, Carleton's novel exhibited the kind of tightly unified plot and characters that made it the most significant literary work that the *DUM* had so far published.

The main character Fardorougha Donovan—his name in Irish, "fear dorcha," suggests blindness—is a miserly gombeen man, or usurer, with a kindly but meek wife Honor. After years of marriage, they have a son, and the miser's love of money finally gets challenged by his equally powerful love for this child. Fardorougha's inability to restrain his passionate avarice, however, as manifest in his irrational fear of starvation, keeps thwarting his family and leaving them too much at the mercy of outside forces. A violent and treacherous group of Whiteboys complicates the life of the Donovans; and Fardorougha's weak health finally fails him, although not before he counsels his family to drive a hard bargain on his funeral arrangements. Since the peasants have so little control over their violent impulses, whether as a group or as individuals, the novel suggests that personal triumph comes only from a religious humility and acceptance of fate, a view of life best shown by Honor Donovan. Through the strength of Honor and her son, the novel achieves happy resolutions to its multi-level conflicts and thereby asserts the value of traditional virtues, especially spirituality, simplicity, and submissiveness. As a child, Carleton had witnessed Orange yeomen breaking into his family's home to search for weapons. Just a few years later, in 1817, he saw the tarred, rotting bodies of Whiteboys swinging from a gallows. But his plea for nonviolence in *Fardorougha the Miser* went far beyond personal memories of the past, appealing as well to those Protestant readers of the *DUM* who feared that the tithe agitation of the 1830s might actually be a prelude to full-scale Catholic revolution. In its most typical moments, the *DUM* responded to these fears with anti-Catholic diatribes; in its finest moments, however, as in Carleton's sympathetic portrayal of an Irish peasant spending his life worrying about his very survival, the magazine's literary and political responses recognized the humanity of all classes and religions.

x

Although not of the stature of *Fardorougha the Miser,* Joseph Sheridan Le Fanu's work from this period approaches Carleton's in its literary complexity and wholeness. Le Fanu, himself the editor of the *DUM* from 1861 to 1869, began his literary career in the January 1838 issue of that magazine with a short story entitled "The Ghost and the Bonesetter." A piece remarkable only for its four separate narrative layers, this story nonetheless inaugurated a series that Le Fanu continued until 1840 and that finally appeared in book form in 1880 as *The Purcell Papers.* The central theme in many of these tales is noble ambition ending in failure, "sacrifices and efforts made with all the motives of faithfulness and of honour, and terminating in ruin . . ." (June 1838, 713). In the second tale, for instance, "The Fortunes of Sir Robert Ardagh" (March 1838), the title character saves his ancestral castle but only through a Faustian pact with a demon who ultimately destroys him. In a further experiment in narrative technique, Le Fanu then offers us a variation on Ardagh's fate. The first, detailing a grisly struggle in the darkness, has arisen out of local rumors, the narrator tells us, while the "true" second version shows Ardagh calmly preparing for the death he knows must come.

In their Gothic sensationalism, deceptive narrative techniques, themes of ruined ambition and decayed grandeur, and overall sense of the world as treacherous, these tales defined for Le Fanu the styles and subjects that would occupy him for the rest of his career. Throughout the 1820s and 1830s, *Blackwood's* had already demonstrated the popular appeal of sensationalist fiction as a magazine staple. Within a narrower and more immediate sphere, though, Le Fanu could have found all these elements readily available within a series of one long and five short tales called *Chapters of College Ro-*

*mance,* then appearing in the *DUM* under the authorship of "Edward Stevenson O'Brien." Le Fanu felt the need to impress the editor of the *DUM* in order to get his own work accepted for publication.[17] What better way than to pattern that work after the editor's own fiction? For "O'Brien" was none other than Butt himself, serializing his tales from November 1834 to November 1837 (8 installments), nearly the whole period of his editorship. Perhaps recognizing its literary shortcomings, Butt did not issue *College Romance* as a book until 1863. Still, the tales merit attention, not only because of their possible influence on the much better writer Le Fanu, but also because of what they reveal about their author.

Butt draws each of his tales from his college memoirs, a framing device that contains rich descriptions of Trinity College life in the early nineteenth century, but that also tends toward repetition. The second chapter, "The Murdered Fellow" (March 1835), is typical of the rest: a promising young scholar named Wallis strikes up a friendship with the wrong man, a fellow student who leads him into atheism and gambling. A consuming passion for money blinds Wallis to his love for his fiancee and even leads him eventually into murder. Only then does the friend reveal that he has, from the start, been in league with hell in order to lead Wallis to damnation. Wallis's inescapable punishment and death only underscore the story's warning that ambition should never outweigh principle. The narrator O'Brien often apologizes for his grim subject matter but justifies it on the grounds that the common lot of humankind is harsh and sorrowful. And besides, O'Brien adds, these things really happened: he either recounts his own experiences or, in the case of "The Murdered Fellow," has access to authentic, first-hand documents.

Because of its narrative technique, Faustian conflict, atmosphere of guilt and evil, a tale of promise ending in ruin, and a sense of the world as treacherous, "The Murdered Fellow" reads much like a

---

17. W. J. Mc Cormack, *Sheridan Le Fanu and Victorian Ireland* (Oxford: Clarendon, 1980), 55.

model for a Le Fanu story. Moreover, *College Romance* also reveals deep ambiguities in Butt's own view of his Trinity College life. His scholars in these tales frequently disappoint their parents' hopes, for college almost inevitably corrupts their morals in some way. "Few persons but those who have experienced them can ever conceive the mingled feelings which enter into the pride and the ambition of a young man, successful in his first entrance into College" (Aug. 1837, 500), O'Brien tells us, knowing that ambition precedes ruin in all of these tales, and surely knowing as well how this sentence must have applied, five years earlier, to the undergraduate Isaac Butt. At first glance, the college life that O'Brien describes always appears deceptively simple and promising; only later do his characters encounter those bewildering complexities of life that stretch even a firm religious faith out to unreliable limits.

One of the last works that Butt handled as editor, running from March until August 1838, was a long, six-canto poem entitled *The Rubi, a Tale of the Sea*. Recounting the exploits of a seventeenth-century pirate ship, the poem wallows through the usual romanticized heroism and bravery of pirate life, then ends with a half-hearted disclaimer against any wish to identify vicariously with such criminals. Butt surely recognized the superficiality of both the glamour and the piety here. Nonetheless, one could not glorify lawless violence during Ireland's Tithe War and then pretend total political innocence. At a level deeper than the usual forms of Anglo-Irish conservatism, *The Rubi*'s adolescent tastes in adventure may indicate, if not a sympathy with the "wrong" cause, then at least an awareness on the part of the *DUM* that there were genuine ambiguities woven into the tangled web of Irish religion, politics, and economics.

Butt tackled these ambiguities directly in the longest tale in *College Romance*, "The Bribed Scholar" (Sept. and Oct. 1836; Aug. 1837). A Trinity College election occasions the conflict in which the central character, Butt's usual promising but penniless young student, votes for the Catholic Emancipation candidate in return for a bribe that will save his father from bankruptcy. Sounding the same hollow notes that rang at the end of *The Rubi,* the tale moralizes against deluded betrayals of principle. As the narrator O'Brien makes clear, however, the student's ethical dilemma has simply outgrown the kinds of explanations and guidelines his traditional values could give him; it is the principles that fail the student, and not the other way around. O'Brien himself, moreover, as Butt's voice in *College Romance,* also supports the Liberal/Emancipation candidate, moving the story even further outside the customary ideological boundaries of Protestant ascendancy.

"I still love my Popish countrymen," Samuel Ferguson had claimed in "A Dialogue between the Head and Heart of an Irish Protestant" (Nov. 1833, 593). And indeed, Ferguson's reputation as a spokesman for Ireland would endure more impressively than would Butt's, for whom expressions of praise always seem qualified. For his biographical study, for instance, Terence de Vere White chose the title *The Road of Excess* and described Butt's personality as combining an earnestness of tone with a "childish streak in his character that never wholly deserted him."[18] The *DUM*'s successor, the *University Magazine,* perhaps recalling that Butt had been hampered by debt throughout the 1860s or that he had fathered at least two illegitimate children, complained that "the general impression left by his career is that of the man of promise rather than performance" (June 1879, 710).

Yet the performance is impressive, in large part because of Butt's engagingly human struggle with his own limitations. The editorial that inaugurated his first issue as editor of the *DUM,* less than a year after Ferguson's "Dialogue," states: "We love Ireland, we love our Roman Catholic brethren . . ." (Aug. 1834, 128). Later during his term, Butt took note of the wide range of favorable reviews lavished on the *DUM,* not only from the "leading Protestant journals of Ireland" such as the *Evening Mail,* but even from the "radical" and politically hostile *Freeman's Journal.* Such praise, Butt remarked,

18. Terence de Vere White, *Road of Excess,* 22.

"could almost revive the dream that once filled our minds in our younger and more enthusiastic days—a dream that all party distinctions might one day be obliterated, and all Irishmen unite together in the bonds of fraternity and peace" (Dec. 1835, 711). Near the end of Butt's "gloomy chapters," as he came to call his *College Romance,* an older friend consoles a young student, devastated by the death of his father, by saying that "the world is far better than you might think, considering the wickedness that's in it" (Nov. 1837, 502). To Butt's thinking, even though the abstractions of Catholicism might well be wicked, Catholics themselves were obviously different. And if the Protestant principles of his own clergyman father contained such unsettling ambiguities, were those of the Catholics really so wrong after all? To love all of Ireland in such a time, a person of Butt's youth, intelligence, and sensitivity had to leave behind the small, familiar Protestant garrison and enter a world that was bewildering and dangerous, but also inspiringly rich in experience and humanity. The same love that would later make Butt the political leader of a much broader Irish constituency had already in the 1830s set down seditious roots.

3

# PRINCIPLES OF MORALITY AND RELIGION

I

Terence de Vere White claims that the four years of Isaac Butt's editorship represented the "highest peak of excellence" in the *DUM*'s long career.[1] Whether we accept this judgment or not, the *DUM* indeed did undergo distinct changes after Butt left, gradually developing some of the politically more moderate features that it would continue to cultivate under Charles Lever's editorship several years later. The person most responsible for shifting the emphasis within the *DUM*'s corporate identity was James M'Glashan, its editor from late 1838 or early 1839 to March 1842.[2] Having begun his career with Blackwood's publishing house in Edinburgh, M'Glashan came to Dublin to work for publisher William Curry in 1830, becoming a partner in the firm in 1837. When Curry died in 1846,

---

1. Terence de Vere White, *Road of Excess* 9.
2. For a discussion of the exact date when M'Glashan's editorship began, see *Wellesley Index*, 4:195, n. 11. Michael Sadleir, "*Dublin University Magazine*, Its History, Contents and Bibliography," *Bibliographical Society of Ireland Publications* 5, no. 4 (1938): 64, claims that James Wills took over the editorship immediately after Butt and held it "for a very short time," but the *Wellesley Index* believes this to be incorrect.

M'Glashan continued to operate the publishing house, even during the severe financial pressure of Ireland's famine years.

M'Glashan had taken an interest in the *DUM* from its outset. After only six issues, he had convinced Curry, already involved as the *DUM*'s publisher, to assume financial control, and M'Glashan had also encouraged Lever's contributions to the *DUM*. Upon becoming editor, while he would keep a very low personal profile, he would also change the contents of the magazine in distinct ways.

In a retrospective essay at the end of the *DUM*'s first year of operations, then-editor Charles Stuart Stanford had made a particular point of acknowledging the magazine's women readers, promising always to have "their improvement and entertainment in view" and never to print anything that might violate their "principles of morality and religion" (Insert for Dec. 1833, 6). For its first few years, however, the magazine seemed not to make any deliberate effort to address women's interests. The fiction of Le Fanu and especially Carleton portrayed women in strong and complex roles, natural players within a human drama rather than role models for a special group of readers requiring a particular market strategy. Under James M'Glashan, however, such a strategy quickly developed, built in large part around the new editor's sense of prudence and moderation. While this editorial emphasis tended to trivialize the offerings more frequently than under Butt's guidance, and while the cautious optimism sometimes rang hollow, M'Glashan also succeeded in avoiding much of the bigotry and belligerence that had previously marked the *DUM*.

II

One contributor who exemplified the magazine's new style and heightened interest in women was Mary Anne Browne. She was best known as a poet, publishing eight volumes of her verse between 1827 and her death in 1845, and her poetry appears more often than any other writer's in the *DUM* for this period; the *DUM* also praised her work in several reviews and in her obituary for March

1845. Her major single work in the *DUM,* however, was a fictional series of prose sketches called *Recollections of a Portrait Painter* (Aug. 1839–July 1841, ten installments). These sketches typically portray a woman as either narrator or main character, frequently both, and they typically recount a romance that ends tragically. "The Member's Lady" (March 1841), for instance, tells of a married woman who runs off with her lover, taking with them the child of her marriage. The husband, a wealthy member of Parliament, discovers her whereabouts and has the child returned to him, thus plunging her into depression and, quickly thereafter, the realization that her lover has now tired of her. Failing in an attempt to see her child again, she gains her husband's pity to the extent that he sets her up in quiet anonymity until he can arrange for a divorce. She lives on, in remorse over her actions, but mostly in grief over the separation from her child. When news reaches her of her ex-husband's remarriage, however, the shock kills her.

The story's conclusion, like its title, asserts that the woman's identity comes primarily from her husband: once he remarries, he obliterates all of her status, however tenuous, as the member's lady, and she has no life left in her. Yet the woman has never cared very much for her husband and quickly forgets her shallow lover. Since the enduring passion in her life is for her child, she seems well insulated from any marriages that either of the men might now undertake. Her seemingly incongruous fatal shock, however, serves to underscore the stark and rigid terms that have always defined the woman: the story never allows her any identity except in relation to someone else, whether as wife, mistress, mother, or—as the closing words of the story would have it—a "guilty and unhappy divorcee." The *DUM* had made the points often enough before, and would make them again, that passion is never a reliable guide to behavior, and that individuals must accept the norms and traditions of their society. While Browne's story tests these lessons against a specifically female experience, it does not challenge their legitimacy.

The *DUM* under M'Glashan's editorship had a number of things to say about women beyond what was implicit in Browne's work. A review entitled "The Women of England, their Social Duties and Domestic Habits" noted that English women had enormous power over men and that they lacked imagination and strong emotions (April 1839). This generalization clearly failed to account for the member's lady, but perhaps she more closely resembled her Irish counterpart, described in a sequel review the next month entitled "The Women of Ireland." Anticipating Matthew Arnold in the same way that Samuel Ferguson had done in his Hardiman essay, the *DUM* found that it was Irish women who possessed the imagination, emotion, and poetic sense lacking in England. On the whole, in fact, "the Irish temperament is best suited to women" (May 1839, 591). A Scot himself, M'Glashan did not have to pause from calculating the responses of the *DUM*'s women readers to wonder how any of this applied to his own temperament.

For calculate he did. Charles Lever, working on his novel *The O'Donoghue* in 1845, wrote to M'Glashan to ask for advice regarding the conclusion of the work: should it end in Irish defeat and tragedy, or in uplifting, but possibly trivial, romanticism? Despite Lever's feeling that the novel so far seemed to be developing toward the tragic ending, M'Glashan disagreed, arguing that "the ladies wouldn't like it."[3]

The contents of the *DUM* from 1838 to 1842 indicate that someone was indeed making a deliberate and concerted effort to publish what the ladies might like. Along with the ongoing "Gallery of Illustrious Irishmen," with its biographies of figures from the past, the *DUM* now ran "Female Portraits" as well as a third series, "Our Portrait Gallery," begun in October 1839 and presenting biographical sketches of living Irish figures.[4] Along with their sympathetic and

3. Edmund Downey, *Charles Lever: His Life in His Letters* (Edinburgh: Blackwood, 1906), 1:183.

4. The "Gallery of Illustrious Irishmen" ran from January 1836 to December 1847 (thirty-three installments), while "Our Portrait Gallery" ran from October 1839 to March 1854 (seventy-two installments), then returned for a second series from February 1874 to December 1877 (forty-seven installments).

detailed portrayals and their reproduced sketches—and eventually even photographs—of their subjects, these biographical series also carried what their titles suggested: reassuring associations of the respected country house with its long-standing family heritage proudly on view. "Female Portraits" lasted but five installments (Feb. 1839–Jan. 1840). Still, Anna Maria Hall did break into "Our [previously all-male] Portrait Gallery" (Aug. 1840), and women were getting more coverage in the DUM than ever before. Another series presented the journal of a young aristocratic woman who described court life in mid-eighteenth-century Poland (May–Nov. 1839, five installments). Maria Frances Dickson published a series, in the travelogue style of reports to a friend back in England, entitled *Letters from the Coast of Clare* (March–Dec. 1841, nine installments). Mrs. Margaret Hutton, noted as a translator from the German of works on art history, dealt frequently with questions of aesthetics in her *Letters from Italy* (Jan.–Dec. 1842, eight installments). And Joseph Sheridan Le Fanu's ongoing stories were joined in the DUM by a review written by his mother and a short story, in Irish dialect, by his sister.

The DUM's interest in a woman's point of view even extended into some of its political commentary. In May 1839 the slim Whig majority faltered, leaving Sir Robert Peel to attempt to form a new government. When Queen Victoria refused to accept Peel's nominations for the women who were to form her household, however, Peel withdrew, leaving the Whigs once more to assume power in the wake of what came to be called the Bedchamber Crisis. Frustrated by how close the Tories had come to resuming power, the DUM blamed the queen for continuing to surround herself in her immediate court with the wives and daughters of Whigs instead of Conservatives. Such behind-the-scenes manipulation of the queen left the center of British government depending on "the paltry acts of female intrigue, and the variable changes of girlish caprice" (June 1839, 757). Still concerned a year later about Queen Victoria's youth and inexperience, another article asked, "How Long Are We To Live Under a Petticotocracy?" (Feb. 1840). Such condescension need not have insulted the *DUM*'s women readers; from their own conservative vantage point, they could easily imagine themselves in the role of much more reliable and valued advisers to Victoria.

### III

Not all of the *DUM*'s work for this period seemed wholly consistent with either Stanford's original promise to women readers or with M'Glashan's caution to Lever. A published lecture by Rev. Robert Walsh presented the cases of several people who had suffered from various parasites such as maggots. The kindly domesticity of Walsh's title, "Our Fellow Lodgers," did little to blunt his horrifying descriptions of bodies in an advanced state of corruption, literally crawling with worms, and still alive to feel and see the advance of death (June 1840). *DUM* readers with more delicate sensibilities could also shudder at the sensationalist story "A Legend of Ulster in 1641" (March-Nov. 1840, four installments). Following the lives of several Protestant characters, the story details how they are hunted down, tortured, and murdered by priest-led Catholic mobs that subject their women victims to the same horrible fate as the men.

As a general rule, though, M'Glashan's *DUM* avoided such evangelical reminders of the body's tendency toward corruption, moderated the violence of its former political commentary, and sought instead to stress the more settled, hopeful times. The Whigs might continue to control Parliament, but in the closing years of the 1830s, the Conservatives found themselves making consistent political gains. In Ireland, with agitation over tithes resolved by the Rent-Charge Act of 1838, political involvement by the Catholic clergy had correspondingly diminished. Although Daniel O'Connell founded the Repeal Association in 1840, demands for repeal would not become a serious threat to the Union until early 1843. O'Connell's political base was broad indeed, but he was also frequently hampered by the need to gain further electoral reforms for the Irish masses and also by the disparate and fragmentary nature of those potential voting groups. Even within the countryside, the economic issues of the cottiers, the "landless men," differed greatly from those of the farmers who enjoyed secure leases. Protestants, by contrast, managed to sustain a more cohesive political unity. While the Orange Order was officially dormant, it was effectively replaced by groups like the Protestant Operatives' Associations, founded by the Protestant working-class hero—and Trinity College product—Rev. Tresham Dames Gregg. So long as the issue of repeal had not yet gathered sufficient political energy to help in the organization of a cohesive Catholic movement, as emancipation had done in the 1820s and tithe payments in the 1830s, the political crises menacing Irish Protestantism seemed to keep their distance.

Specific political issues addressed by the *DUM* reflected this general moderation of public events. No longer did the magazine raise the apocalyptic specter of repeal as an emergency measure that onetime Unionists themselves might need to employ. Instead, it could consider matters less threatening to the Union, such as the Municipal Corporations Act, the Corn Laws, or national education. On the first of these, the *DUM* argued that the proposed municipal reform would reduce the representation and security of Protestants, who currently dominated local government (June 1840). A further article on this topic included lengthy citations from Isaac Butt's speech before Parliament in opposition to the measure. Nonetheless, the Act passed into law in 1840, and while significant changes at the municipal level were slow in developing, the Act did open up local government to democratic elections in Ireland.

On the Corn Laws, as well, the *DUM* defended current policies and opposed suggestions for their repeal. As early as 1834, the magazine had warned that "if the Corn Laws be repealed Ireland would be ruined" (June 1834, 719). A lengthy and detailed economic discussion in 1839 argued that domestic agriculture needed the protection of the present system. In the event of removal of tariffs, "[e]very farmer in England and Ireland would instantly suffer the most severe distress, and, in many cases, utter and remediless ruin" (March 1839, 353). Insofar as tariffs on imported grain protected and stabilized the price of domestic grain, the existing Corn Laws also helped to protect the independence of the Empire. While the *DUM* would return to this debate at several points during this period (see especially Feb. 1842), the Corn Laws remained in place until mid-1846, when the question of their repeal would become caught up in the larger issues of the Famine.

For the time being, though, nothing seemed to merit the crisis mentality of the magazine's earlier years. Mountifort Longfield contributed a four-part series on banking and currency in England (Jan.–Dec. 1840). An article entitled "Modern History Philosophically Considered" concluded "that God reigneth in the affairs of men, and that the end of the divine government is man's improvement" (May 1839, 573). Against such principles of universal order, the petty messes that the Whigs kept making seemed harmless enough: "The spirit of Christianity has arrested the progress of revolution" (Aug. 1839, 241). No one was paying enough attention to developing Ireland's railways, the magazine complained, but surely that would come in time as well.

The most serious threats envisioned by the *DUM* grew out of foreign-policy blunders by the Whigs, especially by Foreign Minister Lord Palmerston. Canada might gain its independence, France might once again wage war, even Russia looked menacing. The spiritual mistake leading to these erosions of the Empire's material strength had been England's failure to represent Protestantism adequately and to carry out its "high and holy office of protectrix of the Reformation" in its dealings with foreign governments and peoples (Jan. 1839, 11). An 1841 essay on "England and Her Foreign Relations" warned that England's "hour of extinction as a nation is at hand, if the hour of her redemption from her present thrall to unprincipled revolutionists draweth not nigh" (April 1841, 516). The Biblical artificiality serves to emphasize how out of practice the *DUM* had grown in whipping up a persuasive crisis mentality. The millennialist sentiments did have a more specific function, however, signalling a strategic heightening of tensions in advance of the general election in 1841.

In June 1841, the *DUM* offered "A Few Words on the Crisis" and concluded with the belief that "the Whigs have managed to reduce the affairs of the country to a state of embarrassment unparalleled in the modern history of England" (777). Next month's article, simply "The Crisis," shortened the title and lengthened the period under consideration: "We believe that the annals of history, ancient and modern, present no parallel to the diabolical wickedness of the wretched men who now hold a convulsive grasp of the reins of power." Urging Protestants to vote in the upcoming election, the *DUM* threw its strongest support behind the Conservative forces led by Sir Robert Peel (July 1841, 119). And in August 1841, the *DUM* could announce that "we are saved." Despite numerous incidents of voting-day violence against Protestants in Ireland, that "blessed instrument" the Church of England had brought about the desired outcome, ably assisted by Conservative elements of the press (Aug. 1841, 237 and 244).

In back-to-back articles for February and March 1842, the *DUM* set about suggesting an agenda item for the new government, an issue that had remained central to the magazine since its outset: education. Six major articles from M'Glashan's editorship analyze this subject, each one based on the *DUM*'s fundamental premise that "all experience demonstrates, that education, without religion, is an evil rather than a good" (Feb. 1839, 128). In stubbornly opposing the work of the National Education Board, the *DUM* could finally take new heart from Peel's electoral victory. While a government would ideally offer financial support only to the Established Church, the *DUM* recognized the impossibility of implementing such subsidies. Therefore, since governmental involvement in education had the effect of squeezing out the Established Church, Parliament should simply remove itself from the business of funding education and leave matters of support up to the various religions (March 1842). In making this proposal, the *DUM* continued faithfully to believe that the truth—Protestant truth—would conquer if given a fair chance. The Church Education Society, founded by the Church of Ireland in 1839, had after all demonstrated, in immediate and dramatic ways, that it could operate successfully, opening schools and recruiting pupils, without government assistance.

IV

As it had done before, the *DUM* again turned toward Ireland's cultural heritage as a way of clarifying the dilemmas of current history. A review of Edward Bunting's *Ancient Music of Ireland* (1840) first noted the "often disgraceful contentions of sects and parties amongst our countrymen, and the want of a philosophical national spirit" that could bring unity. "Our music," however, soon dissipates these "present distractions" of the political arenas, and "we are again not only Irish, but Irish to the heart's core, glorying in the national mind of our country . . ." (Jan. 1841, 5). A national spirit or heart, a national mind—that was the missing element, the quality that could unify Belfastman and Dubliner, Protestant and Catholic, landowner and peasant, all coexisting in peace, none facing the threat of exclusion from an emerging Irish nation. One could sense this spirit, this mind, in the airs to be gathered at an assemblage of the old Irish harpers. But could one also define it, and in words that wouldn't occasion yet another divisive election or ugly exchange of pamphlets? Could one define it as, say, a national literature?

The *DUM* felt itself in a position to try. In an 1841 retrospective, a "Postscript to Our Hundredth Number," the magazine asserted that

> we have had from the beginning one aim especially fixed before us; and that was the creation of a literature, which should be NATIONAL without degenerating into mere PROVINCIALISM. Ireland and Irish topics have commanded the first place in our favour; her welfare and her interests been the chief and dearest object of our exertions. By all legitimate means we have striven to nourish into life and being that, without which no people ever yet were truly great . . . *nationality*. . . ." (April 1841, 531)

The distinction here was crucial to the *DUM*. In theoretical terms, the magazine's opposition to provincial and uncivilized dullness opened the way for a Coleridgean breadth of vision into how a nation's literature might help to shape the rest of its social experience. In more practical, political terms, the magazine was seeking, not just to nourish, but indeed to sustain, its very life. A provincial Ireland would leave but a meager place, if any, for its minority Protestants and their traditions and interests, many drawn from cultural sources in England or the Continent. From its outset, the magazine had regarded the Union as Ireland's main link to the modern world, since it gave to the Irish the status of being citizens of "the most enlightened and commanding nation in modern times" (June 1834, 721). Under the publisher and bookseller M'Glashan, the *DUM* was even more aware of how cultural insularity might affect literature. Writers already had difficulty in finding a native publishing industry and readership and in resisting the financial lure of the London market. In the retrospective of April 1841, the *DUM* took particular pride in having retained much of the literary talent that otherwise "had sought some other market" (531). But if the net of Irish provinciality were now to start drawing even tighter, a potential national literature would be subject to suffocating pressures.

The retrospective "Postscript" rendered this distinction more concrete in terms of the *DUM*'s growing readership:

Independent of the almost exclusive possession of the Irish market, we enjoy an extensive sale throughout England and Scotland: nay, there is not a single colony, where the language of Great Britain is spoken, into which our merits or our title, or it may be both, have not won us admission, and a demand continually increasing. (528)

Here indeed was the ideal balance: to be lionized at home and respected abroad, a combination bringing both financial reward and artistic recognition, both a national and an international reputation. Yet success also sharpened the *DUM*'s protective instincts against a future dominated by Ireland's Catholics. That people like O'Connell would tolerate a magazine's trafficking with imperialist influences was inconceivable.

Keeping Irish writers engaged within the Irish market thus emerged as a key unifying strategy for the *DUM*. The optimism of the "Postscript," however, ignored a number of key defectors, including the *DUM*'s own William Carleton. In an 1838 letter to the London publisher Richard Bentley, Carleton had asked seventy pounds for his novel *Fardorougha the Miser* instead of the fifty pounds Bentley had offered. "The truth is," Carleton added, "I would listen to no such terms at all were it not that I am anxious to get into the London Market."[5] Carleton's anxieties and allegiances run a bewildering gamut during these years, his writing at various times supporting and opposing virtually all of Ireland's warring factions. Nonetheless, the *DUM* described him in its "Portrait Gallery" as being "free from party bias," for literature "is of no party" (Jan. 1841, 72 and 70). After all, Carleton had not yet begun work for the militantly nationalist *Nation*.

His story "Three Wishes: An Irish Legend" appeared in November 1839, a trivial and predictable piece about a rogue who succeeds in tricking the devil but who then is tricked himself by the parish priest. "The Misfortunes of Barney Branagan" (Jan.–May 1841, five installments) was somewhat more serious, although still not close to the quality of Carleton's *DUM* novels. Barney has the unshakable reputation of being hopelessly unlucky, even though his misfortunes always result in some unforeseen net gains for him. His double in the story, a gambler named Cassidy, invariably loses at all of his ventures, disgraces his parents, and sinks into criminal degradation. The story contrasts the innocence of the country with the city's corruption, emphasizes one's parents and family as a center of value, and shows how love can outlast everything except death. Appearances invariably deceive, the British characters especially emerging as con men and villains.

5. Gordon N. Ray, "The Bentley Papers," *The Library*, 5th ser., 7 (Sept. 1952): 186, includes this letter from Carleton to Bentley.

Like Samuel Lover's Barny O'Reirdon, from the *DUM*'s inaugural issue, Barney Branagan is essentially an innocent whose success arises from pure, blind luck. To this extent, he also bears some remarkable similarities to Daniel O'Connell, at least as the *DUM* portrayed O'Connell in its "Portrait Gallery" for March 1841. While acknowledging that "Roman Catholics, in the early part of this century, had strong provocations to shake their chains against the Government," the *DUM* still failed to understand how O'Connell could now employ such unscrupulous means and still "be crowned with such unexampled success" (March 1841, 314 and 318). Defying logic, justice, and reason, these Irish—O'Reirdon, Branagan, O'Connell, even the hero of Carleton's "Three Wishes"—somehow kept on winning, meanwhile stringing together indefinite postponements of their day of reckoning.

v

Not all the rogues escaped. The *DUM* reviewed a work on the notorious duellist George Robert Fitzgerald, known as "Fighting Fitzgerald," who was eventually executed in 1786 for an especially outrageous act in a life built around excess. The *DUM* described him as a disgrace to his Irish gentry class, but also as disturbingly representative of it in the latter half of the eighteenth century, when "the pride of the Irish squirarchy was only equaled by their ignorance and uselessness" (July 1840, 4).

Still, the unusual length of the *DUM*'s review of Fitzgerald (July–Sept. 1840, three installments) revealed some romantic fascination lurking beneath the moral and civic outrage. Furthermore, Fitzgerald bore more than a little resemblance to the popular heroes of the novels Charles Lever kept serializing during these years. *The Confessions of Harry Lorrequer* ran until February 1840 and promptly gave way, the very next month, to *Charles O'Malley, the Irish Dragoon* (March 1840–Dec. 1841, twenty-two installments), whose narrator casually resorts to duels on several occasions. As he would later do during his own editorship, Lever thoroughly dominated the literary portion of the *DUM* during the M'Glashan years. Besides these two novels and several reviews, Lever also published "Continental Gossipings" by "Harry Lorrequer" (April–July 1839, three installments) and began two other works, *Nuts and Nutcrackers* (Jan. 1842–May 1844, twelve installments) and *Our Mess; Jack Hinton, the Guardsman* (March–Dec. 1842, ten installments), both of which he continued after M'Glashan stepped down.

One of the better novels that Lever produced in his career, and one that made W. B. Yeats's list of best Irish books, *Charles O'Malley* recounts the adventures of a young Irishman who adheres closely to the demonstrably successful literary formulas of his supposed friend and editor Harry Lorrequer. Edward Lascelles, Henry David Inglis's novelistic persona, had already been wrongly regarded by the *DUM*'s readers as a real person. Besides following Lascelles's example in narrating a loosely connected series of military exploits, the fictional narrators Lorrequer and O'Malley also succeeded in blurring the identity of their author. The most complex set of fictional boxes surrounds a tale told in the novel by another friend of O'Malley's. Lorrequer, in the role of a desultory editor of O'Malley's manuscript, adds a footnote to the reader explaining that this friend habitually invents all kinds of detail with which to embellish his experiences, and that O'Malley has here been gulled by just such a hoax (March 1841, 382).

Despite the similarities to Inglis, however, William Hamilton Maxwell provided Lever with a stronger model to work with, too strong, according to some hostile readers. Charles Gavan Duffy, reviewing Lever's work for the *Nation* in 1843, had frequent recourse to terms such as "poaching" and "pilfering" to account for Lever's literary influences.[6] Indeed, Lever's sketch of Maxwell for the *DUM*'s "Portrait Gallery" reveals other striking connections beyond what Duffy pointed out. In disregarding the wishes of his family

---

6. See "Mr. Lever's 'Irish Novel,'" reprinted in Deane, ed., *Field Day Anthology*, 1:1255–65. Knighted in 1873, Duffy would later become—and is now more commonly—known as Sir Charles Gavan Duffy.

that he study for the law at Trinity and in being drawn to a military career instead, O'Malley followed the pattern of Maxwell's own life. Moreover, Lever's descriptions of Maxwell's literary style apply quite nicely to the novel *Charles O'Malley*. Maxwell excelled at the "easy portraiture of the Irish gentleman," Lever felt, in works that achieved a "strange mixture of recklessness, and feeling of acuteness, and simplicity of jovial abandonment to pleasure, with a heart bounding in ambition. . . ." In providing a "graphic description of the more striking vicissitudes of a soldier's life," Maxwell had struck on a brilliant plot device, the connection of "the great events of the late war [with France] with a thread of fictitious narrative," the whole then overcast with "the glowing imagery of romance" (Aug. 1841, 222).

In Lever's extensive battlefield scenes, the romance runs high indeed. At Waterloo, O'Malley is captured by the French and interrogated by Napoleon, recaptured by the British and debriefed by Wellington, then assigned a mission that will prove pivotal to the success of the whole battle. Along the way, he saves the life of the father of Lucy Dashwood, the woman whom he has loved with no hope of success since the beginning of the novel—it seems superfluous to add here that they finally marry.

The constant undercurrent of humor in the novel is sustained by Mickey Free, O'Malley's dedicated but hot-tempered Galway servant, and by the pranks and pratfalls of the officers themselves. At one point stationed in a boring and desolate Irish village, two officers amuse themselves by finding trivial issues around which to build spirited arguments. When a stranger arrives in town, one officer maintains that he is a spy for the United Irishmen, the other that he is a Protestant rector. The argument unintentionally degenerates into a fistfight; the stranger actually turns out to be their new superior officer; and both men are confined to quarters, where they dismally await their discharge from the service. The new officer proves to be "really a trump," however, and dismisses all charges.

Thomas Flanagan, in his pioneering study *The Irish Novelists*

*1800–1850* (1959), found the primary message in such stories to be directed at a British readership, the Irish novel thus serving as "a kind of advocacy before the bar of English public opinion."[7] More recently, Seamus Deane follows Flanagan's lead in his own sense of that literary message: "It was, finally, a way of saying that the Irish were scamps, not rebels."[8] As the *DUM* often noted to its readers, however, the London market was not the only game in town. The other major audience to which the writers played was Ireland's conservative Protestants and Tories, those whose interests lay in Protestant ascendancy. For these readers, a novel like *Charles O'Malley* would appeal as a nostalgic recreation of a simpler time, with a more manageable set of experiences.

In the kind of carefree life that O'Malley enjoys, dour Protestant rectors and spies for the United Irishmen really turn out to be nothing more serious than military comrades who appreciate high-spirited fun. A "mess" is not an ordinary state of chaos but a systematic arrangement of soldiers. Political disagreements become petty and irrelevant, resolved through the higher standards of justice and loyalty administered by the officer class, wise and generous heads of a noble family. O'Malley writes, "[t]he warm affection, the truly heartfelt regard, which existed among my brother officers, made of our mess a happy home. Our veteran colonel, grown gray in campaigning, was like a father to us . . ." (July 1841, 736). Battles bear striking resemblances to foxhunts, and when O'Malley finally retires from the military, he takes up his duties, like an officer taking up a new commission, as the head of a Galway estate. For Daniel O'Connell and Irish nationalists, the Napoleonic Wars had been an occasion for hope, another case of England's difficulty being Ireland's opportunity, with the French losses at Waterloo then dashing those hopes. In Lever's novel, by contrast, O'Malley's faithful tenants have served his landowning family for generations and would not dream

---

7. Thomas Flanagan, *The Irish Novelists 1800–1850* (New York: Columbia University Press, 1959), 38.

8. Deane, *Short History*, 114.

of supporting France in any wars against England. When O'Malley returns to his estate, they welcome him, a war hero, in triumph.

The darker sides of the novel edge into view at those times when O'Malley fears that his military code has somehow failed to maintain order and meaning in the world. He feels depressed at the death of a fellow officer, at the humiliating treatment of captured prisoners, at the cruel sacking of an enemy fort, at the discovery that an opponent in a duel has secretly worn a chain-mail shirt. "Many a bright dream has been dissolved, many a fairy vision replaced, by some dark reality," O'Malley reflects (Sept. 1840, 345). His disillusionments never last long, however, and the code of honor repeatedly resolves his doubts. On two separate occasions, he helps French prisoners to escape, and with no sense that he has acted wrongly. Sustaining the honor of the battlefield is more important than winning any particular battle. Once the war ends, O'Malley returns to the financial complexities of an Irish estate that is badly encumbered by debt and promptly sets about saving it. In these simpler times, an Irish landowner's bold resolution and shrewd management could still win such battles.

The *DUM* at one point renewed its old fight with Samuel Lover, lashing his "furious faction and political and religious rancour" (Sept. 1839, 333), even though Lever's earlier review had mentioned Lover with admiration (July 1839, 97). The hostile review provides a rare exception to the general tendency for Lever's nostalgic vision to cast a softening influence over most of the *DUM* from this period. His friendship with G. P. R. James, the writer of numerous historical romances, also led to James's first contribution to the *DUM*, a highly contrived short story called "The Banker's Daughter" (Feb. 1841), and James would later contribute several more items to the *DUM* under Lever's editorship, including the novel *Arrah Neil*. In personality and lifestyle, James closely resembled W. H. Maxwell, another of Lever's friends whose easygoing ways stood out in waggish relief against the stern, evangelical side of the *DUM*'s original character.

VI

James Clarence Mangan continued, during the M'Glashan years, to publish his two series *Anthologia Germanica* and *Literae Orientales,* supplemented by such miscellaneous and extravagant contributions as "A Sixty-Drop Dose of Laudanum" (March 1839) and "A Polyglott Anthology" (April 1839). This last piece, a dialogue between the traveler Herr Hoppandgoon von Baugtrauter and the critic Herr Poppandgooff von Tutschemupp, appeared under the pseudonym of "The Out-and-Outer" and is laced with frequent puns, lines of poetry, and quotations in different languages. The combination here of the scholarly and the satiric extended and refined a pattern that he had begun to establish several years earlier. In 1831, along with Samuel Lover and several others with a liberal agenda, Mangan had helped launch the *Comet,* a newspaper that then carried much of his more gossipy and eccentric material. At about the same time, the Dublin *Satirist* was publishing his German translations of the kind that would later find a home in "Maggy" (as the *DUM* was known to Mangan and his friends).[9]

The list of names and titles alone provides a glimpse into the wide range of Mangan's contributions to the *DUM*, his wild fluctuations between poetic brilliance and self-deprecating parody. On the one hand, his *Anthologia Germanica* has been described by Patrick O'Neill as "the most representative selection of German verse ever published in Ireland."[10] On the other hand, David Lloyd's psychocultural analysis of Mangan and Irish nationalism reveals patterns that led the poet into "the repeated production of an inauthentic subject who continually eludes identification in or with his writings...."[11]

9. A recent study by Ellen Shannon-Mangan, *James Clarence Mangan: A Biography* (Dublin: Irish Academic Press, 1996), adds a great deal of new detail to our knowledge about Mangan's life; in comparison to earlier studies, Shannon-Mangan also tends to portray Mangan as a more deliberate artist in his approach to his career decisions.

10. O'Neill, *Ireland and Germany,* 97.

11. David Lloyd, *Nationalism and Minor Literature: James Clarence Mangan and the*

For Lloyd, this pattern originates in Mangan's sense of alienation from both Young Ireland nationalism and Protestant-ascendancy conservatism. The writer whose work appeared in the *Nation* throughout the 1840s and in the patriotic anthology *The Spirit of the Nation* (1843) at the same time opposed "nationalist expectations that the poet identify with the nation."[12] The scholar whose translations of German, Oriental, Spanish, Islamic, and Celtic literature appeared frequently in the *DUM* at the same time mocked the very basis upon which any translation could rest. German literature of the *Sturm und Drang* period, like the passionate ballads of the ancient Irish poets, was included in the *DUM,* Lloyd argues, as "evidence of the susceptibility of the primitive to cultivation." Such literatures thus provided models "for the cultivation of the Irish people away from emotional Jacobinism and toward constitutional order by means of that cultural education which the *University Magazine* hoped to promote."[13] For Mangan, however, the scholarly apparatus of his articles simultaneously parodies the serious pursuit of truth, undercutting any beliefs in orderly material progress.[14] Robert Welch's study *Irish Poetry from Moore to Yeats* (1980) also sees Mangan's work as a self-conscious "poetry of failure"[15] and defines the nature of the translations as renderings or versions rather than attempts accurately to capture the original. While Mangan's German translations were generally faithful and accurate, his knowledge of the other languages was either rudimentary, as with Gaelic, or nonexistent. He thus often drew his inspiration and material from the translations of others, from Samuel Ferguson's essay on Hardiman,

---

*Emergence of Irish Cultural Nationalism* (Berkeley: University of California Press, 1987), 188. In addition to this study, see also John Hutchinson, *The Dynamics of Cultural Nationalism: The Gaelic Revival and the Creation of the Irish Nation State* (London: Allen and Unwin, 1987), for a discussion of various theoretical conceptions of cultural nationalism and of the relationship between cultural and political nationalism.

12. David Lloyd, *Nationalism and Minor Literature,* 190.
13. Ibid., 130.
14. Ibid., 118.
15. Robert Welch, *Irish Poetry from Moore to Yeats* (Totowa: Barnes and Noble, 1980), 77.

for instance, in the case of Gaelic. In contrasting Mangan's translations with those of Ferguson, Welch argues that Ferguson's "impersonality" or "self-effacement" makes him an "excellent translator."[16] Yet accuracy of translation was hardly the central issue for the *DUM*. After all, Ferguson's knowledge of Gaelic was inferior to Hardiman's. Ferguson's advantage rather lay in the beauty of his language and, of even greater significance, in the ideological identification of his work with Protestant ascendancy.

To this end, the act of translating thus assumes a metaphorical significance as well. Seamus Deane notes that Mangan problematizes the whole concept of translation and thus "questions the very basis of Irish cultural nationalism, which, after all, assumes the translatability of Irish spirit into English words."[17] For the *DUM*, the raw material of ancient Gaelic literature needed to undergo a civilizing transformation, out of the language of poverty, backwardness, Catholicism, and revolution, into the language of the Protestant establishment and the economic and social growth of a modern nation. Only then could that raw material become part of the respectability that the *DUM* saw as a crucial ingredient within its vision of an Irish national literature. The civilizing authority of such a literature would ideally have two functions: it would give renewed heart and spirit to Irish Protestantism, and it would lead the Catholic masses to recognize and accept Protestantism as a legitimate and valuable cultural presence in Ireland. The immediate significanceof non-Gaelic translations such as Mangan's *Literae Orientales* lay, not in any scholarly basis it might have, but in the fact that readers of a monthly periodical in Ireland could learn about Persian or Turkish poetry just like readers in London.

The cultural benefits attached to this aspect of the *DUM* resemble those of its frequent travel articles. By including features on Irish scenery alongside those describing the landscape, history, or cus-

---

16. Ibid., 130.
17. Field Day Anthology, 2:6.

toms of India or Australia, the *DUM* could locate Ireland within an empire respected throughout the world. Letters from the coast of Clare found their way to the pages of the *DUM* alongside letters from Italy, such combinations implicitly asserting Ireland's status as a nation in its own right on the international scene. Respectable Irish could enjoy more than a mere colonial or provincial role in the world, and both travelogues and translations came to serve as a means and claim to that greater role.

It was thus crucial to conservative unionists and supporters of Irish Protestantism that their own members gain control of the translation enterprise. Ferguson did not need four lengthy installments in his assault on Hardiman simply to make the claim that *Irish Minstrelsy* was a shabby piece of work. He also needed to establish his own rights and credentials within the field and to set down the criteria by which future efforts like these would be judged. In the wrong hands, after all, translation could define Ireland too narrowly, as separatist and revolutionary, for instance, or as Catholic and provincial. In the right hands, translation was not unlike that other process so important to Protestant Ireland, namely, conversion of the Catholic masses. When set alongside the bigoted sermons of Protestant controversialists such as those associated with the *DUM*, the verbal extravagances and eccentricities of James Clarence Mangan seem harmless indeed.

## VII

Rounding out the *DUM* contributors from the M'Glashan period, Henry Ferris helped to sustain the magazine's general interest in occult and spiritualist subjects in articles such as "German Ghosts and Ghost-Seers" (Jan.–Feb. 1841). The Irish ballad writer and hedge-school product John Keegan published three stories under the title *Legends and Tales of the Queen's County Peasantry* (Sept.–Nov. 1839). In his only known contribution to the *DUM*, Henry Robert Addison's *Dramatic Doings* provided an inside look at the London theatre scene (Dec. 1840–Jan. 1842, five installments).

In the previous years of the *DUM*, such a title as Addison's would have touched off discussion of some ongoing crisis in the Irish countryside or some new folly in the Whig government. While such doings continued to get coverage in the *DUM* under M'Glashan, the emphasis had changed. Just as Addison wove an atmosphere of easy familiarity around his subject, the *DUM* as a whole sought to portray a more comfortable and accommodating world. If the results tended occasionally to trivialize the magazine and drain it of intellectual energy, they also removed from it much of the earlier sectarian rancor. Catholicism was "still the same relentless foe, which it ever was, to the freedom of the human mind" (Dec. 1839, 714), and democracy would always remain "unfavourable to the happiness of man" (Nov. 1840, 563). But in July 1839, well before Peel's electoral victory in 1841, the *DUM* felt able to offer a vision of change for Ireland, a hope that "the progress of civilization and education may introduce better morals, and render the Irish a happier people." The optimism of this article represents an even greater variance from the *DUM*'s standard editorial line when it extends into the admonition that Protestants "now should bear with patience some injustice from the Roman Catholics, who are now the ruling party." While the *DUM* had shown past flashes of such sympathy for Catholics, it was now blazing new ground: "If O'Connell appears regardless of truth and justice in his persecutions of the Protestants, let them recollect what must have been the feelings naturally excited in his soul by the laws to which he was subjected in the earlier part of his life" (113). Despite Ireland's legacy of conquest and injustice, of hostility and persecution, the *DUM* dared to offer a message of conciliation and dared to hope that the present generations might yet rise above the political traditions of their unhappy past (113).

## 4

## GENIALITY UNDER STRAIN

I

In July 1843, Mortimer O'Sullivan looked back over the past several years, a hopeful time of "halcyon calm" for Irish Protestantism, O'Sullivan felt, because the Conservative electoral victory in mid-1841 had restored Robert Peel to power. Now, however, the country was once more "agitated from its surface to its lowest depths" (July 1843, 106), for 1843 had been designated by Daniel O'Connell as the "Repeal Year." As a specific rallying point, "repeal" covered a wide range of political strategies for O'Connell. Gaining total separation from England was not possible nor even, from his point of view, entirely desirable. The general prospect of independence from Great Britain, however, served both to inspire mass support at home and to create pressure at Westminster for further concessions to Ireland.

The year 1843 thus brought with it what began to seem like an endless series of outdoor rallies, perhaps forty in all, by O'Connell's followers. Menacingly termed "monster meetings," they drew crowds so huge that their numbers defied estimate. At Tara, supporters claimed, a million people gathered around O'Connell's platform to roar approval at speeches urging repeal. By even conservative accounts, attendance at these rallies regularly approached half a million. Even more unnerving to Protestant Ireland and the British authorities, the crowds remained peaceful and orderly. It was bad enough to have the usual barbarians at the gates, but what might they not achieve having been molded into waves more organized and disciplined than the defending army itself? At the very least, O'Connell's troops carried out many of the functions of an alternative and independent government; at worst, they might well shake the Empire, as O'Sullivan observed, to its very depths.

Such an historical backdrop of crisis and cataclysm seemed more appropriate to that period in the *DUM*'s career when its editorship was held by the politically minded Isaac Butt and its editorial policy characterized by bold controversialists such as Mortimer and Samuel O'Sullivan. Instead, the magazine was now under the quite different guidance of Charles Lever, who had taken over from James M'Glashan in April 1842, full of hope, energy, and carefree wit. These were, after all, still the halcyon times, with Irish troubles still under Conservative control. The editorship of a magazine like the *DUM* felt exactly right for an easygoing man of the social world like Lever. Shortly before he set aside his career in medicine and moved from Brussels back to the scene of his Trinity College escapades, he described Dublin as a "changed city" and hoped "that a moderate Government with Tory leanings would be the fairest chance for peace in so disturbed a country."[1]

The success of his novel *Harry Lorrequer* convinced Lever that he could easily continue to increase the circulation of the *DUM*. Indeed, during his editorship, it rose to the unprecedented level of 4,000 copies per month, a figure that it would never hit again and that compares favorably with the circulation level of 10,000 for *Bentley's Miscellany* for the same period. In *Lorrequer*'s wake, the publishing house of Richard Bentley had also sought to tempt Lever into its stable, which already included Charles Dickens, W. H. Ainsworth,

---

1. Charles Lever to Alexander Spencer, 14 Nov. 1841, in Downey, *Charles Lever*, 1:153–54.

and G. P. R. James, by offering him the editorship of its *Miscellany*. Lever rejected these overtures, in part because he preferred Dublin to London, perhaps too because he suffered from what his biographer Lionel Stevenson regards as "a sincere lack of belief in his own ability" as an author.[2] Still, the competition from the London market allowed him to bargain with M'Glashan and Curry for an editor's salary of 1200 pounds per year, with half profits on all he wrote, compared to Bentley's offer of 800 pounds.[3]

Almost immediately, however, the serenity and hopefulness of the enterprise began to pale. Lever discovered that his editor's "salary" was in fact a sum that included what Curry had already promised him for the novel *Jack Hinton, the Guardsman*, so that the editorship itself brought him much less than he had assumed.[4] The work itself also required unexpectedly long hours and attention to detail in return for very little satisfaction. Critics accused the *DUM* of sinking into dullness under Lever's hand, of pandering to the English collectors of stage-Irish trivia. While he could expand the magazine's subscription list, Lever still never managed to bring into focus the various intellectual energies and resources that he hoped to find in Dublin. In an essay entitled "Charles Lever and the Outsider," Tony Bareham describes Lever's "efforts to make his house at Templeogue into one of the premier literary and social centres of the capital, perhaps to re-create a now dead period of the city's convivial greatness."[5] Instead, Lever soon came to despair of greatness even within the columns of his own magazine. He had praised his stable of writers in his inaugural "Editor's Address" in April 1842 (423–24) but soon came to regret such puffery. Already by June 1842, the writ-

2. Stevenson, *Dr. Quicksilver*, 92 and 186; see also Downey, *Charles Lever*, 1:68, for a further biographical consideration of Lever's inferiority complex.

3. Downey, *Charles Lever*, 1:154–56, especially Lever's letter to Alexander Spencer, 14 Nov. 1841.

4. Charles Lever to Alexander Spencer, 4 Feb. 1848, in Downey, *Charles Lever*, 1:273–74.

5. Tony Bareham, "Charles Lever and the Outsider," *Charles Lever: New Evaluations*, ed. Tony Bareham (Savage, Md.: Barnes and Noble, 1991), 103.

ers whose contributions he depended on seemed to him "as groggy a set of screws as ever marched in harness."[6] For a man like Lever, who prized geniality and sociability and who harbored doubts about his own literary talents, the times were indeed agitating.

## II

Despite all of the problems facing him, Lever identified the magazine with his own style and personality in ways that no previous editor had done and that only Joseph Sheridan Le Fanu would later achieve. In its pre-Lever period, the *DUM* had used fiction as the lead item in perhaps only one or two issues per year. Throughout 1842 and 1843, by contrast, virtually every issue begins with an installment from one of Lever's serialized novels.[7] One of these, *Loiterings of Arthur O'Leary,* draws even more attention to itself by occupying only a single column, a rare departure from the *DUM*'s customary double-column format. Moreover, Lever involved his family in the magazine as well, with brother John contributing a religious review (July 1842) and wife Katherine adding two short stories, "Pauline Butler" (Aug. 1842) and "A Queen for a Day" (May 1843). As was frequently the case in her husband's work, Katherine Lever's stories also focus on the themes of deceit and confusion over identity. In the title character of "Pauline Butler," by contrast, she portrays a woman with much greater complexity and depth than Charles Lever's novels had achieved.

For sheer volume, as well, Lever's presence dominated the magazine throughout his editorship. He published frequent reviews, usually on subjects connected with the continent and thus not calculated to win him much nationalist favor at home. A series that he had begun even before assuming the editorship, *Nuts and Nutcrackers*

6. Downey, *Charles Lever,* 1:160.
7. Lever was also unusual among *DUM* editors for his thorough bookkeeping habits. The "Lever Notebook" at the Pierpont Morgan Library in New York contains the "Lever Records" that allowed the *Wellesley Index* to base many of its attributions for this period on external evidence.

(Jan. 1842–May 1844, twelve installments), characterized one aspect of his magazine in its rambling framework: a typical entry consists of several short essays with Lever's thoughts about various subjects of general interest. In *Continental Countries* (Oct. 1842–July 1844, four installments), he brought more focus and method to his subject, discussing the history and society of several European countries but without illustrating his observations in his usual offhandedly anecdotal manner.

Lever's main contributions to the *DUM* remained his literary works, however. *Our Mess: Jack Hinton, the Guardsman* (March–Dec. 1842, ten installments) maintained the picaresque tradition of Harry Lorrequer, and in fact opens with an introductory note from Lorrequer emphasizing the haphazard quality of the narrative. Upon its conclusion, *Jack Hinton* immediately gave way to a similar work, *Loiterings of Arthur O'Leary* (Jan.–Dec. 1843, eleven installments), which also begins with Lever's typically deceptive narrative frame. Supposedly under pressure from magazine readers to produce an account of O'Leary's famed adventures, Lorrequer composes a substantial portion of the manuscript, since he knows his subject so well. O'Leary discovers and burns this version, however, furnishing in its place a motley collection of scraps, fragments, memoranda, and notes that Lorrequer must then use in constructing the "true" story of O'Leary. Set primarily in Europe, the novel follows O'Leary in his random wanderings and inconclusive adventures, some in the style of military tales, others as simple travelogues. The final installment achieves a resolution that touches on some of Lever's own experiences as editor of the *DUM*: two brothers, facing each other on the dueling field, are happily reconciled. In the very same issue, as it happened, a *DUM* review entitled "Modern Conciliation" attacked a political pamphlet by Samuel Carter Hall (Dec. 1843). After Hall published an open letter criticizing Lever's editorship, Lever responded by challenging him to a duel but then, at the last minute, apologized.

With *Arthur O'Leary* concluded, Lever would not produce another significant series until a year later, when he finally began *Tales of the Trains* (Jan.–May 1845, five installments). Subtitled *Some Chapters of Railroad Romance,* the series proposed at its outset to develop an idea that the *DUM* periodically raised: the beneficial effects of expanding the railways. In the narrative voice of "Tilbury Tramp," a government courier, Lever wrote: "The steam-engine is not merely a power to turn the wheels of mechanism—it beats and throbs with the heart of a nation, and is felt in every fibre, and recognized in every sinew of civilized man" (Jan. 1845, 2). For all of its progressive sentiments here, however, *Tales of the Trains* developed little more than some of Lever's—and the *DUM*'s—most long-standing themes: deception, disguise, mistaken identity.

While Lever may have admired the ways in which modern technology could rearrange the surface of the old con games, his deeper fascination lay with the unalterable rules of those games, the patterns that defied history and change. His short story "Carl Stelling—The Painter of Dresden" (July 1842), for instance, opens within a distinctly contemporary framework, but its plot and atmosphere soon shatter the constraints of time. According to an introductory editorial note, Stelling was a talented painter who is now confined to an institution for the insane in Dresden, Germany. Before losing his reason, however, Stelling told his story to a friend, who in turn passed it on so that the *DUM*'s editor could present it here. So far, Lever's usual narrative devices were proving adequate for his needs.

In its exploration of aesthetic obsession, however, the story very quickly expands, coming more to resemble a tale of Edgar Allan Poe's than of Lever's. Having long been fascinated with a miniature that he possesses, a depiction of a beautiful woman and stern older man, Stelling gradually comes to realize, to his horror, that the man has demoniac powers, that the woman has fallen under the man's control, and that they have both lived, vampire-like, for centuries. Now it is Stelling's turn to come under the spell of *La Belle Dame Sans Merci,* the mysterious and eternal embodiment of art who consumes the artist. Seeking escape, he gives himself up to aimless wandering, a humorless and driven version of Lever's other rambling heroes. But Stelling has slipped so far out of the contemporary world that insanity is the only true escape left to him.

A many-layered narrative frame, a Gothic atmosphere and surroundings, an old tutor who secretly posses demoniac power, a young woman who is both the eternal slave of sinister forces and the "beautiful destroyer" of the passive hero (who is also given to fainting spells and sickness and who frequently feels his identity slipping away from him)—all of these elements characterize "Carl Stelling." They also, as it happens, turn up in "Spalatro" (March–April 1843), Joseph Sheridan Le Fanu's short story printed a year later in the *DUM*.[8] Le Fanu by this time had fully developed his own techniques as a student of sensationalism. "Spalatro," for instance, describes a decapitation in grisly detail, and its settings have a nightmarish quality that Lever's more delicate sensibilities eschew. But the striking similarities between Le Fanu's fiction and earlier work by both Isaac Butt and Charles Lever suggest that his contributions to the *DUM* grew out of some awareness of the tastes of its editors.

### III

"Spalatro" remains, however, Le Fanu's only known contribution to the *DUM* during Lever's editorship. Among the regular contributors, Lever managed to retain many other familiar names from past issues of the magazine, such as John Anster, William Archer Butler, James Clarence Mangan, Digby Pilot Starkey, and John Francis Waller. After an absence from the *DUM* of nearly four years, Samuel Ferguson returned with articles on topics such as the Ordnance Survey, Robert Burns, and Elizabeth Barrett. The Irish physician Robert Gordon, who had published poetry in the *DUM* since 1838 under the pseudonym "Coul Goppagh," now contributed two prose works as well. William Johnston continued to keep the *DUM*'s readers in-

---

8. "Spalatro" was first recognized as Le Fanu's in Mc Cormack, *Sheridan Le Fanu*; see pages 64–69 for Mc Cormack's analysis and discussion of the story.

formed about behind-the-scenes doings in Westminster, and Henry Ferris kept turning out eccentric pieces on mystic lore and demonology, including a short story (by "George Hobdenthwaite Snogby") and a three-part series on mesmerism. Maria Frances Dickson returned with a short series entitled "Rambling Records of People and Places," joined now as a travel writer by Louisa Stuart Costello.

Lever also added several significant new names to the *DUM*'s list of contributing writers. The economist and novelist Harriet Martineau, whose *Illustrations of Political Economy* had not impressed the *DUM* in the early 1830s, now had a review of a work on education in which she reflected the *DUM*'s standard line in opposing the National Education System in Ireland (June 1844). John Fisher Murray, better known as a contributor to *Blackwood's* and for his Young Ireland associations, published a short story in the style of Harry Lorrequer (May 1843). John Edward Walsh contributed several essays under the title "Ireland Sixty Years Ago," a title he would use a few years later for a noted book on Irish history. In a more striking case of the article preceding the book, Eliot Warburton contributed a series of sociological travel pieces on Asia, received warm encouragement in them from Lever, and subsequently decided to write a two-volume version of his wanderings. Under the title *The Crescent and the Cross, or Romance and Realities of Eastern Travel* (1844), it became one of the most successful travel books of the nineteenth century.

Still more articles on the East were contributed by another Irish writer, William Cooke Taylor, whose Whig politics and support for the National Education System did not rule out his appearance in the *DUM*. Not only were political credentials less crucial during the cosmopolitan period of Lever's editorship, but Taylor's subject was of considerable interest to the *DUM*. In reviewing a travel book on Turkey, Lever noted that "The East has become to us what France and Germany were to our grandfathers" (March 1845, 331). Heightening the travel interest was England's war in Afghanistan, and the *DUM* devoted a number of articles to the Afghan conflict from a pro-Union perspective, as well as an unlikely sonnet by Sir William Rowan Hamilton. A mathematician and astronomer, educated at Trinity College and then appointed to a professorship in astronomy there, Hamilton was then at the midpoint of a career that had earned him a considerable international reputation. His *DUM* sonnet of January 1843 celebrated the news of British military victories in Afghanistan as well as new economic agreements with China. In the same issue but in more prosaic fashion, Samuel O'Sullivan's article "Successes in the East" hailed the discomfort such news must now be creating within yet another revolutionary group, the "Irish Afghans" who kept urging repeal.

Hamilton contributed several poems during the Repeal Year of 1843, and poetry commanded generally more attention during Lever's editorship than before. In addition, and in ways consistent with Lever's frequently rambling approach to his subject, the *DUM* published a number of essays that rummaged through fragments of poems, translations, or literary allusions, often drawing on several different languages. The titles are depressingly similar in their suggestion of the intellectual gadfly: Robert Gordon's "An Hour in the Clouds," Zachariah Johnson's "June Reminiscences," Samuel Hayman's "Fragments of a Dreamer's Note-Book" and "Some New Jottings in My Note-Book," Digby Pilot Starkey's "Chips from the Library Table." As a lightweight intellectual and aesthetic miscellany, these pieces recall Mangan's "A Polyglott Anthology" from 1839.

Mangan's most significant poetry would not appear before 1846, and then in the *Nation* and not the *DUM*. During Lever's editorship, Mangan continued to offer translations from German poetry, most frequently in his *Stray Leaflets from the German Oak*, most typically in the same satiric tone of his "Anthology." The February 1844 installment of *Leaflets*, for instance, blends Mangan's own poetry with renderings from a variety of minor German poets, masking the original work under the German name of "Selber" ("Himself"). His biographer Ellen Shannon-Mangan suggests that "Selber" represented Mangan's "fantasy of himself as the [*DUM's*] suave, satirical, young poet-translator, master of the cutting criticism and the unique rhyme."[9] The style that Mangan brings to such work, moreover, recalls both the irony and the prosody of Byron's *Don Juan*. A rendering of a German poem about Bluebeard ends with a stanza describing Bluebeard's last wife several years after her rescue from her murderous husband:

> However, she's rich still—just forty-three—
> And quite the ton; she drinks Aesthetic Tea,
> And latterly thinks Blue a much less shocking
> Colour, particularly in a Stocking. (182)

Mangan's own work as "Selber" relies on many of the same Juanesque verbal effects, such as the anapests, colloquialisms, enjambments, and feminine rhymes:

> And though my wisdom, like Sancho Panza's,
>    Consists entirely of bits and scraps,
> I'll bet you fourpence that no man plans as
>    Intense a poem as I on Schnapps. (176)

As one line plunges into the next, it conveys improvisation and authorial whimsy, the off-handed asides swinging the tone from the sublime to the ridiculous.

Mangan was not the only one contributing such verse to Lever's *DUM*. John Francis Waller, involved in the magazine since its earliest issues as "Iota," now contributed poems as "Jonathan Freke Slingsby." Michael Joseph Barry (as "Beta") had also published poems in the *DUM*'s first year. Beginning in January 1842, then, and contributing irregularly until 1847, he began a poetic series known as *The Kishoge Papers*. While Barry would receive more attention for his later involvement in the Young Ireland rising of 1848 than for his poetry, his *Kishoge* series—like Waller's "Slingsby" poems or like other pieces by Charles Hervey—does manage to evoke the style of *Don Juan* with some skill.

9. Shannon-Mangan, *James Clarence Mangan*, 225.

A *DUM* review by poet Digby Pilot Starkey (Dec. 1842) suggests that the magazine's echoes of *Don Juan* were more than mere coincidence. Since Byron's death in 1824, Starkey claimed, English literature no longer had any great poems or poets. An 1844 review of Robert Southey similarly complained that "the world" has become "thoroughly unpoetical within the last twenty years" (April 1844, 458). In reviewing Elizabeth Barrett's work (Feb. 1845), Samuel Ferguson objected to her artificiality of tone and diction, a characteristic that he also regretted in current British poetry as a whole. To complete the circuit, William Archer Butler, looking toward the poets and poetry of America, pronounced that "Genius" is "not there" (Aug. 1843, 230).

Although a September 1850 review would give strong praise to William Wordsworth, the *DUM*'s main response to the perceived dearth of great poetry was to continue publishing derivative and minor offerings. Butler himself worked on a *Prelude*-like series under titles such as "The Boyhood of a Dreamer" or "Recollections of a Poetic Childhood." While he made Wordsworth's acquaintance in 1844, Butler had been chronicling the growth of his own poetic mind since 1836 in the *DUM*, stressing from the outset the "cause of Christianity" as an important but frequently neglected force in poetic visions (July 1836, 32). In its serenity, nostalgia, contemplation of death, and celebration of peaceful scenes in nature, Butler's work typifies one style of poetry in the *DUM* for this period, with the *Don Juan* imitators supplying the other.

Even more than on Butler, though, the *DUM* continued to rely on Mary Anne Browne for its supply of poetic sentimentality. In 1842, she married James Gray, a nephew and friend of the Ettrick Shepherd James Hogg, and her work appears often throughout 1843 and 1844 under her married name. Following her death in late 1844, the magazine sought to place her work within the context of the poetic times: "Among the striking features in the intellectual history of the present age," the *DUM* noted, "none is more remarkable than the unprecedented increase in the number of our female writers"

(April 1845, 397). While the "female mind" in general seemed to the magazine "essentially ill-adapted" for "mental analysis, and the patient process of abstract reasoning," Mrs. Gray was one of those admirable women who knew and observed her limits: "She wrote to please, not to instruct. Her poetry was the spontaneous language of the heart . . ." (397). As a writer, she indeed did possess only a minor voice; for this period of the *DUM*, however, no other poet could lay claim to anything better.

IV

Not surprisingly, given his own literary bent and his various London connections, Lever did a better job at rounding up fiction writers who commanded considerable popular attention. While they were accustomed to higher rates of pay than the *DUM* could offer, they had one advantage over regular hands such as the O'Sullivans, at least in Lever's eyes: politically, they were quite inoffensive. Catherine Gore's "A Chapter on Grandmothers," for instance, blends fiction with social commentary in praise of the civilizing effects grandmothers have on society in general (Feb. 1844). In her story "Uncle Moseley and the Railroad," industrial progress triumphs over individual selfishness and isolation (May 1844). The optimism, the cultured mood and atmosphere, the sense of one's moving easily and gracefully within fashionable society—all of these elements run through Gore's *DUM* pieces, as well as much of her immense novelistic output through the middle of the century. More than any other Victorian writer, she controlled the "silver fork" school of fiction. Before he took over the editorship of the *DUM*, Lever had sniffed that her novels were little more than "translations with a newly invented title."[10] A few years later, and having been forced by the limits of the *DUM*'s stable to lower his standards by several notches, Lever could only have welcomed her contributions.

10. Charles Lever to Alexander Spencer, 2 Nov. 1841, in Downey, *Charles Lever*, 1:152–53.

A far more significant contributor, one who was then enjoying considerable popular success, was Lever's London friend G. P. R. James. Lever had first gotten a literary hand from James back in February 1841, after fire destroyed part of the manuscript of *Charles O'Malley*. To help fill the place that M'Glashan had held for the scheduled installment of *O'Malley* in the *DUM*, James contributed "The Banker's Daughter," a highly contrived short story adequate for a fire sale but little else. Like Gore during this period, James produced a staggering number of novels, and by the end of the 1840s, his literary stature would be badly tarnished by one of William Thackeray's parodies in *Punch*. At the time when his novel *Arrah Neil* ran in the *DUM*, however (July 1843–Aug. 1844, fourteen installments), he brought the status of a genuine literary celebrity to Lever's magazine.

Following James's standard formula, *Arrah Neil; or, Times of Old* is a historical romance. It takes for its setting the same backdrop used in *Love and Loyalty*, the first novel ever to run in the *DUM*: England during the early 1640s, the time of civil conflict between Royalists and Puritans. In a further similarity, both novels sympathize with the Royalists, a partisan alignment not entirely predictable from standard *DUM* politics. The Puritans, after all, had advanced the Protestant Reformation in England, and Oliver Cromwell's subsequent invasion of Ireland had crippled Irish Catholicism and vastly expanded Protestant power throughout the country. But Puritanism had followed the impulses of the heart rather than the guidance of the head. Furthermore, insofar as they also represented revolution and violent social upheaval, the Puritans did not warrant much sympathy from those Protestant members of Irish society who now valued the realities and privileges of the status quo above those ideals of the past that had produced passionate assaults upon established authority.

Ultimately, however, the novel complicates any search for neat political messages. Readers in both England and Ireland, for instance, would have the knowledge, unavailable to characters within the novel, of how the Royalist forces ultimately fell before the Puritans. Moreover, in James's own life and in much of his other work, he cultivated a cavalier manner. He would hardly set such a style aside for the readership of a conservative, Irish-Protestant magazine, especially when the editor of that magazine was himself so genially cosmopolitan, meanwhile serving as the target of so much criticism for his editorial and literary policies. In placing a novel with the *DUM*, then, an established writer like James could have analyzed the magazine's "expectations" in several different ways.

A further interpretive complication arises out of the theme that dominates *Arrah Neil* and that figures so prominently in the fiction running throughout the *DUM*'s whole career: uncertain identity. The title character, a homeless sixteen-year-old girl, harbors a mysterious birthright, one that even she only dimly suspects and that lurks in the background from beginning to end. To the surprise of a few of the novel's characters, but certainly none of its readers, she is ultimately revealed as a person of high birth. More generally, the theme of uncertain identity serves to structure people and events at nearly every level in *Arrah Neil*. Almost without exception, for instance, Puritans are described as "hypocritical," a charge that continued to cling to Cromwell's historical reputation and that required *Arrah Neil*'s readers always to speculate on what hidden motives the various Puritan characters might be harboring. Other characters frequently assume false identities in order to protect themselves at a time when the battle lines of the civil war—itself a national identity crisis—are still confusing and constantly shifting. The main military figure, an heroic English Captain named Barecolt, has changed his name from Cobalter and at another point pretends to be French, meanwhile charging one of the Puritans—who is truly a villain—with being an imposter.

While all of these roles within roles resemble some of the patterns used by Charles Lever, *Arrah Neil* is more solemn and tragic than Lever's historical novel *Charles O'Malley*. Both portray battle scenes and skirmishes, but Lever creates a broader panorama whereas James focuses more intently on the minor, local actors. Characters who rise to prominence, for Lever, do so on their own heroic merits, whereas James attributes their stature to the accidents of history. Within the wider scheme of things, and propelled by the same cataclysmic events, James's minor characters take on a significance equal to that of the kings and Cromwells. Lever's military nostalgia has no appeal to James, and whereas Arrah Neil and her lover enjoy a few brief weeks of married happiness near the end of their novel, it continues just long enough to see them both cut down by the ravages of war. While Protestant readers might have disagreed on historic precedents for the novel's political allegiances, the overall message was clear enough: violent action, especially of the civil kind, is never a good solution.

v

Such a point was hardly new to the magazine, not even as the thesis of a literary work, since *Love and Loyalty* had issued a similar warning as far back as 1833. In the shadow of the repeal banners, however, Ireland's privileged minorities had renewed reason for concern. O'Connell's movement, whether it expected indeed to end the Union or simply to gain another round of British conciliations to Irish Catholicism, led the *DUM* to expand its political coverage beyond the levels that M'Glashan had found adequate. Of primary interest, of course, was the issue of repeal itself. For three days in late February and early March 1843, Isaac Butt debated Daniel O'Connell on a repeal proposal before the Dublin Corporation, the occasion on which O'Connell proclaimed 1843 as the key year for repeal. For Butt, the significance of both the issue and the opponent marked this event, according to Butt's biographer David Thornley, as the "zenith" of his career as a spokesman for Irish conservatism.[11] Meanwhile, within the pages of the magazine that Butt had once

---

11. David Thornley, *Isaac Butt and Home Rule* (London: MacGibbon and Kee, 1964), 15.

edited, Mortimer O'Sullivan would contribute six major political essays on repeal during 1843 alone.

In his series, O'Sullivan cautioned his readers against getting lured into support for O'Connell. Conservative Protestants had considerable reason for concern, since Young Ireland had already claimed the Trinity College graduate Thomas Davis. An even more alarming defection would come in January 1844, when the Protestant landlord and parliamentarian William Smith O'Brien joined the Repeal Association. Despite O'Connell's assurances of protection and respect for all religions, O'Sullivan warned, repeal would ultimately lead to the dispossession of Irish Protestants. As basis for this warning, O'Sullivan pointed to the nearly complete involvement of the Catholic clergy, bishops as well as parish priests, in O'Connell's movement.

By August 1843, after a summer's worth of monster meetings had built up considerable political momentum, O'Sullivan's patience with Peel began to run thin. In the face of a movement that amounted to "revolution" and that threatened "the destruction of the British Empire," the government continued to allow demonstrations and showed signs of offering further concessions (Aug. 1843, 243). By September, however, O'Sullivan's position had shifted slightly. Despite his claim that "the ample range of history" showed "no example of a struggle like this by which Ireland is now agitated, and the British empire threatened with convulsion and ruin . . ." (356), he now expressed support for Peel's tolerant, wait-and-see approach to the repeal meetings.

O'Sullivan's ambivalence at one level shows simple political prudence: who could reasonably have advocated violent military confrontation with mobs such as those that O'Connell could command? At a more humanistic level, however, O'Sullivan continued to support the social force that the *DUM* had always valued over all others: education. Its power gradually but eventually to transform a society, the *DUM* felt, arose from its basis in spiritual and scriptural truth. Articles by Samuel Ferguson (Aug. 1844) and John Anster (Jan.

1845) voiced concerns about abuses attendant upon rapid industrial development, especially the resulting alienation of the individual and the barriers that arose between social classes. In an essay entitled "The Factory System of England," the *DUM* offered, as a solution to such problems, "secular and religious instruction" (Oct. 1843, 437). To educate, the *DUM* pronounced, "we must infuse not merely knowledge, but a sense of duty and of moral responsibility" (Dec. 1844, 683). In analyzing violence in Tipperary, the *DUM* noted that such conditions restricted the availability of capital in the whole economy because investors felt reluctant to incur major risks in a lawless country. Again, the answer was scriptural education, "the vitalizing knowledge of the life and immortality which is alone brought to light by the Gospel. And where that knowledge is effectively communicated, it never fails to impart to the human being that elevating consciousness of his destiny . . ." (May 1845, 624). The Pope, by contrast, represented the "spirit of darkness permanently enthroned at the Vatican" (June 1842, 743). Refusing to allow its believers a knowledge of the Gospel's light, Catholicism only encouraged them further along the path of violence and degradation.

In perhaps the *DUM*'s most oversimplified account of how Catholicism blinded and deprived its own people, Samuel O'Sullivan complained that Catholics had to make do with religious services conducted in a language that they could not understand. O'Sullivan contrasted Protestants with Catholics to suggest that, "in this one particular, there is a difference between these two classes of people which would account fully for every other difference by which their social condition is distinguished . . ." (Jan. 1844, 139). If the Protestants of Ulster were denied their regular services and left with only Latin masses instead, they would soon begin acting in the same vicious manner that typified a Tipperary Catholic.

Mortimer O'Sullivan developed other examples of Irish Catholics suffering under the darkness of their religion. Historically, the Catholics themselves had sold out the rights and status of their native countrymen, and it took the benefits of the Union finally to redress these self-inflicted injustices. Catholics mistakenly believed that Emancipation had been granted them because of the threat of physical force; in fact, England's sense of mercy had produced reform. O'Connell might rail against British domination, but "for every evil and adversity of which he complains," the Church of Rome "is answerable" (April 1843, 480). The repeal agitation, too, grew out of religious animosities fed by the Catholic clergy rather than out of any real political or economic differences.

Whether one considers Samuel's narrow view here or Mortimer's broad one, the effect is the same: feeling the pressure of repeal, the *DUM* on one level continued to cling to the same irrational and partisan religious views with which it had begun twenty years before. M'Glashan's editorship might have allowed for a period of general moderation, and Lever might subsequently have brought a more cosmopolitan experience to the whole enterprise. But religious issues had not yet lost their power to turn hysterical in the magazine.

VI

It is thus not surprising to find the general subject of education once again leaning toward the more specific goal of proselytizing. The British military successes in Afghanistan and China, for instance, now provided what the *DUM* saw as an ideal career opportunity for Protestant missionaries, and Samuel O'Sullivan laid out a carefully staged strategy for them to follow (Jan. 1843). In an article on "Romish Missionaries," John Scouler criticized the Jesuits for providing potential converts with little more than "ceremonial observances" and belief "without reasoning." Protestantism, by contrast, sought to effect an internal "moral change" and trusted that "intellectual freedom and increased physical advantages will be the result of the renewed mind . . ." (Feb. 1843, 212). Mountifort Longfield, in adding his voice to the same chorus, saw even greater physical advantages arising out of a successful campaign of proselytizing. If England carried out its holy duty in bringing religion to the world, "Her peaceful, contented colonies will be a market for her manufactures," and her "redundant inhabitants" could also emigrate to the colonies, thus relieving a rate of population growth that the economist Longfield already found disturbing (April 1843, 520). The O'Sullivans might bring the most consistent expressions of Protestant religiosity to the *DUM*, but they were hardly unique in their fervor.

Closer to home, the *DUM* considered the examples of several Protestant groups that had introduced "colonizing systems" into Ireland itself. After braving the hardships of isolation and the threats and even violence from local Catholics, such colonies gradually won the respect and acceptance of their neighbors. Moreover, the evangelical mission of the colonies was producing growing numbers of converts, thus demonstrating that "Ireland is ripe for conversion" (June 1845, 748).

Pressing upon such faith, however, was the fear among Ireland's Protestants that education and proselytizing might simply not have enough time left to work their beneficial effects. The *DUM* thus sought to establish other lines of defense that would secure the country for purposes of long-term pacification. In July 1843, for instance, during the height of the repeal meetings, Mortimer O'Sullivan suggested that the Protestant yeomanry be reconstituted as a defense force against political agitation and the potential for much greater violence. More importantly, though, the magazine began to emphasize a social group that had received little attention prior to the Lever years: Ireland's landed gentry. The *DUM* urged them to take advantage of their unique place within Irish society and to serve as a rallying point for the forces against repeal: "The same activities and precautions by which Irish landlords guard their own rights, privileges, and interests, will defend and secure the permanency of British connection" (Feb. 1843, 167).

More than ever before, the *DUM* defended landlords against charges of rackrenting, excessive evictions, and indifference to the suffering of their tenants. The current agitation in Ireland had little to do with economic discrepancies, the magazine argued, especially since the country had made so much economic progress in the past few years. In several key articles, the gentry enjoyed much of the same concern and moral encouragement that had previously gone to the Protestant clergy. Several reasons may explain this shift of emphasis. Ever since the 1838 Tithe-Rent Charge Act, landlords rather than clergymen bore the responsibility of collecting tithes for the Church of Ireland. More recently, Peel's government decided in 1843 to investigate landlord-tenant relations as one way to address Irish agitation. Called the Devon Commission, the investigation would not publish its massive findings until February 1845. While the *DUM* would reject the conclusions and proposals of the Commission (see April and May 1845), it was also possible to detect in such inquiries the beginnings of agrarian reform. More and more, the British parliament placed secular above religious interests, a utilitarian hierarchy within which a Protestant clergyman in Catholic Ireland seemed increasingly expendable.

VII

Then, suddenly, the crisis evaporated. In October 1843 the government issued a proclamation forbidding an imminent monster meeting at Clontarf. With no good alternative available to him, O'Connell obeyed, still convinced that the cause of repeal would thereby win a moral victory. But Peel was not finished yet, and within a few days the government would charge O'Connell and several other repeal supporters with sedition. More quickly than many observers, the *DUM* saw in these events new signs of hope for Protestant Ireland, since O'Connell, having quit the field at Clontarf, could no longer present himself as "the general of the physical force of the Irish people" (Nov. 1843, 633). Without the threat of violence behind it, repeal began to collapse as a movement, its energy spent in a long series of O'Connell's personal legal maneuvers. In January 1844, the government first packed its jury and then tried him on charges of sedition. Convicted in mid-February, he would have to wait until May to receive a sentence: one year in prison. Even though this sentence was reversed in early September, Peel by then had clearly won a decisive victory over his old enemy.

While 1844 provided a brief and welcome respite from political battles, the *DUM* soon had its attention drawn to yet another Irish Catholic dragon, the disturbing prospect of the government tripling its annual grant to Maynooth College. As a national seminary for the education of Catholic priests, Maynooth had always provided the *DUM* with a convenient target. In April 1844, for instance, the magazine criticized a proposal by Lord John Russell to increase aid to Maynooth, but it regarded this as little more than just another irresponsible gesture from the Whigs. When Peel himself brought the same measure forward one year later, however, conservative Protestants moved quickly to prepare counter-measures. In Exeter Hall in London, a public meeting of Protestants took place in March 1845 and produced the Anti-Maynooth Committee, an organization dedicated to resisting any further endowment and sanctioning of the Catholic Church and its clergy.

The *DUM,* with major articles in May and June 1845, readily threw its own weight behind such efforts. In Europe, the *DUM* argued, Catholicism was properly tolerated as a religious force but held in check as a political force. In Ireland, however, the government seemed willing, not just to tolerate both aspects, but even to encourage them. Expanded support for the "rookery" at Maynooth would grant it further political legitimacy: "Maynooth is to be enlarged, established, and endowed, but it is not to be ventilated by the airs of heaven" (May 1845, 515). If left to its own corrupt devices, and in a fair contest with Protestantism, Catholicism would wither away. Instead, even the conservative forces in England now offered it friendly support, preventing enlightened Catholics from reforming their faith and gullible Protestants from realizing just how bad Catholicism really was.

Peel had tried the magazine's patience by allowing the monster meetings to continue for so long before he took action. With the success of that action, however, the *DUM* could finally regard his delay as judicious, calculated to let repeal expose its true nature and also to exhaust itself in endless gatherings and speeches. As the magazine itself noted, its only significant disagreement with Peel so far, then, had centered around his continued support for the National System of education in Ireland (Aug. 1844). By bringing forward his proposal for the Maynooth College Act, though, which passed into law in June 1845, Peel left the magazine with a renewed sense of how narrow a political base it occupied in Ireland. If even a conservative government in Westminster refused to defend the best interests of Irish Protestantism, to whom did one turn?

### VIII

Most frequently during Lever's tenure, when the *DUM* gave voice to its various political concerns, it relied on the high-pitched tones of one or the other of the O'Sullivans. At the same time, however, it published a novel, apparently by none other than Mortimer O'Sullivan, that remains largely free of sectarianism even while portraying Irish political turbulence: *The Nevilles of Garretstown—A Tale of 1760* (July 1844–June 1845, twelve installments). Sprawling, panoramic, at times barely coherent in its plotline, the novel opens in the town of Tipperary on the day of the assizes, the landed gentry in particular serving as the center of the festive but chaotic atmosphere. Even though the gentry is represented by Catholics as well as Protestants, these differences of religion are accepted as a natural part of daily life. While Catholics face "the odium of the penal code," the society has "neutralized the effect of severe laws by the charities of social usage" (July 1844, 27).

Still, the events of the novel are always close to nonsectarian violence, at one point even erupting into a faction fight at a funeral. Various characters regularly launch into tales or expositions of their own, and many of these recount duels or military battles. The novel does not romanticize this period, praising from the outset the "advance of civilization" since that time, particularly as shaped by the

"Christian principle" (July 1844, 2). Nonetheless, the old-style gentry class continues to represent order in a benevolent fashion that the novel clearly finds attractive.

Neville Garret, a young man in his early twenties, is presented as "in some sort the hero of our story" (April 1845, 439), a description that aptly reflects its author's off-handed sense of aesthetic control. Moving in and out of the plot in unpredictable fashion, sometimes under the alias of "Carleton," Garret seeks to recover his inheritance from an unjust and illegitimate relative. His quest provides only one example to develop the novel's general theme of legitimacy. Catholics plot against British rule in Ireland, against Protestant domination of Irish Catholics, or against the penal laws. Others seek to restore the Stuarts to the British throne, perhaps through rebellion in Ireland or through intrigue in Paris. Characters are exiled, take on false identities and aliases, and are mistaken for other characters. Rosicrucians attend secret ceremonies in disguise. An informer is tricked by the government authorities, only to turn the tables on those who double-crossed him by lying for the greater good of all. Even the Garretstown house, the object of disputed occupancy and ownership, is said to be haunted. At the end of the novel, George III ascends the throne and issues general pardons for those involved in the conspiracies, an act of leniency that the novel praises. But by then, most readers will have lost track of just who might have been expected to end up in prison anyway.

Even apart from its many layers of deception and its bewildering publication history,[12] *The Nevilles of Garretstown* seems very strange.

12. When the novel first appeared in book form, in New York editions in 1844 and 1845, *The Nevilles of Garretstown* was attributed to Charles Lever. Later published in 1860, because of its centennial link back to 1760, it appeared anonymously but was attributed by some readers to Anne Marsh-Caldwell, the author of the preface for the 1860 edition (see, for instance, Stephen J. Brown, *Ireland in Fiction*). And there was also a German translation, already in print by 1846. The main case for its attribution to Mortimer O'Sullivan is given by W. J. FitzPatrick, who writes that "the real writer, as I was once at no small pains to discover, was the Rev. Mortimer O'Sullivan . . ." (*Notes & Queries*, 7th ser., 6 [Aug. 11, 1888]: 111). While one wishes to know more of the nature of FitzPatrick's pains, he provides no further information. The *Welles-*

The Protestant controversialist Mortimer O'Sullivan was an unlikely novel writer in the first place. Even less likely was the prospect that he would portray a full-blown Catholic insurrectionary movement and then praise the authorities for leniency once the conspirators have been exposed.

But perhaps the novel doesn't represent such a major anomaly after all. Under Lever's editorship, political and religious differences no longer mattered quite so much to the *DUM,* and many earlier hard-line positions got redefined to fit Lever's gentler vision of the world. Thomas Moore, the poet and historian who had endured so much rough treatment in the magazine's earlier reviews, now found himself added to "Our Portrait Gallery" with the *DUM*'s praise and pride (April 1842). In its lead article for April 1844, the magazine shrewdly and generously identified Ireland's three major needs: "Poverty is to be relieved—ignorance to be instructed—lawlessness to be restrained" (402). Explicitly recognizing the ways in which it was departing from earlier *DUM* doctrine, the article placed its greatest stress upon economic problems, attributing "many, if not most of the evils of Ireland to poverty and its consequences" (403). While Charles Lever's notebook records fail to provide conclusive evidence on this particular article, the *Wellesley Index* still finds good reason for attributing it to Lever himself.[13] In both style and content, too, it demonstrates the kind of humane concern for Ireland's poor that Lever acquired early in his career when serving as a doctor during a cholera outbreak in County Clare. A dozen years later, in the mid-1840s, he still recalled his experiences with a sense of pain but also with a recognition of the heroism and kindness in the people he had served.[14]

---

*ley Index,* 4:260, accepts O'Sullivan as the author but also does not explain its rationale.

13. The "Lever Records" suggest that no one was paid for this piece. In such cases, the author was usually the editor himself.

14. Stevenson, *Dr. Quicksilver,* 39-40.

IX

A great many of Lever's experiences and writings from his time as editor of the *DUM* suggest that he was simply too nice a person for the job. Besides the usual demands on an editor—the requests for professional favors, the complaints about editorial neglect of unsolicited manuscripts—Lever also faced a steady barrage of criticism against what were deemed distorted portrayals of Irish character. In late 1843, Lever complained to Samuel Hayman that "No man, barring a dog, could live under the heap of abuse the daily post opens upon me. . . ."[15] Nor could Lever avoid trouble once he had dealt with his mail for the day. William Thackeray visited the editor during his Irish tour in June 1842 and subsequently dedicated his *Irish Sketch Book* to Lever. Returning the favor, Lever praised the work in the *DUM*'s lead article for June 1843. Since a number of Thackeray's published observations showed Ireland in a satiric light, however, Lever then had to face the outrage voiced by Irish nationalists and even by such long-standing *DUM* supporters as Samuel Ferguson. The Catholic *Dublin Review* wrote: "Lever, not withstanding his ephemeral popularity . . . knows nothing of Ireland. His ideas of Irish character are borrowed from the recollection of worn out rakes and superannuated militaires" (June 1844, 290).

Even more trying must have been the opinions of William Carleton, who would have nothing to do with Lever's magazine and instead used the *Nation* as a vehicle for a stinging attack in 1843. Lever's work, Carleton charged, offered "disgusting and debasing caricatures of Irish life and feeling," all because this "buffoon" wished so slavishly to impress his British readership.[16] Carleton was not finished yet, the next month expanding his attack to include Lever's magazine: since the *DUM* "came, unluckily, into his hands, it has, month after month, degenerated into such indescribable dul-

---

15. Downey, *Charles Lever*, 1:174.
16. *Nation*, Sept. 23, 1843, in O'Donoghue, *Life of William Carleton*, 2:60.

ness, that it is, even with the best intentions, impossible to read it."[17] Following Lever's departure as editor, Carleton rejoined the *DUM* in 1846 with his serialized novel *The Black Prophet*. In the meantime, his defection to the *Nation* was costing the *DUM* one of its best literary voices ever.

In her history of Irish periodicals from the nineteenth century, Barbara Hayley regards 1842 as a pivotal year, for now "the country's intellectual energy went into the militant journalism of their *Nation* and other newspapers rather than magazines—the topical rather than the reflective, the active rather than the leisured."[18] While the *DUM* would continue for many years to publish writers like Carleton, Ferguson, Le Fanu, Lever, and Mangan, the *Nation* indeed emerged as the more vibrant voice during the 1840s. Founded in 1842 by John Blake Dillon, Thomas Davis, and Charles Gavan Duffy, the intellectual core of the Young Ireland movement, it resembled the *DUM* both in combining politics with literature and in tracing its intellectual roots to Trinity College. Davis and Dillon had both been active at the end of the 1830s in the Trinity College Historical Society, the same organization to which several of the *DUM*'s founders had belonged just a few years earlier. Unlike the *DUM*, however, the *Nation* was militantly nationalist and could command a readership of perhaps 250,000. In the face of this journalistic monster meeting, the *DUM*'s ability to respond with forceful criticism was limited; after all, some of its own writers had helped to create the crowd.

Most often, though, Lever ended up making conciliatory responses anyway, as he did to resolve his dispute with Samuel Carter Hall. A year after Carleton's scornful words, the *DUM* still gave his work high praise and compared him favorably to Dickens (Sept. 1844). More time-consuming was the matter of Edward Vaughan Hyde Kenealy, a convert from Catholicism, an Irish barrister who would defend the Fenians Burke and Casey in 1867, and—unfortu-

---

17. *Nation*, Oct. 7, 1843, in O'Donoghue, *Life of William Carleton*, 2:61.
18. Hayley, "Irish Periodicals," 84.

nately for Lever—an occasional contributor to the *DUM*. In January 1844, Kenealy published a "Portrait Gallery" sketch on the late William Maginn, a brilliant Irish writer who contributed extensively to *Blackwood's* and later helped to found *Fraser's*. Alongside such accomplishments, though, Maginn also led a dissipated personal life, suffering greatly from alcoholism and debt. Kenealy's sketch treated all of these problems in a fairly frank manner, including a detailed account of how Maginn's savage review of the novel *Berkeley Castle* had led to a duel with author Grantley Berkeley. Believing that Kenealy's manuscript insulted a number of people and that portions were distinctly libelous, Lever edited out much of the offensive material before publishing it.[19] At this point, Kenealy regarded himself as the injured party and presented Lever with his own challenge to a duel.

While Lever managed to end the Maginn controversy amicably, his problems with Kenealy were not yet over. In May 1845, Kenealy contributed the first installment in a projected series on the recently deceased Romantic poet Thomas Campbell. Kenealy described his subject as a "miserable dwarf": "He was, perhaps, the most icy-hearted man that ever lived, wrapping himself up in selfishness as in a robe which he rarely laid aside . . ." (560). Predictably, Campbell's friends and family objected to this treatment. Under new fire, and with the Maginn controversy barely a year old, Kenealy wrote to the *DUM*'s publisher Curry with the suggestion that they terminate the series, an offer that Curry presumably accepted.[20]

By this time, though, Lever had removed himself, not only from the *DUM*'s editorship, but from Ireland itself. His experiences there had subjected him to severe strains—on his health, his equanimity, and his view of the world—and from this time on his work often falters and changes direction under the conflicting pressures that he

19. Downey, *Charles Lever*, 1:183–84.
20. Thomas Campbell to William Curry, June 11, 1845, in the *Wellesley Index*, 4:263. Kenealy's letter was, however, written too late to stop the second installment of this series, which then appeared in June 1845.

faced. Three years after Charles O'Malley was shown fighting for Wellington and then taking up his duties as an Irish landlord, Lever published *Tom Burke of "Ours"* (1844), a novel whose main character represented the other side as an ardent Irish nationalist who served under Napoleon. *St. Patrick's Eve* (1845), from the same time, expressed political views that some might have regarded as radical concerning the status of Ireland's tenants.

"The career of Charles Lever," according to Tony Bareham, "suggests very strongly a man striving to be at the centre of things, but constantly being impelled towards a periphery, a position of 'outsiderness.'"[21] Bareham points to *Tom Burke* as a pivotal work in Lever's career, its "reclusive, discontented" hero becoming painfully aware that Ireland has failed to provide him "with any centrality."[22] Even in his early work for the *DUM*, though, these same tensions and contradictions are already at work, the resolutions to his novels frequently feeling like artificial formulas that seek to impose some hollow harmony. Lever had, for instance, described the title character in his 1842 novel *Jack Hinton* as "an *exceedingly English* young Guardsman coming over to Ireland,"[23] then becoming caught up in the contrasts between the two countries. As critic W. J. Mc Cormack notes of such situational dilemmas, "the comic irony of Lever's early novels is that the hero is officially travelling *at home* within the United Kingdom and his bewilderment is an index of the Union's failure." The marriages that conclude these works, moreover, contradict this irony by reinforcing the political metaphor of the Union.[24]

Mc Cormack's analysis places the novels within a broadly social and political context; but at a personal level as well, there is a fundamental uneasiness here that characterizes, not only much of Lever's

21. Bareham, "Charles Lever," 96.
22. Ibid., 112 and 122.
23. Charles Lever to Alexander Spencer, Nov. 2, 1841, in Downey, *Charles Lever,* 1:153.
24. Mc Cormack, *From Burke to Beckett,* 186–87.

work from this period, but indeed his whole literary identity. On his use of the persona of Harry Lorrequer, Lever wrote that "in England, where I am more read and prize the repute higher, Charles Lever is as much a pseudonym as Harry Lorrequer, for indeed H. L. is believed to exist, and no one cares whether C. L. does or not."[25] In Dublin, by contrast, a city to which Lever had returned for its "keen relish for joking and the sharp readiness of Irish wit" as much as for the *DUM*'s editorship, people now bickered constantly over religion and politics.[26] In February 1845, then, he was eager to leave, and by March had settled in Brussels. His editorial records indicate his role as editor for the April and May issues of the *DUM;* by July, the magazine was under the editorial management of John Francis Waller.[27]

Having put the *DUM* behind him geographically, however, Lever still never managed to divorce his sympathies from the magazine. Even twenty-five years later, he fondly remembered the enterprise this way:

If the men who wrote for the *University* were all more or less engrossed in their several careers as churchmen, barristers, and physicians, and there was consequently less of that bond of professional spirit which they who make literature a career possess, there was on the other hand a great breadth from the diversity of daily occupations, vast variety from the divers contrasts of experiences, and a total absence of all the rivalries and jealousies that unhappily attend men when seeking distinction by the same road.[28]

If the romantic nostalgia is typical of Lever, it is also true that he continued to be one of the *DUM*'s most faithful contributors for more than a dozen years after leaving the editorship. For its own part, when it finally came to write his obituary, in July 1872, the mag-

---

25. Charles Lever to Alexander Spender, Dec. 17, 1841, in Downey, *Charles Lever,* 1:155.
26. Lever's "impressions to Sir Hamilton Seymour" are reported in these terms in Stevenson, *Dr. Quicksilver,* 103.
27. For information establishing the dates surrounding Lever's closing months as editor, see *Wellesley Index,* 4:201.
28. Stevenson, *Dr. Quicksilver,* 111.

azine remembered Lever as its most popular editor ever, looking back with particular fondness to the social gatherings over which he had then presided: "The re-unions at his country residence, not far from Dublin, were delectable. The brightest, the wittiest, the most scholarly men, were sure to be met at his table . . ." (105–6). In his praise for the *DUM*'s breadth and variety as particular strengths, as well as in his service at encouraging such talent to even brighter heights, Lever provides us with a good part of the explanation for the magazine's long career.

5

# A NATIVE PERIODICAL IN A TIME OF FAMINE

I

After Charles Lever's departure from Dublin in February 1845, the *DUM* entered into a period in which the editorial center of the magazine is difficult to locate. In part, this uncertainty arises because Lever managed to divest himself only gradually of the editor's duties. As his notebooks indicate, he had a hand in preparing the magazine through the May issue, with John Francis Waller officially taking the helm by July. But Lever's own leave-taking, "A Word At Parting," doesn't appear until August 1845, with an editorial note explaining that it should have been published in the previous issue. Forced now to rely on agents and mail deliveries for his literary business with the *DUM*'s publisher William Curry, Lever also saw his old Dublin connections adding to his troubles. In late 1846, while negotiating some payments with Curry, Lever noted of his dealings, "I have been outrageously rogued and robbed throughout."[1] After 1845, he never again used a Dublin publishing house for any of his novels, and he would not resume regular contributions to the *DUM* until May 1847.

1. Stevenson, *Dr. Quicksilver*, 159.

A similar pattern of uncertain editorial authority characterizes Waller's connection to the magazine in the ten years after Lever's departure, until December 1855. While he occasionally writes under the standard editorial pseudonym of Anthony Poplar, he more commonly adopts his long-standing pseudonym of Jonathan Freke Slingsby, and on one occasion even appears as Iota, his original pen name in the *DUM*. In Lever's case, such shifting masks may betray some underlying doubts and insecurities; for Waller, however, they rather indicate the playfulness that he brought to his role as editor and also the extent to which that role was shared by James M'Glashan. Through all of the editorial turmoil, M'Glashan served as a strong thread of continuity within the magazine, and he continued, throughout Waller's entire tenure as editor, to serve as a kind of behind-the-scenes manager. Starting with "May-Day Melodies" in May 1850, then, Waller's most characteristic entries were the frequent columns in which he portrayed himself as Slingsby and M'Glashan as Anthony Poplar, sometimes accompanied by another character named Bishop.

These columns tend to breeze cheerfully through a handful of recent novels or volumes of poetry, or to present a smattering of original poems and an occasional short story, often by Waller himself. A sample from "Thoughts in the Woodlands" typifies the mood, style, and theme in his verse:

> Manfully bear we then
>     All trials given
> Thankful for life and food
>     Morning and even.
> Let each, with strong control,
> In patience keep his soul,
> Still speeding towards the goal
>     Whose gate is heaven. (Aug. 1850, 237)

Whether the form was that of a conventional review, an essay-style letter, or an imagined dialogue, the world view of Waller's work never wavered or changed. His book publications from this period include *The Slingsby Papers* (1852) and *Poems* (1854), and in reviewing this latter work, the *DUM* praised the "peculiar pensive Christianity" underlying his voice (Jan. 1854). At the same time, Waller's writing contains an element of almost aggressive triviality, present in his own contributions but also running throughout much of the magazine's other offerings during his entire tenure as editor.

John McBride's dissertation study of the *DUM* emphasizes 1852 as a point of conclusion. After that year, McBride argues, "the emotional and intellectual commitment to a sense of communal identity which characterizes the earlier period is never again matched."[2] Waller's own columns, indeed, show little commitment of any kind, his style combining middle-class values, mid-Victorian smugness, and late-collegiate wit in a depressingly consistent fashion. Notes of dreariness inevitably give way to expressions of optimism and hope, and meditations inspired by the seasons always stay firmly attached to the comforts of a country-house garden.

Yet the magazine not only survived this wave of banality, it continued—albeit in diminished fashion—to advance its original goals. An overview of the *DUM* on the occasion of its twenty-first year noted that, when the magazine began its life, Ireland

> had no national literature, few names which made themselves known through the world, and of those few the majority were so known through the medium of English or foreign publications. What we wanted was not genius, or wit, or learning, but we wanted that which should collect, intensify, and expound it. . . . We wanted an exponent of our own thoughts, our own aspirations, our own tastes and feelings, in politics, in science, in *belles lettres*, in poetry, in music. We wanted, in a word, A NATIVE PERIODICAL. (Jan. 1853, 2)

In language that echoed the categories of a similar essay in April 1841, the *DUM* distinguished between a national and a merely provincial literature, proudly laying claim to the former: "We have, in truth, created a periodical literature in Ireland, and for Ire-

---

2. McBride, *"Dublin University Magazine,"* 1:343.

land . . ." (6). While the magazine under Waller's editorship published a great deal that was trivial and transitory, it also offered more than enough of the material that justified such claims.

II

The Dublin poet and translator Denis Florence M'Carthy, one of the few Irish writers to gain a place in Leopold Bloom's personal library, was heavily represented in the *DUM* under Waller, and his poetic voice in many ways corresponds with Waller's. An earlier contributor to the *Nation* and a supporter of repeal and Young Ireland, M'Carthy began his connection with the *DUM* in April 1847 with the translation of a Gaelic ballad, "The Foray of Con O'Donnell." The stately verse of "The Voyage of St. Brendan" (Jan. 1848) continued his interest in Ireland's past, but most of M'Carthy's verse in the *DUM* never rises above trite superficiality, as in the final lines of a poem in August 1849:

> Ah! I shall love!—and love!—and love!—
> Since Love is but the Life of All! (152).

M'Carthy's prose offered even worse fare. In "April Fancies," the *DUM*'s lead article for April 1853, we find: "The revival of nature in Spring is one of those rare phenomena of the exterior world, which never presents itself to our observation or imagination, without perpetually renewing feelings of wonder and delight" (395). In a short story, "The Angel of Toil" (Aug. 1848), M'Carthy anticipated much of the banality of Coventry Patmore's 1854 poem *The Angel in the House*. In M'Carthy's story, a struggling young artist sees in a dream how men all over the world—and especially a shipload of Irish migrant workers—are inspired in their work by the love of their women back home. Where love is absent, the men sink into vice, their work debased and meaningless. When the artist awakens, his own beloved, Enna, stands by his side, informing him that she will agree to marry him and also that his portrait of the Virgin Mary, inspired by Enna, has just won a major competition.

Along with Waller and M'Carthy, the other major purveyor of the sentimentality of nature in the *DUM* from these years was Marian E. Martin, of the same family that later produced the Irish novelist Violet Martin. Between 1848 and 1856, Martin contributed some two dozen pieces, many of them expository essays in which she meditated on or felt inspired by plants, "Thorns and Thistles, and Their Comrades" (April 1854), for instance. Lightweight, breezy, sprinkled with poetry, these extended reveries on nature or life in general further helped to refine the recurring style of Slingsby in Waller's magazine. While most of this work evokes the hothouse air of an English or Irish country garden, Percy Boyd takes this vision of oppressively playful leisure on the road in his accounts of German student life or his European travelogues, such as "A Scamper in the Long Vacation" by "Geoffrey Briefless, Barrister-at-Law" (Nov.–Dec. 1846).[3]

Even the short fiction that seeks to offer matter for serious thought seems mired in Slingsby-esque banality. A series of five stories between 1845 and 1850, by an unidentified author, appeared under the subtitle of "A Story of Gold." All are set in Ireland, and all demonstrate how greed for money leads to personal tragedy. Another short story, "Grace Kennedy" (Sept.–Nov. 1850) by the Irish writer Samuel George Cotton, portrays a young girl adopted into a peasant family whose Catholic mother brutalizes her. The girl is eventually restored to her rightful place, her sterling character in no danger from her newfound riches, just as her manner of speech has avoided contamination by the coarse brogue of her foster family. The mother, meanwhile, is packed off to prison, and good riddance to her.

Similar values emerge from five short stories by Dinah Maria Mulock, later Mrs. Craik. Beginning with "The Rosicrucian—A

---

3. Boyd's title anticipates those of later popular Victorian travelogues such as Edward Whymper's *Scrambles Amongst the Alps* (1871) and Leslie Stephen's *The Playground of Europe* (1871).

Tale of Cologne" (Feb. 1847), Mulock did most of her work for the *DUM* before the success of her first novel in 1849. In the story "Philip Armytage; or, The Blind Girl's Love" (June 1847), for instance, she accomplishes the remarkable feat of having her heroine Stella go blind twice during the narration, once from a disease (which is curable), later from a stroke of lightning (which is not). The title character is so inspired by his love for Stella, however, that they manage to triumph over all of their hardships until she finally dies in childbirth. Philip lives on, longing for Stella and waiting for death as a welcome relief from the unlikely events with which Mulock has surrounded him. All of these writers exhibit Waller's tendency not only to pensive and sentimental Christianity but also to didactic triviality. It is easy to dredge up such specimens from any editorial period of the *DUM*. At the same time, the magazine under Waller's guidance touches bottom more frequently and aggressively than under any previous editor.

### III

It would be easier to endure the *DUM*'s extensive trafficking in trivia during this period if not for the fact that the first half of Waller's ten-year editorship, from 1845 to 1850, found Ireland suffering the ravages of the Great Famine. The *DUM* had considered the issue of hunger in the land since the magazine's outset, although never out of any consistent position. In January 1835, the magazine defined a typical Irish cabin as "a seminary for the education of pigs" and went on loftily:

> Much of the misery in Ireland is apparent, not real; and many of the privations under which the people labour, and which, to a stranger, would seem to imply so much suffering, proceed from an utter indifference about comforts and decencies, which, in England, would be deemed indispensible, and which a very ordinary effort of industry or ingenuity would be more than sufficient abundantly to supply. (2)

In contrast with such crass snobbery, the *DUM* just over a year later argued for legislation to address the "appalling misery and destitution" in Ireland (April 1836, 349), going on to note that "[t]he destitution in some districts has reached the utmost limit of human endurance" (350).

During the 1840s, the *DUM* continued to mix insensitivity with sympathy. In February and again in August 1846, fear of widespread hunger was dismissed as the "potato panic." In January 1847, however, the tone changed drastically: "We are, indeed, involved in the greatest National Calamity" (141). The magazine criticized England for its refusal to help out more fully during this crisis, and it defended the landlords who had been forced to assume so much responsibility for famine relief. Then, in April 1847, Isaac Butt published one of the longest essays ever to appear in the *DUM*. Entitled "The Famine in the Land," it was followed in May by a companion piece, "Measures for Ireland," in which Butt reviewed many of his points from the previous month. The first of these pieces, especially, reprinted that same year as *A Voice for Ireland,* stands as one of the most profound analyses of the Famine written during the period.

Butt began by describing the Famine as "a calamity, the like of which the world has never seen. Four millions of people, the majority of whom were always upon the verge of utter destitution, have been suddenly deprived of the sole article of their ordinary food" (April 1847, 501). He was also bitterly aware of the ironies of the situation:

[I]n a country that is called civilized, under the protection of the mightiest monarchy upon earth, and almost within a day's communication of the capital of the greatest and richest empire in the world, thousands of our fellow-creatures are each day dying of starvation, and the wasted corpses of many left unburied in their miserable hovels, to be devoured by the hungry swine; or to escape this profanation, only to diffuse among the living the malaria of pestilence and death. (501–2)

The answer, Butt argued, was a massive relief effort financed by the British government, to include enough imported food to replace the blighted potatoes and enough payments to individuals to purchase that food.

Butt criticized the Tory party in general for having long denied the existence of any genuine famine, although he praised the early efforts of Sir Robert Peel, who had wisely imported Indian corn during the winter of 1845–1846 to prevent widespread famine then. While Peel's efforts had been too limited, he was still, as Butt saw it, the only major official able to understand the nature of the crisis. In July 1846, however, Lord John Russell's Whig government returned to power determined to minimize government intervention in Ireland and instead to leave relief assistance to private enterprise, a position that Butt attacked as foolhardy, irresponsible, and cruelly self-serving. He felt that Ireland's landed gentry and tenant-farmers had so far acquitted themselves well in responding to the crisis, yet they were slowly being driven into bankruptcy because they were forced to finance too much of the relief effort for the poor by themselves. While England's main legislative gesture toward relief had merely been to provide for public-works projects, even these were woefully inadequate. Butt pointed out the extensive work on roads that led nowhere at a time when other projects, such as the Irish railway system, could well have profited from such government assistance. In addition, the pointlessness of the relief efforts encouraged negligence and indolence when the peasantry might be learning better work habits, respect for law and order, and some useful alternatives to the old barter economy.

Butt urged Irish landlords to take a more active role in promoting further government action and also in assisting their tenants to emigrate to alleviate the distress. In developing a general concept of Irish federalism, though, he also raised the vague threat that British heartlessness would swiftly increase support for repeal since "Britain is now branded as the only civilized nation which would permit her subjects to perish of famine, without making a national effort to supply them with food" (508). The events of the Famine, and the response of British hypocrisy, left Butt further removed from his political conservatism than ever before. "Civilization" had been the cultural goal for Ireland that the *DUM* had been striving for since its outset, yet in the case of Union with England, civilization had failed Ireland totally.

While the *DUM*'s most explicit pronouncements on the possibility of repeal came from Butt during these years, his was hardly an isolated voice. In January 1847 the magazine published "Rogue and Rapparee," a short story about the eighteenth-century Irish highwayman Redmond O'Hanlon. Outsmarted by a Quaker, O'Hanlon still befriends his intended victim, and they part within a general atmosphere of comedy and good fellowship. A second article in the same issue warns against popular pamphlets that inflame the violent passions of the masses. One example, the writer notes, seemingly unaware of contradicting the short story, even romanticizes such villains as the notorious highwayman Redmond O'Hanlon. As the Famine wore on, the issue of respect for authority became increasingly complex for the *DUM*, and Butt was not the only conservative Irish Protestant to challenge England. In April 1848, when the Protestant Repeal Association was founded, Samuel Ferguson joined up, and Butt came close to adding his support as well.

The *DUM* occasionally reverted to its previous hard-line stance. A review of Daniel O'Connell's life, for instance, deplored "the present state of social disorganization in Ireland" (Sept. 1848, 343), going on to urge that "[a]*ll agitation* for a Repeal of the Union should be made highly penal" (353). The more common articulation of the *DUM*'s position on repeal, though, occurs in a June 1849 article citing a letter of Isaac Butt to the Earl of Roden. Butt foresaw the possibility that repeal might come as a way for England to divest itself of its problematic Irish connection. Ireland should thus prepare for such an eventuality, not because it was desirable necessarily, but because it might happen. The magazine approved of Butt's sentiments, for it had itself endorsed this position in earlier articles. In October 1847, for instance, the *DUM* observed that "when Repeal of the Legislative Union has been brought to pass, Ireland shall have, within her own limits, among her own sons, the materials of which a legislature can be constructed" (496). Another piece, in January

1848, had contemplated repeal in a similar fashion. Absent from all of these discussions and forecasts is the *DUM*'s previous note of hysteria that had arisen at the prospect of repeal. British compassion for Ireland might well be dead, but the magazine was not about to waste further time in bemoaning this loss.

IV

In the latter part of 1846 and early months of 1847, through such measures as the Labour Rate Act of 1846, the British government kept distancing itself from Ireland's plight. Relief for the Irish destitute increasingly became the responsibility of local property owners, with relief sponsored by the British government, whether in the form of public works or food shipments, simply closing down. Most immediately, then, Butt's essay was a response to these significant policy shifts, albeit a response that did nothing to discourage British abandonment of Ireland. In June 1847, shortly after his essay appeared in the *DUM*, the Irish Poor Law Extension Bill passed, one of its provisions requiring anyone holding more than a quarter-acre of land to give up that holding in order to qualify for relief. Termed the Gregory Clause after its sponsor William Gregory, the quarter-acre provision facilitated clearances of marginal holdings throughout Ireland. By the end of the century, the Gregory Clause would be infamous for having helped to break apart rural Irish society and would prove embarrassing for Gregory's widow, Lady Augusta Gregory, in her efforts to launch a national literature. In 1847, however, the Bill did not distinguish between Ireland's social classes as much as it did between partners in the Union, for now the Famine was entirely the responsibility of Ireland. In his economic study *Why Ireland Starved* (1983), Joel Mokyr calculates that the British government spent about 9.5 million pounds on famine relief; just a few years later, by contrast, 70 million pounds would go to finance the Crimean War.[4]

4. Mokyr, *Why Ireland Starved*, 292, cites Jonathan R. T. Hughes, *Fluctuations in Trade, Industry and Finance* (1960), 26.

In part, such policies developed around the abstract principles of *laissez-faire* economics. England did not adhere to a pure *laissez-faire* line in its response to the Famine, as shown in R. D. C. Black's classic study *Economic Thought and the Irish Question* (1960). Still, the tendency within British economic policy was to highlight the limits and abuses of Famine relief and to let independent market forces establish their own balance as far as possible, even if this required considerable human sacrifice. Painfully aware of concrete effects lurking within the theoretical abstractions, Butt's essay in the *DUM* had questioned whether the Irish people were being allowed to starve "by a deliberate compact to the gains of English merchants . . ." (April 1847, 507), since the net result seemed to be only higher food prices and greater profits for the middlemen.

Irish hopes for aid from England suffered another blow in July 1848, through a futile insurrection attempt largely headed by the Young Irelander William Smith O'Brien. The movement toward this uprising had grown out of a widespread pattern of European unrest beginning with the Paris revolution in February 1848, the same month in which Marx and Engels published *The Manifesto of the Communist Party*. Looking back on the year, the *DUM* noted, "[f]rom its centre to its extremities, Europe has been convulsed" (Jan. 1849, 134). Even though Young Ireland's skirmish proved embarrassingly feeble in its lack of any widespread support, it still helped lead British patience, in the winter of 1848–1849, simply to run thinner than ever. To a British eye, the whole of Ireland seemed to hold one hand out beseechingly while preparing for rebellion with the other.

British policies gained further impetus from the conviction that Ireland needed a good lesson from its Famine experiences. Irish peasants were perceived as lazy and incompetent; Irish landlords as irresponsible absentees. While the *DUM* itself saw absenteeism as a serious problem, it devoted considerable space to the defense of Irish landlordism, particularly in its attacks on the Poor Law provisions that taxed landholders for relief of the poor. Terming the system a "cruel and unjust imposition on the landed interest" (Feb.

1849, 226), one that encouraged pauperism and indigence while failing to end suffering and starvation, the *DUM* speculated that England might well intend to wipe out Irish landlords. As late as January 1850, in "Ireland Under the Poor Law," the magazine continued to support the position that Butt had developed in his essay but that still seemed out of touch with the most up-to-date circles of British political economy: England itself should give Ireland more financial assistance. Within the context of continued Irish resistance to British rule, the argument failed to persuade.

More compelling long-term forces had begun to assume shape, however, which would later come to conduct the argument upon the different—that is, more separatist—ground of Home Rule. The Franchise Act in 1850 changed the composition of the Irish electorate, making it more middle class, more politically coherent, more capable of making its wishes known in Westminster. K. Theodore Hoppen claims that the Act "laid a time bomb into the nest of Irish politics," one that gave Irish nationalism a "crucial modernizing thrust."[5] In 1850, such long-range effects could not yet be foreseen. Even harder to predict would have been the specific connections, not fully apparent until the 1870s, between this electorate and the future Irish leader of those same Home Rule forces, Isaac Butt.

v

In the late 1840s and early 1850s, even while settling itself realistically to face complete abandonment by England, the *DUM* still published no more than a handful of articles that mentioned repeal, with these doing so only tangentially. The interests of Ireland's Protestants remained too firmly linked to England for the magazine ever to launch any full-scale campaign against the British connection. Given the cataclysmic effects of the Famine on Ireland, the *DUM* also devoted surprisingly little space to this subject. In *Heath-*

---

5. Hoppen, *Elections*, 33.

*cliff and the Great Hunger*, Terry Eagleton notes that literary representations of the Famine during this period are scarce no matter where we look, finding in this paucity a pattern of "oppression or evasion."[6] The *DUM*, in its turn, tends to support Eagleton's generalization, since Butt's essay "The Famine in the Land," for all of its depth and power, was the only major piece of nonfiction to consider the Famine. The other splendid exception to the *DUM*'s dearth of coverage, however, was William Carleton's novel *The Black Prophet—A Tale of Irish Famine* (May–Dec. 1846, eight installments).

Carleton had absented himself from the *DUM* ever since May 1841, keeping a scrupulous distance throughout Lever's editorship. Now he returned with one of the most significant works ever to appear in the magazine, a novel that Carleton himself, "in his later years," regarded as "his best work."[7] By the end of the century it would appear on W. B. Yeats's list of "The Best Thirty Irish Books."[8] At the time of the novel's writing, Carleton was enjoying a period in his life that his biographer David O'Donoghue describes as "the most fertile" and energetic of his career.[9] Not only was his novelistic output especially prolific during this decade, but the literary quality of the work, Vivian Mercier writes, "offers brilliant insights into the politics of its time,"[10] while Robert Lee Wolff claims that *The Black Prophet* in particular "attains an impressiveness as a social document unmatched by any other fictional treatment of the Irish Famine."[11] When Carleton published *The Black Prophet* in book form in 1847, he dedicated it to Prime Minister Lord John Russell and further added a

---

6. Terry Eagleton, *Heathcliff and the Great Hunger: Studies in Irish Culture* (London: Verso, 1995), 12.
7. O'Donoghue, *Life of William Carleton*, 2:86.
8. This list appeared in the Dublin *Daily Express* for 27 Feb. 1895, while a similar list, also including *The Black Prophet*, appeared in *The Bookman* in October 1895. One convenient source for both lists is Phillip L. Marcus, *Yeats and the Beginning of the Irish Renaissance*, 2d ed. (Syracuse: Syracuse University Press, 1987), 285–87.
9. O'Donoghue, *Life of William Carleton*, 2:72.
10. Vivian Mercier, *Modern Irish Literature: Sources and Founders*, ed. Eilís Dillon (Oxford: Clarendon, 1994), 59.
11. Wolff, *William Carleton*, 110.

preface blaming the government for its failure to respond to the misery of the Famine and also hoping that the novel itself might help to change British minds. Even without benefit of preface, however, the polemical character of the work is heavily apparent in the serialized version.

It is this combination of the polemical and the fictional that lends to the novel both its emotional force and its aesthetic flaws. The general praise for *The Black Prophet* needs to be set alongside Terry Eagleton's response to the frequent passages of "bureaucratese" in which the style becomes artificially inflated and abstract. For Eagleton, such stylistic features betray fundamental evasions within the novel: "The language, in short, is collusive with the very political power finally responsible for the suffering it portrays; if what is represented belongs to one political culture, the means of representation are drawn from another."[12] While Eagleton reads the novel in valid and powerful ways, another response to *The Black Prophet* would see such discrepancies between the English/rational/abstract style and the Irish/emotional/concrete subject matter as a heightening of its effects, an underscoring of the inability of language to express such horror. The force of Famine breaks down bodies, social conventions and relationships, even language itself. Christopher Morash considers such possible responses to the novel in relation to its author, describing the Famine as a "terminal crisis in Carleton's aesthetic," "a crisis of authenticity" that would cripple his subsequent output as a writer because the experience of the Famine victims "lies beyond the bounds of representation."[13] The range of possible responses here maps out the tensions, contradictions, and ambivalences surrounding *The Black Prophet,* inherent in its very creation. While such a novel might well reveal subconscious collusion or occasion a crisis of authenticity or representation, it

---

12. Eagleton, *Heathcliff,* 210.
13. Christopher Morash, *Writing the Irish Famine* (Oxford: Clarendon, 1995), 178–79.

also exemplifies the difficulties facing an Irish writer in the midst of such human and social catastrophe. On top of all that, then, a conservative Irish magazine uneasily allied to a union with Great Britain still needed to provide the novel with a forum.

Setting *The Black Prophet* during the famine in 1817, Carleton could draw upon his own memories of such events in Ireland's history; in a lengthy footnote, he further credits another source, D. J. Corrigan's 1846 pamphlet "On Famine and Fever as Cause and Effect in Ireland" (Sept. 1846, 353–54). The novel thus seeks to recreate for its readers the experience of famine, to bring the abstract statistics, disconnected anecdotes, and dry government reports to life. Its narrative line drags us through one cabin after another, all "untidy and dirty" through neglect, showing little more than "the marks and tokens of gradual decline" (May 1846, 611). The natural landscape also appears invariably "deplorable," a "dreary and depressing" atmosphere in which grain lies beaten flat and rotting under the nearly constant rain. During the short periods between downpours, a "brooding stillness" oppresses the land, with the halflight casting a "spectral hue" over everything. Even as such weather adds to the human misery below, the clouds simultaneously seem to shape themselves to accord with the events that they overshadow: "Hearses, coffins, long funeral processions, and all the dark emblems of mortality were reflected, as it were, on the sky, from the terrible works of pestilence and famine, which were going forward on the earth beneath them" (Sept. 1846, 335).

Such a generalized backdrop further sets the stage for the narrator's long commentaries. At the exact midpoint of the novel, and opening the September installment, a chapter entitled "National Calamity" presents a panoramic and bitterly ironic overview:

Day after day, vessels laden with Irish provisions, drawn from a population perishing with actual hunger, as well as with the pestilence which it occasioned, were passing out of our ports, whilst, singular as it may seem, other vessels came in freighted with our own provisions, sent back through the charity of England to our relief. (Sept. 1846, 337)

As with the description of clouds and hearses linked within a mutually reinforcing pattern of gloom, a grim symmetry also unifies this passage, further reflected in other ironies that Carleton's narrator highlights: Despite the famine, one may also find, "studded over the country, a vast number of strong farmers, with bursting granaries and immense haggards," who keep these supplies until prices have been driven to their highest (Sept. 1846, 336).

The main example of such avarice feeding upon human desperation is a stereotyped miser named Darby Skinadre. A kind of evil genius of the famine, Skinadre convinces many people that their own religious and spiritual failures have led them into hardship: ". . . we have brought all these scourges on us by our sins and our thransgressions; thim that sins . . . must suffer" (June 1846, 744). Since Skinadre uses religion to obscure his own profiteering, the novel thus exposes as hypocrisy the theory that the famine has been sent by God as a deserved punishment.

Within the novel's broad sweep, however, people like Skinadre, hoarding grain so that it may then be sold at exorbitant rates, account for but a fraction of the horror. In seeking to explain such misery, Carleton ranges widely, focusing, for instance, on the Irish land system with its complex layer of middlemen, "one of the worst and most cruel systems that ever cursed either the country or the people" (June 1846, 754–55). The landlords themselves are not really to blame, the narrator argues, because they have no control over a system of subletting that keeps dividing the land into increasingly smaller and less viable holdings. Caught in such complex and long-established cycles, the estate owners are just as helpless as the peasants. The narrator suggests that the English legislature might have intervened more aggressively in an attempt to change the behavior of the Irish people, through a better system of public health, for instance. Some government measures, such as the public-works projects, do make a temporary difference in the novel; but since no one attends to the spiritual improvement of the populace, wandering agitators easily stir up more social chaos. The reliance on the potato, too, has clearly left the peasantry vulnerable: "The climate of Ireland is so unsettled, its soil so various in quality, and the potato so liable to injury from excess of either drought or moisture . . ." that there is always some degree of famine or "potato cholera" somewhere in the country (Sept. 1846, 350). Over and over in the face of attempted solutions or explanations, the novel runs up against insurmountable Irish complexities. The very landscape resists the imposition of external remedies, and the question of responsibility for the famine dissipates within the vagaries of Irish weather.

In portraying the peasantry, Carleton frequently uses a romanticized style, praising their willingness to share even in a time of famine: "In this respect there is not in the world any people so generous and kind to their fellow-creatures as the Irish, or whose sympathies are so deep and tender, especially in periods of sickness, want, or death" (July 1846, 92). The pride of some victims keeps them from begging, even to prevent their own death from starvation. Others resist the temptation to strike out at the rich, or they observe their religious duty and attend to those even worse off, despite the danger of contracting typhus or cholera. At other times, however, the novel describes social conditions of a quite different order. The pressures of famine lead to frequent outbreaks of "the insanity of desolation" in which violence rules; "wanton and irrational outrages" cause people "to forget all the decencies and restraints of ordinary life" (Sept. 1846, 351).

Such seeming contradictions draw their terrible logic from a world turned upside down by hunger and fever, in which the narrator can casually weigh the merits of death by typhus versus death by cholera. "Alas! little do our English neighbours know or dream of the horrors which attend a year of severe famine in this unhappy country" (Sept. 1846, 354), the narrator adds, as if to remind us that any expectation of consistency is hopelessly inappropriate for such times. The novel thus deals, not with potential chaos, but with degrees of chaos. Many of the characters are only barely able to control their constant impulse to lash out, and passions frequently burst forth into violence that typically leaves someone wracked with guilt. One young woman becomes pregnant and seeks to marry the father of her child but is instead rejected and disgraced by her outraged parents. When the woman and her new baby subsequently die of famine fever, her parents alternate between their own famine-induced delusions and their clear-sighted remorse over their own intolerance.

Along with Darby Skinadre, the novel's most memorable individual character is the Black Prophet Donnel Dhu M'Gowan, to whom even his own wife says, "you're a hardened and a bad man . . . hard, an' dark, an' widout one spark o' common feelin' . . ." (Sept. 1846, 334). The Prophet's brooding, sinister appearance is reinforced by the famine itself, by the tendency of his predictions to promise disaster, and also by the ongoing atmosphere of mystery regarding an unsolved murder. Now, some twenty years after the crime, the pressure of famine threatens, from the earliest stages of the novel, to force the truth into light, even as that same pressure seems to render individual guilt negligible. The crime occurred over twenty years ago. With death now a commonplace and with survival often possible only at the expense of someone else's life, what purpose is served in seeking to establish the murderer's identity and guilt? In such times, one seems to meet murderers at every turn.

Even with the famine and the various tragic resolutions, the novel still ends in a largely positive manner, primarily by clarifying some mistaken identities. The corpse turns out to have been that of someone other than the presumed murder victim, and the man who all along has believed himself to be the murderer is innocent, with none other than the Black Prophet himself finally exposed as the real culprit. Such acts happen, the novel suggests, because of hasty passions, and people are thus advised to curb their emotions and to guard against moments of rage. The women characters, Mave Sullivan in particular, embody the novel's highest values through their bravery, quiet stoicism, capacity for sacrifice, and loyalty to those they love. Besides seeing justice finally served, then, the novel also asserts the overriding virtue of love, as when the Prophet's wild, beautiful, heroic daughter Sarah remains true to him to the moment of his execution.

Despite the compelling nature of such women characters, the ultimate triumph of justice still feels artificially imposed. First, it relies upon the enlightened intercession of an estate owner who has occupied only the fringes of the novel until at last he emerges to exert the needed power. Then, the novel's conclusion ignores the ongoing human misery occasioned by famine conditions that would continue to revisit Ireland's peasantry. While someone like the Prophet may be more fascinating, our main feelings of sympathy extend beyond individual characters, and the society as a whole remains as vulnerable to famine as ever. As with the uneasy symmetry between vice and virtue, clouds and hearses, incoming and outgoing ships, or as with the discordant combination of the historical with the fictional, the polemic with the aesthetic, the social commentary with the literary portrayal, the novel's resolution feels frustratingly incomplete and fragmented. Individual vignettes may portray the effects of the famine with great power, but any causes or explanations for that famine, any answers to the questions that it raises, are rendered finally futile.

A few months after the conclusion of Carleton's novel, his short story "O'Sullivan's Love" (March-April 1847) would similarly attest to love's ability to triumph over all. Just as in *The Black Prophet*, however, this claim is strained in the short story, where harmony is restored only because of some timely graverobbers. As the Famine wore on through its second year, the growing weight of human tragedy in Ireland made any literary expressions of optimism increasingly difficult to sustain. For the summer of 1847, observers estimated that only one-fifth of the usual acreage of potatoes had been planted, and it was clear that *The Black Prophet* had taught Lord John Russell nothing.

In August 1847, then, the *DUM* began "An Irish Election in the Time of the Forties" (Aug.–Sept. 1847), a sketch in which Carleton portrayed a world of bleak and savage hopelessness. The sketch is set during the 1820s, at a time before the forty-shilling-freeholders (or "forties") lost the franchise through Emancipation in 1829. While this class still had the vote, the narrator states, Irish elections lacked all dignity and, in fact, revealed an awful truth about human nature:

> No man can know until such an occasion as this occurs, the melancholy and humiliating materials of which the mass of society is composed throughout all its grades. It is indeed a painful and a mournful thing to think of it, and to reflect that every day in the week you are surrounded by falsehood, dishonesty, perjury, fraud, venality, and corruption, in their worst forms, and that, although you see them not, unless in the more diminished and less obscurable escapes of ordinary social trial, yet that they are before you, and behind you, and on each side, lying latent and ready to leap into active life whenever the adequate temptation shall present itself. (Aug. 1847, 179)

Within such a futile vision of humanity, the results of such an election are naturally quite pointless. The narrator scorns any possibility of "a domestic parliament" functioning in Ireland until such time as "a sound and truthful education" becomes available (Aug. 1847, 190).

In the same month in which Carleton's sketch began in the *DUM*, the English-sponsored soup kitchens in Ireland started closing their doors. While the times clearly demanded expressions of rage, Carleton had lost all sense of where to direct his efforts, instead lashing out, with indiscriminate paranoia, at the Irish. The values proposed in his sketch similarly missed the mark, since the kind of education that Carleton advocated had so far done little to enlighten mid-nineteenth-century England.

VI

Carleton's position in "An Irish Election," however, was not consistent with the whole pattern of the *DUM*'s political response to the Famine; the magazine more typically assailed the British government rather than the Irish populace. Albeit rarely, the magazine was entertaining the prospect of repeal. More importantly, it had lost all faith in Sir Robert Peel, the statesman upon whom the magazine had previously based most of its hopes for the future of the Union and indeed the whole Empire. At least until the 1850s brought an end to the Famine and a resurgence of prosperity to the Irish economy, the *DUM* thus saw no one within the parliamentary sphere who seemed capable of promoting those interests with which the magazine had identified itself.

From the very beginning of Waller's tenure as editor, Peel had strained the patience of the *DUM*. During 1844 and 1845, Peel's government had introduced a series of bills to simplify the process by which the Catholic Church received gifts and legacies, to increase government subsidies to Maynooth, and to create several new non-denominational colleges in Ireland. All of these measures were designed to conciliate Irish Catholicism, an approach the *DUM* found exasperatingly shortsighted, charging that Peel seemed "fully bent upon the substitution of a Popish for a Protestant Establishment" (July 1845, 63). Although the magazine was grateful that Peel's government had weathered a crisis of confidence and near fall from power in December 1845, its gratitude was mild indeed, and in March 1846 the magazine said of the Prime Minister that "We have nothing to expect from him" (375).

Within his own party and country, Peel faced much stronger attacks centering on his decision to seek repeal of the Corn Laws, the duties that protected the prices of domestic grain. With the prospect of widespread famine in Ireland apparent by October 1845, Peel felt increasingly compelled to remove these duties and allow food prices to fall, a position perceived by the landed classes as nothing less than betrayal. The *DUM* generally supported free trade and the absence of government intervention in the marketplace. Rejecting the *laissez-faire* extremes advocated by the so-called Manchester School, however, which put more emphasis on capital than on land, the magazine argued that protection of home industry was a necessary exception to free-trade doctrine and, in April 1846, denounced repeal of the Corn Laws as "revolution." For all of that, the Corn Laws were nonetheless repealed in June 1846, only days before Peel resigned from office in favor of the Whigs and Lord Russell. Having lost confidence in Peel, the *DUM* observed this transition with no observable concern. From another quarter, Protestants in both England and Ireland were beginning to unite within National Clubs, a trend that the magazine found hopeful.

Sectarian divisions in general got heightened attention in the *DUM* during the Famine, and here, too, the signs seemed hopeful, with scriptural education "every day producing its proper effects" (Sept. 1845, 361). The explanations for this trend echoed long-standing positions: Protestantism encouraged intellectual freedom, and despite the "sad bungle" of the National System, Catholicism in Ireland was "a species of Christian pharasaism in a state of decay and rottenness, which must very speedily vanish before the free preaching of the living word. We say that, in its present state, it is directly obstructive both of religion and civilization" (March 1848, 398). The Catholic clergy could only maintain its status on nationalist and political rather than religious grounds, hence the folly of any legislation that helped to perpetuate "a superstition which is the nightmare of Ireland" (Jan. 1849, 117).

By 1852, the *DUM*'s confidence in the progress of scriptural education had reached an all-time high, the magazine claiming proudly that "[t]he face of the country is becoming Protestant . . ." (Aug. 1852, 244). With the material ravages of the Famine now safely in the past, the magazine could more readily specify "the principal causes of Ireland's miseries" in spiritual terms: "moral degradation" resulting from "a perverted education" (Sept. 1852, 374). The categories came into focus with a clarity that the *DUM* had not felt since the 1830s: "Education, virtue, worldly prosperity and Protestantism, as a general rule hand in hand, and opposed to ignorance, vice, misery, and Roman Catholicism" (Sept. 1852, 376). What next for Ireland? "Protestantise her." Efforts of the Protestant clergy to assist the populace during the Famine, accompanied by varying degrees of proselytism, had indeed resulted in widespread conversions, and the Catholic Church had suffered even more losses through emigration. As Desmond Bowen notes, the period 1849 to 1854 thus became a "short but heady time of Protestant triumphalism" throughout England and Ireland.[14] A Papal Bull issued in September 1850 served as a further Protestant rallying point, since Rome thereby proposed to increase its temporal power in England through a new system of Catholic diocesan organization. But in March 1851, the same month in which the *DUM* attacked this move in an essay entitled "The Papal Aggression," its lead article still expressed unqualified hope for Ireland's future.

Besides religion, new patterns in land ownership also served as the foundation for the more optimistic times. The financial pressures of the Famine had driven many of the large estates into bankruptcy or insolvency, and under the Encumbered Estates Act of 1849, many of them had been broken up and sold. The *DUM* had supported such legislation as early as September 1848, further stating that "the destiny of Ireland rests with the proprietors of the soil" (360). While the statement echoes previous emphases on the centrality of a landed class, the proposed legislation, at first glance, seems inconsistent with the magazine's tradition of support for the gentry and for Protestant ascendancy. Yet the *DUM* was shrewdly cognizant of the fact that the old-style landlords could no longer hold out against the new economic pressures, even as the continued survival of Irish Protestantism seemed to demand a stable landed interest.

Over the course of 1847, in part because of Daniel O'Connell's death in May of that year, in part because of James Fintan Lalor's series of open letters to the *Nation*, the Irish question as a whole shifted from a concern with repeal to one with land. Specifically, what was to be the relationship between landlord and tenant? At the low-

---

14. Bowen, *Protestant Crusade*, 239.

est economic end of the rural structure, the cottier class was rapidly disappearing, victims of Famine-driven evictions, starvation, and emigration. At the upper end, and through the provisions of the Encumbered Estates Act, about a quarter of the total area of Ireland was being sold off. The new landlords represented to the *DUM* a decided improvement, since they were financially more astute, more closely tied to their estates, and, simply, more numerous. As such, they seemed to offer Ireland the kind of civilizing stability that the magazine regarded as crucial.

Previous landlords had failed in this function, according to the *DUM,* because of too high a rate of absenteeism, which the magazine termed Ireland's "chief curse." Not only did the absentee spend money on personal expenses outside of the country, he was less likely to invest capital into his estate. Moreover, his tenants were further deprived of his moral influence and example: "A proper system of education may, and will, do a great deal to civilise Ireland, and to elevate the character of the people; but the example of one good man is worth a thousand books, and a well-spent life will inculcate more moral precepts than an entire library could enforce" (March 1850, 284). Such a man might now just as well be Catholic as Protestant, the magazine allowed. After all, "Civilization depends in quality on the amount of Christian morality generally admitted into the social system . . ." (Jan. 1847, 128). The most important consideration was the landlord's ability to help stabilize the country. At a specific level, this would mean preventing land reforms such as the "Three F's" demanded by the Irish Tenant League: fair rents, fixity of tenure, and free sale, or the tenant's right to sell leases. At a more general level, it would mean preventing the further spread of democracy, the political system that "is avowedly a claim for the ignorance of the country to control its intelligence—it is a formal declaration that property shall be stripped of its legitimate influence, and shall succumb to blind passion and brute force" (April 1848, 523). At the time that this statement appeared in the *DUM,* revolution was spreading from France and across much of Europe. Even in the calmest of times, Irish Protestants had to face their tenuous status as a cultural minority and to seek the best means to shore up that status. Increasingly for the *DUM*, the best strategy seemed to mean emphasizing a coalition of specifically Irish interests rather than relying further on England.

VII

The years of the Famine thus led the *DUM* into new areas of national consciousness. In the essay "Ireland's Industry and Ireland's Benefactors" (Jan. 1849), the magazine urged the country to support domestic manufacturing and production, while "Native Art and National Advancement" gave particular support to Irish artists (Sept. 1846). English attitudes were satirized in "English Notions of Irish Improvement" (April 1850). In a review of the work *Paddiana; or, Sketches of Irish Life, Present and Past*, the magazine complained: "The whole of the English press, without distinction of party, seems animated by the one common object of vilifying and holding up to odium every thing in our unhappy country" (June 1848, 715). More than in previous times, too, the magazine scrutinized the fortunes of the Irish publishing industry. A June 1847 review of a work by James Thomas O'Brien, Bishop of Ossory, criticized him for having it published in London rather than Dublin. Later that same year, the *DUM* jabbed at the *Dublin Review* as "a periodical affecting nationality, though it is printed and published in England . . ." (Nov. 1847, 616). Samuel Ferguson criticized several novels by Carleton and Anna Maria Hall for being written to inform and instruct a British readership and hence for lapsing into didacticism (Dec. 1845). A review of Waller's 1854 volume *Poems* praised him for directing his career and work toward a specifically Irish reading public. As the *DUM* rightfully noted, this was a courageous decision for a literary writer (Jan. 1854). The book version of Carleton's *The Black Prophet*, by contrast, for all the blame it directs at England, was first published by a London press, and not two years after Ferguson's review.

The issue of publishing touched on the *DUM*'s most immediate operations. While Irish fiction had reached its peak of popularity through Lever's work in the early 1840s, the Famine had generally flattened the Irish book-publishing industry. The solvency of the *DUM*'s publisher Curry began to fall apart in mid-1847, with bankruptcy proceedings barely a year away. While the able M'Glashan took over the business as sole owner, he inherited considerable financial difficulties. Waller's own work, with its exasperating flightiness consciously directed at an Irish readership, exhibits the magazine's uncertain market focus under his editorship. Another example comes from the contributions during this period from James Clarence Mangan, who introduced a new series, "Anthologia Hibernica":

> the great and general impulse given to the Irish mind of late has exercised its legitimate influence over us. Slender as our talents are, we have become exceedingly desirous to dedicate them henceforward exclusively to the service of our country. For that country—and we now express ourselves merely in reference to its literature—we see a new era approaching. (Feb. 1847, 239)

The sentiments here serve admirably to define the *DUM*'s broader concerns with a national literature. Reviewing Henry R. Montgomery's collection of translations from Irish poetry, the magazine was equally hopeful of the future: "The mind of Ireland is becoming educated; a taste for the cultivation of her literature and history is daily on the increase; people are no longer quite absorbed in the stormy pursuits of politics" (Aug. 1847, 128). Furthermore, and with remarkable insight, the reviewer acknowledged Ferguson's essay on Hardiman as the starting point of the movement's success. Another review, which could well have appeared in the *Nation,* complained that ancient Irish literature was too often subjected to a mocking or bantering treatment in translation, making it "almost unfit for the serious purposes of a lofty and ambitious native literature" (March 1848, 305).

As with every previous departure from its ideological origins, the *DUM* again wavered, in this case on the issue of just how national it hoped to become. Mangan's idealistic series would run through only three installments (Feb.–July 1847), with his most typical contributions to the magazine going into yet another series, "Lays of Many Lands" (Sept. 1847–Jan. 1849, eight installments). He sent his most famous poem, the explosively nationalist "Dark Rosaleen," to the *Nation;* then, four years after Mangan's death in 1849, the *DUM* reprinted his poem as part of a review of Edgar Allan Poe. There was, the reviewer suggested, a "singular resemblance" between the two poets (July 1853).

Joseph Sheridan Le Fanu's poem "Shamus O'Brien" (July 1850), by the other *DUM* writer who bears comparison with Poe, also exemplifies the magazine's ambiguity on the issue of national verse. Le Fanu had first presented the poem to the Trinity College Historical Society over ten years earlier,[15] and Samuel Lover had been reading it on occasion since then, to the delight of the American lecture circuit. Yet with its ballad style, its defiant speech from the dock, and its complete sympathy with one of the rebels of '98 who escapes from the gallows with the help of a Catholic priest, the poem marks how far the *DUM* was willing to go in the direction of national literature.

The magazine also published the work of Jane Francesca Elgee, already better known as "Speranza" of the *Nation*. The year after one of her more fiery contributions to the *Nation* had led to its suppression for July 29, 1848, the *DUM* published two of her poems (Jan. and April 1849), as well as several reviews scattered over the next several decades. In November 1851, she married William Wilde, the surgeon, antiquarian, and topographical writer who had been covering Irish subjects for the *DUM* for some years. His major contributions to the magazine appeared during Waller's editorship and included the series "Irish Popular Superstitions" (May 1849–May 1850, four installments) and several contributions to the "Irish Rivers" series. This latter series also included essays by Samuel Hay-

---

15. Mc Cormack, *Sheridan Le Fanu*, 51–53.

man and the Irish barrister and historian J. R. O'Flanagan, a typical installment using a particular river as the central structure in a discussion of the history and physical geography of that area. The theme-based series proved remarkably durable, running the entire length of Waller's ten-year editorship (Sept. 1845–Dec. 1855, twenty-two installments).

While the magazine under Waller consciously sustained and developed its Irish character, his interests in literature also led to more detailed and extensive discussions of aesthetic criteria than at any other time, with Irishness as only one of many evaluative guidelines. In general, while the magazine valued literature that "sympathised most intimately with the social questions and difficulties of the age" (Aug. 1848, 152), it opposed didacticism; while it valued accuracy and truth, it opposed a close portrayal of the ordinary details from everyday experience. The noblest object of poetry, according to reviewer William Archer Butler, was "not merely to *please,* nor merely to *instruct,*" but "chiefly and essentially to fill and *exalt* the soul through the imagination" and "to produce high and ennobling emotion" (May 1847, 574–75).

More specifically, this meant that the novels of Dickens did not fare well in the *DUM*'s reviews, that John Ruskin came under frequent criticism, and that England's five best poets of the nineteenth century were declared to be Byron, Shelley, Southey, Tennyson, and Wordsworth. British poetry since the death of Shelley was characterized by "almost universal mediocrity" (Aug. 1848, 151), a "progressive deterioration" related to the decline of the aristocracy and the rise of utilitarianism and industrialization (Oct. 1845, 420). Ireland's best poet of the age was Thomas Moore, its most characteristic genre lyric poetry, and its best novelist Maria Edgeworth, whose realism was not so detailed as to mar the overall effect. Melville's *Moby-Dick* eluded the categories that Waller's magazine sought to establish; its reviewer finally settled on the judgment that "with all [its] glaring defects, it would be in vain to deny that the work has interest" (Feb. 1852, 221).

The *DUM*'s philosophy of literature thus combined a neoclassical taste for nature and common sense with a post-Romantic emphasis on imagination and spirituality. The result—a large amount of mid-Victorian, middle-class verse—was both predictable and undistinguished. Perhaps the most frequently published poet, as well as the most characteristic of the magazine's tastes, was Mortimer Collins, whose first poem appeared in June 1851. One of his works, exemplifying much that the *DUM* admired in verse, portrays a young girl praying for the safety of her brother, a soldier in the Crimean War:

> Rise, rise Heosphoros, by Euxine marge,
> And usher in the great decisive day,
> When our twin chivalry, with headlong charge,
> Shall sweep the countless Scythian serfs away. . . .
> (March 1855, 355)

The passage effects some startling transformations of mundane battlefield geography into sublime mythology. The morning star "Heosphoros," for instance, contains echoes of Bosphorus, the straits at the western end of the Black Sea, in the area where the Crimean War was being fought. But perhaps the most ambitious example is "Euxine," an earlier name for the Black Sea. By using "Euxine," which meant the Friendly Sea, the poem not only avoids lapsing into prosaic modern terms, but it also locates the soldier's present danger safely in the heroic (and friendly) past. The morning star Heosphoros announces the sun, here identified with the onrushing troops of France and England. In opposing Russia, the long-time enemies have merged into a harmonious unity ("twin") and into an embodiment of "chivalry" when they might otherwise be mistaken for cavalry. Within the poem's impulse to translate, even "Scythian" has a classical heritage. "Serfs" might startle with its feudal and monosyllabic bluntness, but surely a modern soldier had nothing to fear from such people. And were they even real people anyway, especially from the point of view of domestic girlhood in mid-Victorian England? While the poem's values thus seem escapist and sentimental, Collins still has employed an ambitious array of verbal filters for such a topical and minor piece.

In May 1849, Samuel Ferguson published a long poem, "Inheritor and Economist," that criticized English doctrines of free trade,[16] and several other minor pieces appeared during this same period by James Clarence Mangan. Of greater interest for Waller's *DUM*, however, is the appearance of William Allingham (Feb., Oct., and Nov. 1853), significant as the later author of the long poem *Laurence Bloomfield in Ireland* (1864). Other poets of note include John Thomas Ball, Michael Joseph Barry, the Irish divine Richard Sinclair Brooke, Stopford Brooke, Aubrey de Vere (July and Aug. 1849, shortly before he converted to Catholicism), the late Mrs. James Gray, William Rowan Hamilton, Samuel Hayman, G. P. R. James, E. V. H. Kenealy, John Fisher Murray, and Sarah Parker ("the Irish girl"). Along with Waller's own frequent verse, writers like these served to keep the place of poetry secure in the magazine, although they hardly advanced its quality.

Drama now received much more attention, largely through the work of John William Cole, the long-time actor and manager for Dublin's Theatre Royal and one of the *DUM*'s most prolific contributors. Besides a number of shorter works, Cole also put together the major series *Leaves from the Portfolio of a Dramatic Manager* (Dec. 1850–June 1852, twelve installments), primarily focusing on the Dublin theatrical world, as well as the series *The Dramatic Writers of Ireland* (Jan. 1855–March 1856, eleven installments). Rounding out the coverage of drama, the historian Archibald Alison wrote on British theatre, and Denis Florence M'Carthy on the Spanish playwright Calderon.

VIII

Despite Waller's interests in poetry and Cole's extensive writing on drama, however, fiction continued to represent the magazine's

---

16. For a discussion of this poem as one that links the fate of the Irish landed gentry with the fate of Ireland itself, see Morash, *Writing the Irish Famine*, 80–84.

main area of literary interest, and again, it was Charles Lever who provided the bulk of this work, beginning with the novel *Maurice Tiernay, the Soldier of Fortune* (April 1850–Dec. 1851, twenty installments). With the character of Tiernay, Lever sought more deliberately than before to create a hero whose experiences would serve as an experiential record of European history over the past half-century.[17] His narrator thus comes of age during the French Revolution of 1792 and, despite the horrors that he has witnessed, he rejects a life of spiritual retreat for one of complexity, worldliness, and public action. Against a constant backdrop of revolution and social change, Tiernay comes to see humanity as bestial, a blind and ravaging mass, in contrast to the life of the soldier who possesses clarity of vision and honorable ideals.

While Tiernay becomes more cynical and world-weary than his counterparts in Lever's previous novels, he is otherwise difficult to separate from the Lorrequers and O'Malleys. Like them, he eventually distinguishes himself heroically in battle and marries a rich aristocrat. But the novel is more aware than its predecessors of the discrepancy between Tiernay's ongoing struggles and his eventual triumph. His experiences keep cycling him through the same patterns, a series of events that repeatedly denies him any sense of meaning acquired or progress gained: chameleon-like, he takes on the characteristics of whatever group he is with at that moment, then learns some bitter wisdom when his cause ends in loss, disillusionment, or disappointment. Finally, a war wound even costs him his leg, an irreversible sacrifice of the kind never required of Lorrequer. By forcing such a set of fragments into a final assertion of harmony and happiness, Lever only emphasizes the unlikely nature of Tiernay's achievement. It is as if an Irish peasant family, ravaged by the Famine, eviction, and emigration, ended up living happily ever after alongside their gold claim in California.

A number of external pressures combined to produce the im-

---

17. Stevenson, *Dr. Quicksilver*, 181.

probable resolution to *Maurice Tiernay*, including Lever's own painful awareness of the Famine, his financial need to produce work quickly, his Dublin critics who attacked him as a happy-go-lucky stage-Irishman, and his London admirers who wanted still more of Lorrequer's reassuring hijinks. Tiernay's links to revolution and Catholicism further emphasize the extent to which Lever's dilemma resembled that of the *DUM* itself: in the wake of Young Ireland and the Famine, what role should the magazine now seek to play? The disastrous Irish Rebellion of 1798 leads Tiernay to say: ". . . I had been disappointed in every expectation I had formed of Ireland" (Jan. 1851, 33). Yet his conclusion disregards the ways in which his own life has paralleled that of Ireland, with its series of rebellions that led nowhere, its expectations that ended in disappointment. In order for Tiernay's life to bring him success, its author must resort to sleight-of-hand plot reversals; but favorable accidents of history were still difficult to come by, even in Lever's novel, and for Ireland during the Famine, they were simply not available.

Tiernay's success was not the only unlikely solution that Lever offered through the *DUM*. In December 1852, with Protestant indignation still high after Rome's attempt to consolidate its power in England, Lever proposed that England establish formal diplomatic relations with the Vatican. While the magazine felt compelled to add an editorial preface to distance itself from Lever's views, it was not about to alienate its most reliable novelist during the 1850s. Lever had already followed *Tiernay* with *The Heirs of Randolph Abbey* (Jan.–July 1852, seven installments)[18] and was well into *Sir Jasper Carew* (July 1852–June 1854, twenty-one installments). Still to come was *The Fortunes of Glencore* (Aug. 1855–April 1857, seventeen installments) and *Gerald Fitzgerald* (Jan. 1858–July 1859, eighteen installments). Lever may often have felt disappointed in his expectations

---

18. Orville Roorbach, *Bibliotheca Americanus (1852–55)* (1939), attributes *The Heirs of Randolph Abbey* to Lever, although FitzPatrick, *Notes & Queries*, III, specifically claims that Lever was not the author.

for Ireland, but he remained remarkably loyal to the magazine with which he had begun his literary career.

### IX

Joseph Sheridan Le Fanu's fiction also appeared frequently in the *DUM* during Waller's tenure, and while his short stories do not approach the volume of Lever's work there, they offer us the most complex and efficient expression during this period of the *DUM*'s wavering ambivalence on such issues as repeal, nationality, and the Union. Le Fanu's metaphors further serve, moreover, to illuminate other problems that the magazine wrestled with during these years: the discordant tensions and uncertainties that unsettled its vision of Ireland; the bitterness, pain, and anger within Butt's essay "The Famine in the Land"; the frustrating resolution at the end of Carleton's novel *The Black Prophet;* the inescapable sense of human futility confronted with the spread of the Famine. The best of these stories is perhaps "The Fatal Bride" (Jan. 1848), narrated by an outside observer to the events he describes, involved mainly because he has stumbled into a complex world of compounded guilt and secrecy. His friend Jennings was formerly married to a terrible woman, who then left him. Like Jane Eyre's Rochester, Jennings now prefers to regard that contract as dissolved and to hide it in his past, especially since he now wishes to marry a Miss Chadleigh. While one of Chadleigh's two brothers knew of the first marriage, his death will keep that secret safe, even from the intended bride. Nonetheless, since Chadleigh's father now forbids this union, she and Jennings must marry in secret, an arrangement that successfully fools everyone while she continues to live at home.

Predictably, the secrets blow up in ambiguous ways, what would normally be good news having disastrous overtones. Chadleigh becomes pregnant, yet this will expose the current marriage. Her brother turns out to be alive after all and on his way back to England, yet this will expose the previous marriage. Before he arrives, she gives birth, an event that precipitates a duel between her other brother and her husband. Or perhaps he isn't her husband. Jennings first explains that he possesses papers showing how the marriage to Miss Chadleigh, through a legal technicality, never actually became final. In his dying moments, however, he claims that these papers are forgeries. Amid all the bewildering differences between the two Chadleigh brothers and the two Jennings marriages, a reader may well feel that the legal status of the Jennings-Chadleigh marriage remains hopelessly clouded, none of which prevents the son of that union from growing up to become a Member of Parliament and heir to the wealthy Chadleigh estate in—naturally—Ireland.

What conclusions are we then to draw? Most explicitly, "The Fatal Bride" counsels prudence, a virtue for which Jennings himself, thoroughly ambivalent about his various marriages, is the strongest advocate. The narrator shares in this ambivalence insofar as he has also felt a romantic and totally irrational impulse to fight on Miss Chadleigh's behalf, even while stressing that his own status as a bachelor is important to his self-identity. Yet he avoids Jennings's personal entanglements more through chance than design, and prudence rises to the didactic surface more through guilty hindsight than persuasive wisdom. Beneath that surface, more powerful forces lend "The Fatal Bride" its main literary energy, forces that had long been combined within the *DUM*'s fiction: guilt-ridden doubts about identity, sexuality, and social legitimacy.

Le Fanu's narrative frame further expands this combination into an elaborate historical metaphor. In the late 1840s, at the time when we learn of these events, the narrator is seventy-five years old. Around 1790, Miss Chadleigh's mother ran off and left her family; around 1805, the above story took place. The narrator does not need to remind us that the Act of Union occurred between those two earlier events, a political marriage built upon guilt and shaken ever since by questions about its legitimacy and legality. The product of that marriage may indeed now occupy a place of prestige on the floor of Parliament, but only because we suppress the facts of his heritage. Mired in the complexities of the past, those facts can perhaps never be fully understood, and prudence offers little help in planning other family events. Le Fanu's metaphor does, however, allow us to foresee that such marriages inevitably contain ruin.

Le Fanu's story "The Watcher" (Nov. 1847), published just two months before "The Fatal Bride," portrays the same themes but more simply and directly. Set in Dublin in 1794, the story concerns a man named Barton whose guilt is also built upon sexual indiscretion. When he plans to marry, his shadow self emerges to terrorize and eventually kill him. Barton believes that "there is a God—a dreadful God—and that retribution follows guilt." In the grip of a system that is "malignant" and "implacable," he suffers "the torments of the damned" (534). In "Some Account of the Latter Days of the Hon. Richard Marston, of Dunoran" (April–June 1848), we meet the same God, one who increasingly seems drawn from the landscape of famine, "a malignant, or, at best, a reckless one, if you will. Why, look around you; see disease—madness—hunger—hatred" (June, 730). Marston participates in the same sexual guilt that preys on other Le Fanu characters, much of it generated by marriages of the same questionable nature. He abandons his wife to marry the family governess, only to learn that she is already married and that her previous husband, posing as her brother and living in the same house, is trying to seduce Marston's daughter. The story prefigures much of the substance of Le Fanu's later novel *Uncle Silas* (1864); Marston resembles Silas just as the governess Mademoiselle de Barras resembles Madame de la Rougierre. But like "The Watcher" and "The Fatal Bride," "Marston" also contains an act of sexual indiscretion that occurs in the 1790s, just in time for the Act of Union. Furthermore, insofar as all three tales are told during Le Fanu's guilty involvement with Young Ireland, they are most immediately concerned with the various and shameful consequences of that Union. While prudence may indeed have led him to sever his dangerous political alliances before they could destroy him publicly, these private experiences still emerged as literary metaphors. In such a form, they may further remind us of similar patterns within

*The Black Prophet.* In Carleton's novel, too, a crime occurs shortly before the Union, a murder spawned by sexual jealousy and spawning in its turn another generation of repressed guilt and suspicion. If a character like Mave Sullivan is an impossibly virtuous heroine, others may be all too realistic, particularly those who fascinate us with their impulse or capacity to destroy. In a letter to Carleton shortly after the publication of *The Black Prophet,* and seeking to patch up a quarrel with his friend, Charles Gavan Duffy wrote: "In a gust of passion you are one of the most unjust of men, and shut your eyes to everything but your wrath. . . . you were as merciless as Skinadre. . . ."[19] Like Stephen Dedalus's Shakespeare, who "drew Shylock out of his own long pocket," the creators of "The Fatal Bride" or *The Black Prophet* could both likewise look within themselves for the tortured villains they portrayed.

A later story, Le Fanu's "The Mysterious Lodger" (Jan.–Feb. 1850), offers salvation to its narrator, whose eventual conversion to Christianity leads him out of his psychological terror. "Some Gossip About Chapelizod" (April 1851) then evokes the lighthearted style of W. H. Maxwell and Charles Lever, while pointing ahead to Le Fanu's *The House by the Churchyard* (1863), by putting the fictional portrayal of guilt and doubts even further behind him. As *Uncle Silas* would later show, however, Le Fanu would always have his Gothic themes within easy psychological reach.

Along with Carleton, Lever, and Le Fanu, the other major fiction writer to appear in the *DUM* under Waller was Michael Banim, with the novel *Clough Fionn; or, The Stone of Destiny* (Aug.–Dec. 1852, five installments). With his brother John, Michael had made up the collaborative literary team "the O'Hara family," and their novels and short stories had provided Irish fiction with its first detailed look at rural life in the West of Ireland. Like Carleton, they could draw on a Catholic background, and with their most important work, in the 1820s, they gave Carleton some useful models for his own writing.

19. O'Donoghue, *William Carleton,* 2:77.

*Clough Fionn* appeared ten years after John Banim's death in 1842, the first novel that Michael had produced since that year, but still, as an editorial note explains, a novel that originated in notes and plans made by the two brothers while John was alive.

*Clough Fionn* relies on several of the character stereotypes that occupied a popular place in both English and Irish conceptions about the Famine: the absentee landlord who understands nothing of his estate and thus contributes to its decline, the unscrupulous middleman who evicts without mercy and thus lives under the constant threat of assassination, the hot-headed peasant who is always on the verge of violence, the dedicated and gentle Irish colleen, and her heart-of-gold lover who finally realizes that violence achieves nothing. This final character, the peasant Patrick Donohoe, defines the novel's ideal response to conditions such as those that Ireland faced during the Famine: one should trust patiently in love, mercy, and justice. Patrick's father Murtoch represents the old code of vengeance, which brings him only loss and failure since his impulse is to challenge established order. Patrick himself, however, through the new code built upon Christian ethics, manages not only to marry the daughter of the middleman Mulcahy, but also to effect a complete transformation of Mulcahy's character. Through his ability to control his passions, Patrick is thus able to help return his village to the idyllic state originally disturbed by Murtoch.

All of this melodrama, nostalgia, and pious counsel severely limit *Clough Fionn*. Characters who speak Irish, for instance, have their words translated into a formal and ornate English; even though the narrator explains that "when the Irish language is used to portray the feelings, it is figurative and poetical, and cannot be translated into common-place language" (Sept. 1852, 340), the effect is still comic. Beyond its trite stereotypes, though, the novel also contains an engaging layer of commonplace detail from rural life. Moreover, in portraying and condemning the actions of the middleman, it offers a powerful critique of the *laissez-faire* belief that the free market would establish its own best course.

## X

At only five installments, *Clough Fionn* was a short novel, and indeed, the whole tendency during Waller's editorship was away from long novels and toward shorter works, especially the two-part short story. Another genre that enjoyed a burst of popularity was the travelogue, including essays on travel experiences as well as reviews of travel books. Inspired by British involvement in the Crimean War, travelogues hit their peak in 1854, averaging two articles per month, including one review of a book speculating about life on other worlds, a possibility that the *DUM* was willing to entertain. While the magazine might have had a sharper sense than before of Irish nationality, at the same time it was also conscious of its cosmopolitan agenda. As a part of the Union, Ireland could further regard itself as a partner in the Empire, especially if an Irish magazine helped to build and maintain that Empire by educating its readers about the British role and presence throughout the world. In criticizing Canada's independence movement, then, the magazine adopted a point of view that identified totally with England, and not at all with repeal: "The empire which has cost us years of contest and diplomacy, seas of blood and mines of treasure to win and to hold, is crumbling in pieces in our grasp . . ." (Feb. 1850, 151).

Even with new methods of communication and on-the-scene reporting now available, the magazine still tended to rely on the old methods, such as travel books, to gain its information and perspectives on world trouble spots like those in the Crimea. The telegraph, for instance, could provide only misleading "scraps of news" about a possible conflict with Russia (March 1854, 253). Better was the railroad. Not only could it function as "a sign" or "an agent of social and national advancement" in ways useful to a colonizing power (Aug. 1855, 137), it could also conduct observers to the scene of action itself. For social and historical commentaries on Turkey and Russia during the period leading up to the Crimean War, then, the

*DUM* relied frequently upon Francis Doyne Dwyer, a major of the Hussars serving in Austria.

Reviewers of more conventional cultural fare included Anthony Trollope (May 1851 and Oct. 1855) and old hands such as John Anster, Samuel Ferguson, William Archer Butler, and John Thomas Ball. Patrick Kennedy, one of Ireland's major authorities on Celtic folklore and the oral tradition, made his first appearance in the *DUM* under Waller. His first collection of folklore, *Legends of Mount Leinster,* appeared in book form in 1855, and he would ultimately publish well over two hundred items in the *DUM*. George Petrie wrote on the musician and antiquary Edward Bunting, the novelist Marmion Savage contributed a dream-vision series, and the novelist James Grant contributed about a dozen short items. Henry Charles Sirr, former British Vice-Consul at Hong Kong, contributed a series on Ceylon. And pieces began appearing from the Irish journalist Durham Dunlop and the lawyer Cheyne Brady, both of whom would go on to serve terms as editors of the *DUM* once Waller stepped down.

The dominating subject throughout 1854 and 1855, however, was the Crimean War. From the beginning, the *DUM* supported British involvement on behalf of Turkey, seeing the conflict as one between "civilisation" and "Russianism" (April 1854, 392). At the same time, the magazine sharply condemned British prosecution of the war, seeing these policies as half-hearted, inefficient, underfunded, mismanaged, indecisive, and generally incompetent. The war might well be offering to England "the providential and salutary storm that may purify our political atmosphere, and restore moral health to the national frame" (June 1855, 651). Not until late 1855, however, did the magazine find anything to praise in the government's war effort.

The criticism was more than justified, and for all of the reasons that the *DUM* seized upon. British forces, badly outfitted and commanded, suffered hardship behind the lines and defeat on the battlefields. Alongside the magazine's clear-sighted assessment of the blunders, however, came the talk about a "rattling good war" that offered only apocalyptic silliness in place of analysis. Driving both of these impulses within the magazine's coverage of the war was the fundamental optimism that had characterized the *DUM*'s view of the world since the end of the Famine.

A July 1851 article, "The Day After the Storm," summed up the optimism about this new stage in Ireland's development: "The electric telegraph, the extension of railways, and the wonderful improvements that have been made in steam navigation, have done more to further the amalgamation of England and Ireland, than all the legislative enactments of the last half century" (108). Besides the technological and industrial progress, social conditions were also ripe for improvement, since party feelings had subsided and the peasants no longer identified their interests so closely and irrationally with the land: "Crime has almost ceased, the poor-rate is decreasing, civilisation is spreading, education is advancing, our manufactures are making gigantic strides, our rich mines are unappropriated, and our lands ready to yield their grateful produce; capital only is wanting" (126). Faced with improved economic conditions throughout Ireland, the magazine did not lament the decay of any traditional institutions. It had always been moderately fascinated with technology, especially the railroad, and had always based more faith on capital than on land. Now, like a middle-class entrepreneur, it entered into a period of boosterism with enthusiasm and shrewdness.

London's Great Exhibition of 1851, with the Irish National Exhibition in Cork and the Great Industrial Exhibition in Dublin soon to follow, were celebrated as monuments to technology and progress, a token that God's hand was manifest in the world. The famous Ballinasloe cattle fair had been a complete failure in 1849; just four years later, in revived form, it proved to the *DUM* that prosperity had reached even to the agricultural districts (Nov. 1853). While tenant-right groups such as the Tenant League, along with their parliamentary counterparts in the Irish Brigade, continued to agitate for land reforms in the early 1850s, they still lacked the unity, discipline, and widespread support necessary to emerge as a real threat. Within the broad and conservative view of social events, the *DUM*'s optimism seemed wholly justified.

On a narrower and more personal level, however, the magazine faced some unsettling losses. In his role as Jonathan Freke Slingsby, Waller might joke about his gray hair, but the *DUM* was showing its age in more serious ways as well. Various public figures associated with the birth of the magazine were beginning to die, Sir Robert Peel in 1850, and the Duke of Wellington in 1852. Death also began striking down some of the magazine's founders, William Archer Butler in 1848, Samuel O'Sullivan in 1851. Waller would be succeeded in the editorship by Durham Dunlop, a younger man by only three years, and Cheyne Brady, only eight years younger than Waller, would succeed Dunlop. But while Slingsby was reporting on the delights of his Irish country-house garden, Brady was prowling through the science exhibits and sending back enthusiastic reports about a new era of science, technology, and progress. The *DUM* seemed to be embracing the modern world as never before, and in ways that left especially its political base, so often defined and clarified by the prolific Samuel O'Sullivan, now murky and unsettled.

In 1855, as well, publisher James M'Glashan, having been closely involved with the *DUM* since its beginning, was showing signs of brain disease and senility. Pathetically, he wrote to Lever: "They have given me a pittance to live on, but taken away the Magazine and all that I care to live for. You have always treated me generously and never made hard bargains with me."[20] With his difficulties regarding the *DUM*'s editorship and Dublin's political infighting now over a dozen years in the past, Lever began building hopes of returning to his old job, writing to his financial agent Alexander Spencer in July 1855 that "events might bring the Magazine into the market. If so, there is nothing I'd make such an effort to obtain. It

20. Downey, *Charles Lever*, 1:342–43.

would be in my hands a property—a great one." Lever's fancy was hardly a passing one, and he wrote Spencer again two months later to see if the editorship might be available: "If I could obtain the Magazine for myself it would be a great object. . . . My fear is that J. F. Waller, at present acting as editor, will step in before any one can interfere, and the assignees may not know that I would willingly resume it—either as editor or owner."[21] The assignees, unfortunately, looked more toward an advantageous liquidation of M'Glashan's assets than toward continuity and tradition within the Irish periodical press. Lever would have represented a strong link with the *DUM*'s past, and he would continue to write for the magazine. But not only did he fail in his attempts to obtain the magazine, it was purchased by the *DUM*'s London distributors, Hurst and Blackett. Having recently taken over Henry Colburn's long-standing firm, Hurst and Blackett were primarily concerned with continuing Colburn's tradition of popular, three-decker fiction. Like M'Glashan's assignees, the firm found little of interest in an Irish periodical. Within only three months, then, the magazine was returned to a Dublin firm, Hodges, Smith, and Co. But the symbolism of these transactions was not lost on the Irish literary world. For the first time, albeit temporarily, Ireland's only national monthly magazine had completely severed its Irish connection.

21. Charles Lever to Alexander Spencer, 5 July 5 1855, and 17 Sept. 1855, in Downey, *Charles Lever,* 1:342 and 344.

6

PRAGMATISM, OPTIMISM, MEDIOCRITY

I

The firm Hurst and Blackett operated the *DUM* out of London for three months, January through March 1856, at which time Digby Pilot Starkey and Cheyne Brady entered their copyright for the magazine and, as of the April issue, assumed ownership. For most of 1856, however, the editorial status of the magazine was complex and uncertain.[1] The *Wellesley Index* concludes that, for the period from January to October, Durham Dunlop probably served as editor, Brady then taking over, as both co-owner and editor, for the November 1856 issue and continuing to direct the magazine until he sold it to Joseph Sheridan Le Fanu in July 1861.

For the first year after it had passed out of M'Glashan's hands, the *DUM* had difficulty maintaining even its physical operations. A magazine undergoing editorial changes, meanwhile moving its headquarters from Dublin to London and back again, would not have reassured prospective contributors with its professional stability. In addition, there was a new and disturbing symbolic fact: even if for only a short time, this Irish periodical had been separated from its native foundation. At the same time, both Dunlop and Brady now present-

---

1. For an account of this murky period, see the *Wellesley Index*, 4:204.

ed a much different editorial face to the *DUM*'s readers. In its vision of religious, economic, social, and political developments, the *DUM* for this period claimed a much greater faith in the future than was usually the case, an optimism that the *Wellesley Index* describes as a tendency towards "secular and liberal pragmatism."[2] The description suggests the extent to which the magazine's new image would pander to a crass Victorianism. For all of its upbeat surface, the energy and vision ran but shallow, keeping the magazine mired in complacency and mediocrity until Le Fanu's editorship.

While the offerings themselves might suffer, the stable of writers still contained some notable names, even under Dunlop's guidance: reviews by Jane F. Wilde (March 1856) and Anthony Trollope (July 1856), a short story by William Carleton (April 1856), a literary satire by the novelist and journalist Marmion W. Savage (June 1856), poems by J. F. Waller, Mortimer Collins, and the "Belfastman" Francis Davis, and a continuation of Charles Lever's novel *The Fortunes of Glencore,* as well as an essay by Lever on the political situation in Italy (Sept. 1856). The *DUM* had now survived for more than twenty years in an increasingly competitive literary marketplace, and Dunlop's editorship shows very few signs that he tried to change any of the formulas or patterns that had succeeded thus far. A journalist born and raised in Ulster, Dunlop also continued to devote approximately the usual space to articles concerned specifically with Ireland.

Shortly before assuming the editorship, Dunlop had returned from the Crimean War, in which he had worked as a volunteer field surgeon. Understandably, then, for the first few months of 1856, while war in the Crimea still continued, it received considerable attention in the *DUM,* from Dunlop, from occasional political analyst Francis D. Dwyer, and from John Frazer Corkran, a journalist who would spend nearly twenty years in Paris and who often published in the *DUM* under the title of "Our Foreign Courier." The magazine called for government investigations into the "mismanagement, in-

2. Ibid., 4:206.

capacity, [and] blundering" that had weakened England's ability to fight in the Crimea (April 1856, 382). Still, the criticisms remained vague and were tempered with praise that the British Tories had risen above narrowly partisan issues during this crisis.

The *DUM*'s spirit of political optimism also took shape from the fiction offerings during the months of Dunlop's editorship. In April 1856, Carleton published "Fair Gurtha; or, The Hungry Grass," an account of how charity, patience, and forgiveness triumph over greed and famine. While the story avoids any sectarian bias, it also suggests that those who suffered from famine had earned their fate. By thus reducing complex social and economic relationships to cause-and-effect formulas, throwing in a dash of Celtic superstition, and concluding the whole with a set of romantic pleasantries, Carleton offered a comfortable explanation for Ireland's recent catastrophe. But he was generally producing very little of substance in the wake of the Great Famine, and this story, with its oversimplified stereotypes, is no exception.

A more ambitious work during Dunlop's editorship was the short novel *The Darragh* (May–Oct. 1856, six installments) by Richard Sinclair Brooke, a Protestant rector who published several stories and essays on literary and Irish subjects during these years. "The Darragh" is an Irish Big House in the 1820s. The setting allows for a wide range of themes standard in many nineteenth-century Irish novels: the decaying luxury of the landed gentry, agrarian unrest, occasional Gothic touches, class resentment, a confusing and thwarted inheritance, and marriage between two characters, one Irish and the other English. The main character, Walter Nugent, attends to a humble clerkship with dignity and honor, even though aware of his aristocratic heritage. Having proven himself through both merit and class, Nugent also ultimately wins back his inheritance. "I am proud and happy," he can finally claim, "to mark the steady advance of MY COUNTRY in enterprize, in industry, and in success; and I rejoice to see her hastening to take her rightful and acknowledged position among the nations. I was with her in the bleak night of her famine, and I hope to live to be with her in the bright morning of her fame . . . (Oct. 1856, 442). As with Carleton's story, falsehood and treachery lose out in the end. But Brooke goes considerably further in linking the fortunes of his characters to those of Ireland itself during these years, a time when the *DUM* indeed saw a steady advance in the country's prosperity.

For estates like "The Darragh," fortunes were mixed but generally good. Landlords and tenants continued to defend conflicting interests and to regard each other as adversaries. Seemingly resigned to their declining role in Ireland's agrarian economic base, many of the larger landlords failed to develop the management approaches and capital investments that might have solidified their estates. At the same time, their strategy may have demonstrated more *laissez-faire* than lethargy, for Ireland's Tories, as K. Theodore Hoppen notes, "were enjoying unprecedented electoral success" in the years of 1857 to 1859, gaining political strength—and peace and quiet on the estates—in large part through a sacrifice of landlord profits.[3] For most of the country, economic conditions slowly improved throughout the second half of the 1850s, particularly for the small farmers and the shopkeepers. As rural laboring class continued to decline, urban centers became increasingly more developed and more diversified, giving a cosmopolitan magazine like the *DUM* ample reason for optimism. Upon hearing of poverty among Donegal peasants, the magazine expressed shock and hoped that relief efforts would be increased, while another article complained that continued acts of violence kept investors from bringing capital into the country. More commonly, though, the *DUM* celebrated the many political changes visited upon Ireland in the nineteenth century, now including even emancipation, as clear reforms by which "the cause of Christianity has been promoted" (Nov. 1857, 568).

The title of one *DUM* article, "Statistics of Irish Prosperity" (Dec. 1858), exhibits the general tone. The article finds evidence of Ire-

---

3. Hoppen, *Elections*, 165.

land's increased well-being at many levels of society: crime is down, the Encumbered Estates Court has resolved the land problems, the peasantry has a much improved relationship with their landlords, and the "rancorous political demonstrations" that would otherwise "mar the prospects of Ireland" have been suspended (726). Another article just two months later employed further statistics to make the same points. The various social policies implemented since 1850 have "been most beneficial to Ireland," having "emancipated her agriculture, promoted her industry, augmented her wealth, and brought comfort home to the mass of her inhabitants. . . ." In addition, the connection with Great Britain had been "materially strengthened," and the effect upon the "general national character" had been "excellent" (Feb. 1859, 213). In other articles, the *DUM* reassured the British public that recent evidence of sedition revealed only the dying vestiges of the old Irish lawlessness. New Ireland observed law and order, prospered through the development of busy industries, and looked forward to continuing its mutually beneficial relationship with Great Britain.

II

The *Wellesley Index* attributes many of these optimistic articles to Cheyne Brady, who took over the editorship of the *DUM* in November 1856. His essays over the next several years, perhaps ten pieces in all, covered such subjects as prison reform, industrial schools, French economic policies, and sundry Irish issues, the broad and varied scope that one might expect of a lawyer turned journalist. Brady's general concern, however, remained the celebration of Victorian progress, and he drew on writers who shared in his optimism and his support for even swifter advances. In reviewing "The Manchester Exhibition of Art-Treasures," William Stokes, the Irish physician and art connoisseur, described the second half of the nineteenth century as the "age of exhibitions" in which industry, technology, science, and art had all demonstrated new levels of achievement. Stokes proposed the creation of a great national gallery in England, since this would further "elevate and civilize the human mind" (May 1857, 619).

As with the Crimean War in 1856, however, scattered events from international quarters continued to trouble such hopeful visions, and new technology also showed itself capable of raising old fears. In 1857, France began to increase its shipbuilding, including the development of ironclad warships, perceived by the British as a major threat. Over the next few years, speculation spread about war in Europe or even an invasion of England. In describing its own perspective on such events, the *DUM* claimed that "we aspire to being little more than monthly gossips, the 'Sarah Gamp' and 'Mrs. Harris' of the political births each month brings forth . . ." (Oct. 1860, 226). In actuality, however, the magazine repeatedly urged British military preparedness in case the war effort in France should show further signs of escalating. As late as February 1861, a *DUM* review entitled "Ships in Armour" continued to warn about French ironclads. Remembering the French strategy of using Ireland as a weapon against the British, the *DUM* sought to undercut such tactics for the future in claiming that "Paddy is the cat whom Monsieur Monkey coolly asks to put its paw in the fire" (Aug. 1860, 131). Interest in France remained a constant element in Brady's magazine; William Blanchard Jerrold, for instance, published a lengthy serial called "The Work-a-Day World of France" (May 1860–Sept. 1861, eleven installments), which examined its subject at a less political level.

Similarly jarring to the *DUM*'s English-oriented political sensibilities was the 1857 mutiny within the Bengal army in India. The lead article for October 1857 blamed the Moslem religion for this event, and further articles on India kept turning up in nearly every issue of the magazine for the next two years. As if seeking the decisively final word on this subject, the *DUM* also held a contest for an essay on "The position which the Government of India ought at present to assume towards Christianity and Christian Missions" (May 1859, 515). The judges were Montifort Longfield, James Lawson, and William Alexander, and the winning essayist was J. B. Heard, the Irish-born divine who had recently begun covering political events for the *DUM* and who would ultimately publish some forty pieces in the magazine, many of them on England's place within a European political framework. It was England's responsibility, Heard's essay argued, to convert India to Christianity, not for further gains to the Empire, but for the benefit of India itself. Once England ceased to occupy the country, as it one day must, it needed to leave India in a position to govern itself properly, that is, to be able to resist external forces and also to maintain internal unity. Since proper government depended upon proper religion, British policy should thus encourage "religious instruction," a phrase that Heard found more appropriate than "proselytizing."

In April 1858, a *DUM* article entitled "Double Government" drew some parallels between the British presence in India and in Ireland, good-heartedly but feebly proposing that any resultant tension be lessened by a decrease in official pomp and ceremony. In its more common stance, though, the magazine sought to distance Ireland's political situation from that of India. The Bengal mutiny had heightened racial consciousness in England, and neither Ireland nor the *DUM* could well afford the resurrection of old prejudices against the "Celtic race." Moslems might cause turmoil in India, but Ireland, within the *DUM*'s vision of the Empire, occupied a superior and much more cooperative place. In assessing the Crimean War, the magazine had earlier welcomed the opportunity there for Irish soldiers to fight alongside their English counterparts, a battlefield conversion that revealed a "sullen foe" actually to be a "generous friend" (Feb. 1857, 256). In similar fashion, then, the *DUM* gratefully thanked Ireland for its offer to assist England with more troops to help suppress the rebellion in India (Oct. 1857).

Meanwhile, and to the further dismay of England, the United States began to edge toward Civil War. In June 1861, Heard hoped that war could be averted in America but also complained of events there: "Never before did democracy so disgrace itself in the eyes of civilized nations; never before did it furnish such complete proof of its utter incompetency for all the purposes of a government" (750). The Irish political scene, by contrast, received virtually no *DUM* coverage during these years. Not only did international events overshadow such local concerns, but Ireland looked politically placid. Beyond the notice of the authorities, however, James Stephens began his celebrated three-thousand-mile walk throughout Ireland. Having been in Paris since participating in the abortive rising of 1848, Stephens now wished to test the mood of the country and to see if any further opposition movement could be created. Deciding that conditions were mixed but ultimately favorable, on March 17, 1858—St. Patrick's Day—he founded the organization that ultimately became known as the Irish Republican Brotherhood, or the Fenians.

Stephens organized in secret, and the *DUM* contains nothing to suggest that its writers were privy to any inside information. Indeed, the magazine's coverage of Ireland emphasized mainly its cultural aspects. Patrick Kennedy continued his prolific investigations into Ireland's folklore and its oral tradition. R. S. Brooke, Charles Henry O'Neill (as "Clanaboy"), and John Thomas Gilbert all published serial features on Ireland's history, culture, and landscape, and Jane Wilde had an essay on ancient Irish culture and its artifacts (March 1861). The magazine participated in an ongoing debate concerning reforms of Trinity College's financial structure. And it considered the status of Irish art. One review complained that "in Ireland, Art has no distinctive school, racy of the soil" (Aug. 1858, 197). The fine arts "were never in a more depressed condition than at present; but let us hope that a brighter prospect is about to dawn, and that Art shall not form an exception in the great social progress which is now taking place in this country" (210). To that optimistic end, a later review of art exhibitions expressed the hope that, in the future, "home talent may be better represented, and foreign somewhat less" (Aug. 1859, 215).

For most of its aesthetic concerns, however, the *DUM* looked toward the British scene, most notably in Frederick George Stephens's reviews of pictorial art. For an Irish magazine interested in promoting "home talent," Stephens posed some difficulties. Also publishing during this period in journals such as *Athenaeum* and *Macmillan's*, he was too professionally established as a critic to praise anything he might consider provincial or inferior. In reviewing an exhibition by the Society of British Artists, for instance, he noted: "Conventional and puerile designs, bad colour, bad or no drawing, hideous faces, impossible draperies, and total neglect of nature, seemed to be the prevailing rule" (July 1859, 94). Movements such as the Pre-Raphaelites, by contrast, enjoyed Stephens' support and encouragement. Stephens would cease contributing to the *DUM* once Le Fanu assumed the editorship, and by June 1861, a post-Stephens review would describe Pre-Raphaelitism as a "soulless naturalism" that suffered from an overly literal rendering of its subject and that had produced little more than "a series of ambitious failures" (687). While he still covered artistic developments, however, Stephens provided the magazine with an astute aesthetic sensibility, albeit not an Irish one.[4]

Another critic of note is Stopford Brooke, son of R. S. Brooke and author of most of the *DUM*'s reviews of fiction for this period, although he also dabbled in more general cultural issues. In "Womanhood and Its Mission," for instance, a long, philosophical essay, Brooke emphasized the differences between men and women along these lines: "We can call to mind no purely intellectual, or physical work done by a woman. Her heart and spirit give the motives of her life" (May 1859, 640). Through such essays, the *DUM* was, at one level, simply updating its old stereotypes about women, ones that had appeared as early as Charles Stuart Stanford's courtly remarks to the magazine's women readers in December 1833 (Insert, 6). Particularly under James M'Glashan's editorship, women's issues and interests

---

4. B. Richards discusses Stephens's contributions to the *DUM*, describing Stephens as "a highly professional critic," one who, under Le Fanu, got replaced by "a provincial amateur." B. Richards, "Pre-Raphaelite Standards in the *Dublin University Magazine*'s Art Criticism," *Long Room* 14–15 (Autumn 1976–Spring/Summer 1977): 15.

had gotten extended attention around 1840. But with its greater awareness of Victorian England during the 1850s, the DUM could also not afford to ignore increased attention there to what was variously known as the "woman question" or even "woman worship." Coventry Patmore published *The Angel in the House* in 1854, and in 1858, the year before Stopford Brooke's remarks, occasional *DUM* contributor Dinah Maria Mulock followed with *A Woman's Thoughts About Women*. The early feminist Barbara Leigh Smith had begun agitating by the mid-1850s and gained the support of such writers as Elizabeth Gaskell, Harriet Martineau, and Elizabeth Barrett Browning. Through his work as a volunteer field surgeon in the Crimean War, too, Durham Dunlop might have been aware of the accomplishments of another figure who had helped advance the position of women, the battlefield nurse Florence Nightingale.

Nightingale was an ambiguous and tricky subject for a magazine such as the *DUM*, especially under an editor like Dunlop, who valued the individual human element within an increasingly mechanical and material society. On the one hand, as a nurse she occupied a traditionally female role, and she humanized the bureaucracy on the Crimean front; on the other hand, she triggered the traditional suspicions against women's involvement in public affairs. In tackling the theme of "the nature of woman," then, the *DUM* conveniently ignored her. In March 1855, an article on the French soldier-surgeon Baron Larrey, probably authored by Dunlop, concludes with a discussion of medical conditions for soldiers in the Crimean War, but with no mention of Nightingale.

On the status of women as writers, the magazine could approach broad social issues on more familiar ground, as in its attention to Elizabeth Barrett Browning's *Aurora Leigh*, the verse novel that portrays the intellectual development of a woman poet. One reviewer argued: "Woman must be ever true to her womanly instincts if she would be the meet helper as well as companion of man" (April 1857, 470), then going on to call E. B. Browning "the greatest female poet of our age" (461), and *Aurora Leigh* her major work. Two years later,

Jane Wilde, pronouncing Thomas Carlyle the age's leader in philosophy and John Ruskin in art, agreed that Browning was "the greatest poetess of this age" (March 1859, 300). A November 1860 review, by contrast, described *Aurora Leigh* as "unpoetic indigestible hodgepodge" (521). As with its position on the Pre-Raphaelites, the magazine's views on Browning lacked the kind of consistency that its earlier and more politically engaged editors had still been able to provide on aesthetic issues.

### III

The *DUM*'s own poetry during this period, suffering from an overly conventional prettiness and sentimentality, could have only profited from a few "unpoetic, indigestible" bits. William Allingham, still several years away from *Laurence Bloomfield* (1864), offered only a handful of slight pieces (Dec. 1857; Feb. and June 1858). Francis Davis, "The Belfastman" who had once contributed to the *Nation*, had about eight poems in all. John Francis Waller published some musical masques along with a number of other poems. Other poets included Mortimer Collins (praised for his "delicate etching of quiet scenery"; June 1856, 671), Thomas Caulfield Irwin, George Walter Thornbury (with several Cavalier songs), and the husband-and-wife team of Rev. William and Cecil Frances Alexander (who wrote in what one reviewer described as the style of "Irish Lake Poetry"). Modern poetry, another review suggested, had now developed beyond Byron, whose passion consumed the heart and thus did not lead to any action. The danger of modern poetry, though, is "that it may destroy action by making too much of the inner life" (June 1856, 667). The quietly melancholy verse that appeared with such enervating regularity in the magazine was an excellent case in point.

The *DUM*'s fiction of the period was hardly much better. Charles Lever serialized two unremarkable novels, *The Fortunes of Glencore* (Aug. 1855–April 1857, seventeen installments) and *Gerald Fitzgerald, "The Chevalier"* (Jan. 1858–July 1859, eighteen installments), besides two essays on current political events in Italy (Sept. and Nov. 1856).

Digby Pilot Starkey serialized the novel *John Twiller* (by "Godfrey Massingberd"; Nov. 1856–July 1857, nine installments). The title character, a would-be poet and fiction writer, spends much of his time in extensive philosophic musings about the meaning of life. While he never accomplishes anything, he still harbors fantasies about being discovered and revered as a great writer after his death.

William Hurton, a miscellaneous writer from Scotland, contributed a number of reviews, essays, and short stories, many on nautical subjects, as well as the novel *Vonved the Dane—Count of Elsinore* (Jan.–Nov. 1860, eleven installments). Hurton's narrator describes the work this way: "Wild and romantic adventures—deeds of daring—the most powerful passions of human nature—the worst and the best emotions of the soul—these formed the groundwork of the canvas, so to speak . . ." (9). Set in the early nineteenth century, bearing a title character who is a romanticized pirate, the work is, as its narrator unwittingly suggests, hopelessly melodramatic.

Even William Carleton was unable to check the slide of fiction into mediocrity. His short story "Utrum Horum? or, The Revenge of Shane Roe Na Sogarth: A Legend of the Golden Fawn" appeared in May and June 1860. The story contains several elements that Carleton had worked with in previous and more successful fiction, such as a detailed portrayal of Irish society and a dilemma to be negotiated, here by the main character, M'Mahon. The Latin portion of the title refers to a choice that M'Mahon must make between his two sons, one of whom will then be killed by the story's villain. In the bleakness of its social vision, however, and in the simplistic nature of its choices, the work fails to support the harmony and resolution imposed on its material at the end. Other short stories from the period include one by Elizabeth Gaskell (Nov. 1858), then near the height of her reputation as a novelist in England, and two stories by Georgina Marion Craik (May and Aug. 1857), remarkable only in that one of them is narrated by a piano.

Another style that appeared frequently in the *DUM* during these years was a kind of High-Victorian, high-society fiction somewhat in the manner of Trollope and Bulwer-Lytton with a dash of superficial comedy. Charles William Shirley Brooks, currently on the staff for *Punch* and later its editor, wrote such a piece (*The Partners,* June 1857–Jan. 1858, six installments), and Richard Seymour Conway Chermside managed two (*Artist and Craftsman,* July 1859–March 1860, nine installments; and *An Only Son,* Feb. 1861–Nov. 1861, ten installments). This passage, from *An Only Son,* catches the recurring flavor of these works: "'What's up at the Locksley's, I wonder,' quoth his Lordship, sauntering into the room where his mother and Lady Constance were, his hairy doggie close upon his heels . . ." (April 1861, 421). The barrister Martin Farquhar Tupper captured a similar tone in "The Rides and Reveries of Mr. Aesop Smith," narrated by "Peter Query." Tupper's series contained short items such as parables, fables, and anecdotes, usually designed to show the folly of current events and experiences. His other *DUM* contribution, "Cheap Security," contains a facetious conversation between characters named Muff, Till, Funker, Dolt, and Wydawake (Aug. 1858). Tupper's occasional book-length publications of such material, while very popular, failed miserably with the critics.

With high-society trivia on one side and Aesop Smith's quaint moralizing on the other, one turns with relief to Robert Curtis, who wrote his short stories as "A Constabulary Officer." Curtis drew on his police experience to give his stories a solid grounding in Irish conflicts at a local level. The stories suffer from a predictable pattern: as in "M'Cormack's Grudge," for instance (Oct.–Nov. 1857), honest people struggle to avoid conflict and wrongdoing, suffer some loss, but then find that, in the end, justice is invariably served. Despite the contrived solutions, Curtis's stories also offer a realistic glimpse, free from any sectarian biases, into the complex circumstances of his characters.

IV

For the first several years of Brady's editorship, the *DUM* followed a consistently nonsectarian policy. The energies of Protestant evangelicalism, quiet for over five years, flared up again in 1859, however, as the sentiments of revivalism once more swept across both England and Ireland. This movement was not as significant as the revival of 1849–1854, and it also had a more formidable opponent than ever before. Irish Catholicism, now shaped so definitely by the Ultramontanist philosophy of Paul Cullen, Archbishop of Dublin, continued to increase its strength and its ability more readily to resist Protestant pressures. The Catholic clergy had now achieved a greater degree of unity than before and more influence within Irish society as a whole, in part through increased numbers of both priests and nuns.

The year 1859 thus saw a sharp increase in the role of religion as a theme in the pages of the *DUM*. Between February and December of that year, the magazine ran a series first called "Essays by Clergymen of the United Church of Ireland," later continued under the title "University Essays." One series contributor of note was the Irish cleric Orlando Thomas Dobbin, who would continue to write religious articles throughout the editorship of his cousin, J. S. Le Fanu. Opening the series, though, was the prolific J. B. Heard, here with a discussion comparing the decline of paganism in the Roman Empire to the current growth of Christianity in India. Striking a note familiar to the *DUM*'s earliest readers, Heard related Protestantism to the advance of Empire: "At once we are called to act as the religionists, the civilizers, and the lawgivers of the East" (Feb. 1859, 138).

The terms had changed a bit, though, as in Heard's insistence on the phrase "religious instruction" over "proselytizing." The choice of a kinder, gentler expression and the vague promise of national independence at some elusive point in India's future, while they fail to mask Heard's imperialist assumptions, still reflect the *DUM*'s preference during this period for the safe, the bland, the correct. Up-to-date and stylish, the language also respects the more enduring traditions and values of mid-Victorian society. A review of Charles Darwin's *On the Origin of Species* similarly captures the magazine's combination of intelligence, knowledge, and intellectual timidity. While the review is written by a geologist, David Ansted, and shows a thorough grounding in paleontology, it finally rejects Darwinian processes as too mechanical, preferring instead to stress "unity of creation" as an explanation of the world (June 1860). Even while preferring proselytism under a different name, the DUM never rose above the evangelical fervor of 1859, and its sectarian limitations during this period reflect its overall quality.

The *Wellesley Index* uses terms like "debacle" and "devastating" to describe the DUM's problems during 1856, the year of Dunlop's editorship following M'Glashan's collapse. Under Brady's editorship, finally, "writers of quality and dependability began to come back and new ones to be recruited."[5] This version of the period tends, however, to give Brady more credit than he may deserve. The entire period from the end of 1855 to July 1861 demonstrates a fairly uniform mediocrity for the DUM as it sought to cling to the old patterns without building upon those significantly. The magazine was shaped by Brady's pragmatic optimism that had no definite ideological foundation to it. It had cast off the old ideological fervor and energy without similarly casting off the trappings of religiosity and faith in proselytizing, and without discovering any new political energy. What changed all of that, what once more restored the DUM to its earlier levels of excellence, was the return of a writer of real stature and quality in Le Fanu. Mangan was dead, Ferguson had ceased publishing in the DUM in 1853, Carleton had exhausted his creative energies, and Lever was now choosing British outlets such as *Blackwood's* and *Cornhill*. Of the major writers ever to be associated with the DUM, only Le Fanu was still available to infuse the magazine with its old quality. Under his editorship, the 1860s would once again see the magazine as the premier representative of Irish literary excellence within the magazine market.

5. *Wellesley Index,* 4:206.

7

# DOUBLING THE UNCERTAINTIES OF AUTHORITY

I

As had been the case under Charles Lever, the *DUM* prospered under Le Fanu in large part on the strength of its editor's own prolific output. Le Fanu had purchased the magazine in July 1861 and soon after began serializing *The House by the Church-yard*. During his editorship, until he sold the magazine in 1869, eight other novels would follow: *Wylder's Hand, Uncle Silas, Guy Deverell, All in the Dark, The Tenants of Malory, Haunted Lives, Loved and Lost,* and *The Wyvern Mystery*. The sheer volume of this list, not even including an additional handful of short stories, reviews, and political articles, indicates the extent to which the *DUM* functioned as a showcase for Le Fanu's own work.

Unlike Lever's fictional heroes, Le Fanu's characters tend to call the entire showcase into question and doubt. In *The House by the Church-yard* and, to an even greater extent, in *Uncle Silas*, Le Fanu developed a psychological complexity in his fiction that also contains a powerful social critique. Beneath the surface of conventions and commonplaces, Le Fanu's characters expose the same ambivalence and paralyzing uncertainties that haunted Ireland's Protestant ascendancy. Whereas Lever and Carleton portrayed society in a more direct and historically specific setting, Le Fanu sought an indirect mode, outside of history and realism, that freed him from various restraints. Through the conventions of sensationalist and gothic fiction, he could present the internal doubts, the confusions, the fears of many Protestants about the legitimacy and authority of their ascendancy status. Even though these literary conventions were already well worn by the time he began to use them in his tales in the 1830s, Le Fanu managed to draw from them a psychological depth that makes his work seem in many respects more modern than that of any other writer for the *DUM*.

Having established his financial interests in Dublin journalism as early as 1840, Le Fanu could draw on this expertise as well as his creative talents in formulating efficient strategies for operating the *DUM*. One such strategy was the maintenance of a relatively limited stable of writers to whom he returned frequently throughout his tenure as editor. J. W. Cole continued his coverage of the Irish theatre; L. J. Trotter contributed perhaps thirty pieces, on a wide variety of subjects, over the first several years of Le Fanu's editorship; J. B. Heard and James Anderson Scott held main responsibility, along with the magazine's editor, for political coverage; Orlando Thomas Dobbin, Irish cleric and cousin to the editor, wrote on such topics as styles of sermons, with O'Dell Travers Hill also covering religious issues. Folklorist Patrick Kennedy published most of his more than two-hundred *DUM* contributions during Le Fanu's editorship. Mortimer Collins, T. C. Irwin, and John Francis Waller—usually in his "Slingsby" role—all contributed poetry. Irwin's reputation in particular grew during this period. He had earlier contributed to the *DUM* under Waller, as well as to the *Nation,* but his first major volume, *Poems,* did not appear until 1866, and the *DUM* claimed that this work presented "unquestionable evidences of genius" (Oct. 1866, 465).

Within a narrow stable of writers, versatility was valuable. Irwin also published a one-act play in the magazine as well as a number of reviews on cultural issues, while Mortimer Collins expanded his repertoire to produce two novels, *Who Is the Heir?* (Dec. 1864–Oct. 1865, eleven installments) and *Sweet Anne Page* (Sept. 1867–July 1868, eleven installments). The first of these, in its title, raises a question common to a number of Le Fanu's own novels from this decade, while the second, perhaps Collins's best work of fiction ever, portrays an heiress who goes insane amidst a passionate tangle of love rivalries. The novel proved somewhat controversial at the time and helped to advance Collins's image as "the King of the Bohemians." Percy Fitzgerald, however, one of Le Fanu's Dublin friends and a writer whose career would include nearly two hundred volumes of fiction and history, best exemplified the ideal *DUM* contributor of the 1860s. Some three dozen of his articles cover a broad range of subjects; he published frequent biographical items on Laurence Sterne and David Garrick, and he added three novels for good measure. *Mildrington the Barrister—A Romance of Two Syrens* is typical, its lawyer hero mired in a highly wrought style whose main advantage was its ability to stretch itself out over eleven installments during 1862 without ever overshadowing the quality of Le Fanu's own novel from this year, *The House by the Church-yard*.

Early in Le Fanu's editorship, L. J. Trotter voiced the concern—frequently made, doubtless true for works like *Mildrington the Barrister*, but still of dubious taste considering the publishing habits of Trotter's editor—that "the serial system has done no good to novel writing as an art . . ." (April 1862, 404). That same year, reviewing Elizabeth Barrett Browning's *Last Poems*, Mortimer Collins suggested that "The function of woman is—not to write, not to act, not to be famous—but to love" (Aug. 1862, 162). The *DUM* would be guided by neither of these critical dicta, and serialized novels by apprentice women writers proved to be one of the defining features of Le Fanu's editorship. Within a few months of Collins's pronouncement, the Wexford writer Annie Robertson began serializing the first of two novels in the magazine. She was soon joined by Le Fanu's oldest child, Eleanor Frances Le Fanu, who used the pseudonym of "Russell Gray" in publishing three novels in the *DUM*, with

Nina Cole adding two more. While these works never rise for long above their overly romantic mediocrity, their adherence to a woman's point of view occasionally results in striking portrayals. And while they were immediately attractive to Le Fanu as a cheap and ready resource for fiction, the DUM did offer a prominent outlet for their work.

None of the above trio of women writers ever achieved any literary prominence. In one further case, however, that of Le Fanu's niece Rhoda Broughton, he helped to launch the career of one of the bestselling women writers in the latter part of the Victorian period. Le Fanu recommended his new discovery to London publisher George Bentley in an 1865 letter that stressed the "great promise and power" of *Not Wisely, But Too Well,* her novel that had just begun its serial run in the DUM (Aug. 1865–July 1866, twelve installments). Near the end of the serialization, Le Fanu again assured Bentley that the novel needed some revising but that he himself had *"great* confidence in it."[1] Le Fanu's confidence, however, was to be severely shaken by the reaction of Bentley's reader Geraldine Jewsbury, who attacked the work as being too audacious and daring for the kind of family readers that made up Bentley's market. As he had already done on occasion with his own work, Le Fanu quietly submitted to Bentley's decision not to publish: "I have communicated with the author of *Not Wisely* and strongly urged the expediency of withdrawing the book. . . ."[2]

By late 1866, though, Broughton herself was negotiating with Bentley, and the writer who could portray powerful emotions and strong wills in her own characters showed herself not nearly as submissive as her uncle. She objected to making changes for the sake of propriety and to padding the length for the sake of the standard three-decker, and she complained that she had hurt her chances to

---

1. Le Fanu to George Bentley, Aug. 2, 1865, and April 21, 1866, in Michael Sadleir, *Things Past* (London: Constable, 1944), 97. Sadleir provides a detailed account of the Broughton-Bentley-Le Fanu relationship.
2. Le Fanu to George Bentley, July 28, 1866, in Sadleir, *Things Past,* 98.

publish by first issuing the novel in the *DUM*.³ In a diary entry for September 21, 1867, George Bentley described her as "wilful."⁴ While she chafed against Bentley's conservative tastes, however, and while her own heroines frequently find themselves caught between the demands of love and of duty, Broughton herself finally did strike a compromise. *Cometh Up As a Flower,* her next novel and one that also first appeared in the *DUM* (July 1866–Jan. 1867, seven installments), was expanded beyond its serial form and so elicited a "generous proposal" and the request that she submit other work.⁵ In all, Bentley would subsequently publish thirteen of her works, helping her to become, in Michael Sadleir's phrase, "almost a national institution."⁶

II

*The House by the Church-yard: A Souvenir of Chapelizod* was Le Fanu's first work as the new owner and editor of the *DUM* (Oct. 1861–Feb. 1863, seventeen installments). The opening installment sets the stage of the novel, Chapelizod in 1767, at that time "about the gayest and prettiest of the outpost villages in which old Dublin took a complacent pride" (Oct. 1861, 387). The broad sweep of characters includes military and professional men, their wives, daughters, and lady friends, servants, minor blackguards, a Catholic priest, a Protestant rector, and the new and mysterious young gentleman Mr. Mervyn, all of them quickly intertwined within a Dickensian plot that resists any hierarchical ordering.

Within the intricacies of the novel, the chatty gaiety and lighthearted courtships conceal several darker currents, the main one

---

3. Rhoda Broughton to Richard Bentley (George Bentley's son), Sept. 20, 1867, in Sadleir, *Things Past,* 100.

4. Royal Gettmann, *A Victorian Publisher: A Study of the Bentley Papers* (Cambridge: Cambridge University Press, 1960), 204.

5. Ibid.,104, with reference to George Bentley's memorandum to Rhoda Broughton, 30 Oct. 1867.

6. Sadleir, *Things Past,* 84.

carrying us ever closer to the true identity of Charles Archer, the suave and polished land agent who lives under the name of Paul Dangerfield. To his neighbors, such as General Chattesworth, Dangerfield seems "the most principled man I think I ever met . . ." (Feb. 1862, 137). To himself, Dangerfield can never escape his earlier identity as the murderer Charles Archer, and at times even doubts the very nature of that identity: "Charles Archer living—Charles Archer dead—or, as I sometimes think, neither one nor t'other quite—half man, half corpse—a vampire—there is no rest for thee: no sabbath in the days of thy work. Blood—blood—blood—'tis tiresome. Why should I be a slave to these d____d secrets" (Sept. 1862, 293). Dangerfield's villainy finally comes to light when his latest victim, Dr. Sturk, regains consciousness through the benefits of a macabre trepanning. Yet the framework of the novel suggests that nothing much, after all, has been gained within a society that continues on its path to the grave whether evil gets exposed or not. The narrator, "Charles de Cresseron," is inspired to tell his story by the discovery of Sturk's battered skull after it has moldered in the coffin for half a century. Over and over, de Cresseron steps aside from his tale to remind us of the mortality of his characters: "Poor Nan! with thy fun and thy rascalities, thy strong affections and thy fatal gift of beauty, where does thy head rest now?" (Oct. 1861, 402).

The setting of the novel arises out of Le Fanu's nostalgia for the first dozen years of his own life, when his father served as Anglican chaplain for the Royal Hibernian Military School in Dublin. For Le Fanu's family, however, the security of this time, centering around the quaintness of Chapelizod and the bright pageantry of viceregal affairs, gave way in 1826 to a new parish assignment in Abington, on the borders of Limerick and Tipperary. In this remote rural village, faced with the relative apathy of the few Church of Ireland parishioners and the inexorable movement towards Catholic emancipation, the Le Fanus found life physically isolated and uncertain at best, violent and potentially apocalyptic at worse times. In *The House by the Church-yard*, the splendid details of an old time and place have suffered a similar transformation: "the earth, or rather that grim giant factory, which is now the grand feature and centre of Chapelizod, throbbing all over with steam, and whizzing with wheels, and vomiting pitchy smoke, has swallowed them up" (Oct. 1861, 388). Within the sinister terms of this vision of hell, the factory that swallows the past becomes merely one more means by which the earth will devour the whole of humanity. "Oh, fair youth!" laments de Cresseron: "The parting from thee was a sadness and a violence—sadder, I think, than death itself. . . . our march is towards the darkness" (July 1862, 49).

This general and recurring mood of darkness serves as backdrop to more mysteries than just Paul Dangerfield's awful past. Mr. Mervyn, who lives in a house once supposedly haunted, unnerves nearly everyone, the rector's daughter, for instance, feeling "uncertain whether he's a man or a ghost" (Jan. 1862, 22). The ill-fated Dr. Sturk, worried mostly about how to conceal his present financial crisis, also hides his suspicion that he once knew Dangerfield under a different name. Several other characters also feel burdened by secrets they reveal only late in the novel, and still others, like Charles Archer, are wrongly presumed dead on occasion. Such identity confusions are carried even farther in Le Fanu's next novel, *Wylder's Hand* (June 1863–Feb. 1864, nine installments). One major character there whom we meet early on soon disappears and is thought to be dead, then alive when he is apparently seen by three other characters, then once more dead when a body that resembles him is found, then alive again when the three "sightings" are publicly announced; finally, as even a court rules in the case, we learn that he has in fact been dead since quite early in the novel.

Following the serialization of *Wylder's Hand,* Le Fanu's next and best-known work, *Uncle Silas,* began its run in July 1864 under the title "Maud Ruthyn," became "Maud Ruthyn and Uncle Silas" for two installments, and finished, from October to December 1864, as "Uncle Silas and Maud Ruthyn." This final switch, moving the emphasis increasingly from Maud to Silas, represented Le Fanu's attempt gracefully to transform his title into the one that Richard Bentley suggested, and got, for the three-decker edition in 1864—*Uncle Silas: A Tale of Bartram-Haugh.*

Even while producing so prolifically during this period, Le Fanu still managed to sustain a high level of quality through these three novels, in part by reworking some old material. *The House by the Church-yard* glances back at some short pieces on Chapelizod published in the *DUM* for January and April 1851, and *Uncle Silas,* set in Derbyshire, had its origins in Le Fanu's short story from the November 1838 *DUM* called "Passage in the Secret History of an Irish Countess." Elizabeth Bowen, following this bibliographic lead, has stressed the essential Irishness of the novel, *Uncle Silas* having "always struck me as being an Irish story transposed to an English setting."[7] W. J. Mc Cormack's biographical study reinforces Bowen's insight in his own reading of the novels, emphasizing the Anglo-Irish continuities and influences within Le Fanu's writing during this period.[8]

The similarities between *The House by the Church-yard* and *Uncle Silas* are indeed crucial. Like the earlier work, *Uncle Silas* develops a central plot whose mysteries begin with whispered scandal and anxious premonitions and then develop to the final revelations of

7. Elizabeth Bowen, introduction to *Uncle Silas: A Tale of Bartram-Haugh,* by Joseph Sheridan Le Fanu (London: Cresset, 1947), 8.
8. Mc Cormack, *Sheridan Le Fanu.* Mc Cormack's excellent study places Le Fanu's life and writings consistently within an Irish context. For a contrasting view, see Jochen Achilles, *Sheridan Le Fanu und die schauerromantische Tradition: Zur psychologischen Funktion der Motivik von Sensationsroman und Geistergeschichte* (Tübingen: Gunter Narr, 1991). Achilles's study argues that Le Fanu's novelistic techniques, characterization, and setting owe much more to "the English tradition of Gothic fiction" and to "typically Victorian moral, political and religious concerns" (271) than to geographical considerations: "Die Herkunft seiner Romanfiguren,—handlungen und—schauplätze ist in sehr viel höherem Maße literarisch als geographisch festlegbar" (12). See also Patricia Coughlan, "Doubles, Shadows, Sedan-Chairs and the Past: The 'Ghost Stories' of J. S. Le Fanu," *Critical Approaches to Anglo-Irish Literature,* eds. Michael Allen and Angela Wilcox (Totowa, N.J.: Barnes and Noble, 1989), 35, who argues that "Le Fanu's construction of the Other in landscape and history owes a good deal to the influence of folklore. . . ."

bigamy, murder, and suicide, all spurred on by Le Fanu's ever-present theme of financial crisis. Silas Ruthyn himself resembles Archer/Dangerfield in the ghastly whiteness of his appearance. Vampire-like, the natures and identities of both men become ambiguous and unknowable, "hoverings between life and death—between intellect and insanity—a dubious, marsh-fire existence, horrible to look on" (Oct. 1864, 426). Faced with such horrors, the characters in both novels can take nothing for granted, not even their own sanity: "[A]m I mad?" Maud Ruthyn asks herself. "Is this all a dream, or is it real?" (Dec. 1864, 672).

These questions are slippery. At one level, they reinforce Maud's credibility for us as the narrator of *Uncle Silas*: If she is able to ask such things, she can't be mad. At another level, we feel superior to her: While she may tremulously wonder if her terror is a dream, we know it is real, even though we have not yet learned its full nature. What we fail to note is that Maud has in fact lured us inside her "real" experience with the same artifice that her creator has used throughout this whole work of fiction: possessing the hindsight that we lack, she narrates these events years after they have taken place, revealing this maturity only in the closing pages. In his frequent interpolations about the veracity of the "documents" he used to construct *The House by the Church-yard,* de Cresseron had done an even subtler job of obscuring the difference between fact and fantasy. Faced with these further layers of narrative deception that Maud Ruthyn or Charles de Cresseron add to their respective tales, the reader ends up more disoriented about the nature of reality than do the actual characters.

Harmony is restored by the end of both works, yet the victory seems hollow and uncertain. De Cresseron obliges with a description of a wedding party but also reminds his readers that the joyous, pleasant faces there "won't smile or blush any more . . ." (Feb. 1863, 167). Maud's own marriage, "happy in the affection of a beloved and noble-hearted husband," has not shielded her from sorrow when her first children die in infancy (Dec. 1864, 679). "Maud is, by nature, a bride of Death," Elizabeth Bowen observes.⁹ When she first comes to Bartram-Haugh and befriends Silas's exuberant daughter Milly, Maud feels a new and delighted sense of freedom and companionship. Yet her experiences there ultimately leave her little of the world beyond her sense of its treachery.

III

Le Fanu's early short stories in the *DUM*, twelve in all, were later collected as *The Purcell Papers* (1880). Largely narrated by a rural parish priest, the stories convey Le Fanu's anxieties about the fate of the Big Houses, the lost causes and heroic defeats, the decay of the social landscape, and the inability of spiritually shaken characters to reunite the fragments of their society. This same world view remains intact for the novels of the 1860s; within Le Fanu's vision of Protestant ascendancy throughout much of the nineteenth century, culture crumbles away through relentless processes very like those that threaten Maud or Chapelizod. One early response to this anxiety was Le Fanu's association in 1847 with the *Nation* and with the Young Irelanders John Mitchel and Thomas Francis Meagher, to whom Le Fanu had promised his support in the formation of a council of nationalist Protestants. He soon recoiled in horror, however, from a political involvement he came to regard as treasonous. By early 1848, the militant rhetoric of the *Nation* threatened to develop quickly into armed rebellion, and England responded by arresting several Young Ireland leaders. Le Fanu hailed the conviction of Mitchel in a June 1848 article in the *DUM*, a reversal of loyalties that, according to W. J. Mc Cormack, reveals "the vehemence of a man denouncing sins which he had all but committed himself...."[10] Other public distancings were still to come, Le Fanu's follow-up article in July 1848 further warning against the seditious impulses of Irish Catholicism, "a dark and sinister theology" (118).

9. Bowen, introduction, 9.
10. Mc Cormack, *Sheridan Le Fanu*, 105.

Glancing back at this period, the *DUM* in 1862 continued to "despise the cock-a-doodle-doo of Meagher, Mitchel, and the other stage rebels" (Feb. 1862, 251).

While Le Fanu continued to harbor his personal anxieties, the *DUM* itself, through its sub-editor James Anderson Scott, presented a more optimistic view in the early years of the 1860s. Scott dominated the political commentary for the magazine through the first half of the decade much like a cheery public-relations man. Analyzing census figures for 1861, for instance, he found that such data offered "strong evidence of returning prosperity" for Ireland and that the country could look forward to being "restored to a wholesome point" (Sept. 1861, 380). In the next issue, in an article entitled "A New Leaf Turned Over," he reiterated his faith in "Ireland's new and prosperous era" (Oct. 1861, 504), a few months later finding "fresh grounds for confidence and hope" (Feb. 1863, 248).

On one point Scott remained wary: the possibility, a distressingly persistent one in political discussions from the very outset of the decade, that the Church of Ireland might lose its legally privileged status. The Established Church, Scott argued in a June 1863 article, had long served as "the principal bond" between England and Ireland; to sever that bond would be to risk "anarchical consequences" (621). If English statesmen "abandon the Irish Church they will cast away Irish Protestantism with it as a political element, and commit the folly and perpetrate the crime of virtually repealing the Union" (623). Within his general position of moderate conservatism and constitutional order, believing as he did that Ireland's various problems were all improving on their own, Scott urged a hands-off policy. In "The Irish Question in 1865," he argued that "if existing evils are being thus naturally redressed, Ireland needs no panacea in the shape of Tenant-right, a new Education scheme, or the abolition of the Established Church. . . . What she really wants is to be let alone" (April 1865, 368). In August and September 1865, Scott had further grounds for confidence, now because of the recent electoral success of Lord Palmerston and the forces of "Moderatism" and constitutional order that would support the Established Church (Sept. 1865, 352). To the *DUM*'s horror, however, by November 1865 Palmerston was dead. The magazine's deeper anxieties, so far confined to Le Fanu's fiction, broke through in Palmerston's obituary: "An awful feeling of uncertainty for the future mingles with the national sorrow" (Nov. 1865, 599).

Le Fanu may or may not have written a lead article for January 1862 on "The Death of the Prince Consort."[11] In any case, he provided no other items on political issues until, like some doomsayer who has kept silent long enough, he emerged from the *DUM*'s shadows to author the obituary for Palmerston and then a series of several more articles over the next few years that, in their political vision, swing wildly between Scott's earlier optimism and a kind of Irish-gothic foreboding. In February 1866, Le Fanu warned against the extremist forces that, in his view, Palmerston had previously kept in check. By July, events seemed once more to have stabilized, and Le Fanu hoped that "the improvement of Ireland has been proceeding with the steady and cumulative action of an established law, while the disturbing influence which has thrown us back during the last ten months is simply one of those occasional checks to which all national processes are in one form or another liable" (July 1866, 116). The language here, however, sounds like the press release of a nervous public official, and its vague generalities and cautious qualifiers ring hollow. When Le Fanu turns, in the same article, to look more closely at that "disturbing influence," Fenianism, the tone changes markedly: "This conspiracy was as cunning and ferocious as any ever yet projected in Ireland. In the elaboration of its mystery and the energy of its internal terrorism it is unmatched" (117). The feeble qualifiers have given way to frantic absolutes in a rhetorical shift that ends up sounding like one of Le Fanu's novels.

---

11. The *Wellesley Index*, 4:318, assigns this to Le Fanu on the basis of internal evidence; it is not listed on Mc Cormack's index of Le Fanu's unpublished writings (*Sheridan Le Fanu* 275).

The *DUM* astutely attributed the birth of Fenianism to the 1861 funeral for Terence Bellew MacManus, only months after Le Fanu had assumed editorial control (April 1866, 467). The huge Dublin procession to honor the dead Young Irelander, perhaps 50,000 strong, clearly showed the physical-force movement to be alive and well. By 1864, James Stephens, as head organizer, had thousands of unarmed troops at his command in Dublin and Cork. In that same year, Archbishop Cullen tempered his earlier opposition to Fenianism by forming a new Catholic political group, the National Association of Ireland. In announcing the Association, Cullen listed the perennial Irish problems: a declining population, widespread poverty, a weak economy. One of his solutions involved disestablishing the Church of Ireland. In March 1867, when the long-awaited Fenian rising finally took place, disorganized, mismanaged, and still largely unarmed, it was easily put down. But the pattern of events was clear, and the *DUM* had been unwilling to read it. In December 1865, a few months after widespread arrests of most of the Fenian leaders who had renewed the threat of an uprising, the *DUM* had claimed that "there is not sufficient internal discontent in Ireland to afford materials for a rebellion above the Cabbage-garden character . . ." (716). A few months later, the magazine recognized the support for Fenianism from America, but discounted its influence in Ireland, since "the great rural population are prepared for the new era of industry and peaceful progress" (April 1866, 480). In the weeks before the 1867 rising, the magazine continued to suggest that the "difficulty" of administering Ireland "may, indeed, be fictitious, as created by the perverseness merely of a distracted population . . ." (Feb. 1867, 231). Political analysis in the *DUM,* frequently capable during its history of great knowledge and insight, had given way to mere wishful thinking.

On the parliamentary front, Gladstone's Liberals came to power in 1868 on promises of change, and he quickly introduced a bill for disestablishment of the Irish Church. In 1869, when the bill passed into law, Irish nationalist forces also gained a new leader, the lawyer who had defended Smith O'Brien in 1848 and Fenian prisoners in the latter 1860s, the *DUM* editor who had first seen Le Fanu into print: Isaac Butt. The first Land Bill, forecasting the eventual break-up of the large landed estates in Ireland, was only a year away. But by that time, the *DUM* had given up the fight. Having defended the status of the Church of Ireland ever since its inaugural issue, the magazine, by October 1868, was reduced to this: "No purpose sufficient to justify the effort would be served by entering, in these pages, into the rude conflict of argument going forward in every part of the country, on the question of the Irish Church" (Oct. 1868, 473). In its growing apathy and discouragement over the course of Irish history, the *DUM* devoted less and less space to political commentary in the closing years of the decade, virtually ignoring the crucial general election at the end of 1868. For 1869, the year when the new government pardoned several dozen Fenian prisoners and when the long-dreaded disestablishment severed the relationship between church and state that had existed for three centuries, only one political article can be found, titled "The Railway Problem in Ireland and Belgium" (Feb. 1869).

IV

At one level, the *DUM* had simply chosen for the time being not to bother with futile public expressions of despair or outrage over further Catholic advances. Protestant evangelical energies had generally faded in Ireland over the course of the 1860s, marked by dwindling support for such efforts as the Irish Church Missions. Once Le Fanu had stepped down as editor, the *DUM* would renew its abuse of Irish Catholicism, a "stagnant system of idolatrous worship" (June 1870, 638). Away from the terms and strategies of public policy, however, Le Fanu could entertain less simplistic views. One of his few personal friends from the 1860s, after all, was the Catholic folklorist Patrick Kennedy. It is thus not surprising that Le Fanu, in 1868, could privately support the selection of a "liberal Roman Catholic" as Irish Lord Chancellor under Gladstone's new administration.[12]

A close reading of his novels from the 1860s also reveals attitudes toward religion quite unlike the usual evangelistic fare in the *DUM*. Like every other potential human value in these works, religion fails to offer his characters any kind of certainty or comfort, becomes instead just one more of many novelistic elements for Le Fanu that, in their totality, project a view of society as one that is fundamentally, radically, and irrevocably treacherous, whether this be Chapelizod or Bartram-Haugh, Ireland or England. Attracted for a time to the religious philosophy of Emanuel Swedenborg, Le Fanu attributed the same interest to three of *Uncle Silas*'s main characters; even as the pattern showcases Swedenborgianism, however, other patterns undermine it, such as the inability of any of these three characters to represent any secure value system within the novel. In the case of her uncle, Maud claims not to know if Silas's Swedenborgianism was sincere or not, professing for herself a more conventional Christianity. Yet her final sentiments reveal her essential confusion and ambiguity: her metaphors reflect the tenets of Swedenborgianism, and she continues to feel both drawn to and horrified by the uncle who tried to murder her.

*The House by the Church-yard* is narrated by de Cresseron as outside observer. In Maud Ruthyn, however, who is both main character and intended victim in *Uncle Silas,* Le Fanu found a narrator who more readily reveals the repressed tensions within his vision. At one level, the shift in the sex of the narrators signals a deeper shift in the gender alignment of the novels. Whereas *The House by the Church-yard* is dominated by male characters, *Uncle Silas*, like *Wylder's Hand* and every other Le Fanu novel of this decade, places much more emphasis on women. They have become more active participants now and, as in *Uncle Silas,* frequently control events in ways that the

---

12. Le Fanu to Lord Dufferin, 7 Dec. 1868 (Public Record Office of Northern Ireland, Belfast; the Dufferin and Ava Papers), in Mc Cormack, *Sheridan Le Fanu*, 217.

men cannot. Despite his formidable atmosphere of mystery and evil, Uncle Silas lacks the ongoing vitality of Archer/Dangerfield and often remains secluded offstage, more threatening as passive and potential villainy than as an active force. His son and partner in crime, Dudley Ruthyn, is but a crude and insensitive bungler, albeit a nasty one. In the most horrifying case of mistaken identity from these novels, Dudley finally murders his own accomplice, the wicked but unsuspecting Madame de la Rougierre, as she lies sleeping in Maud's bed. Madame herself has succeeded more consistently at intimidating Maud, largely because of her coarse sexuality. The other women too, like Monika Knollys, Milly Ruthyn, Meg Hawkes, or Mary Quince, join Maud in defining the novel's main center of energy as a female one.

Even more unlike *The House by the Church-yard*, *Uncle Silas* is an interior, "written" novel. De Cresseron ranges widely throughout Chapelizod and its environs and gives his story the feel of a spoken tale. He begins this way: "We are going to talk, if you please, in the ensuing chapters, of what was going on in Chapelizod about a hundred years ago" (Oct. 1861, 387). De Cresseron's magisterial confidence leads him boldly through his sprawling material, and at its end he calmly pulls on his night-cap and wishes "pleasant dreams" to his readers. *Uncle Silas,* just two years later, has murdered sleep, and in more ways than for the hapless Madame de la Rougierre. Lacking de Cresseron's secure position outside of the events that he will describe, Maud never thinks of casually asking for the indulgence of her reader. She seeks instead the kind of cathartic symmetry that will allow her to make sense of her terrifying experiences and thus brings to her tale a highly confined structure, both geographically and formally. Whereas de Cresseron, in his exterior role, eschews symmetry for seeming shapelessness, Maud holds fast to her central point within the events, places, and characters she describes, and the psychological effects of all these on her interior consciousness give *Uncle Silas* its focus and power.

In her 1992 dissertation, Julia Williams discusses Le Fanu's handling of interior space in *Uncle Silas* as one that "reflects his recognition of the dimensions of Anglo-Irish space within the colonial situation." Williams argues that the novel characterizes interior space as feminine and thus—because of Maud's immaturity and sheltered childhood—as threatened by a hostile outside world. In addition to the suspense engendered through the limitations on Maud's point of view as narrator, we also share Maud's "fear that the boundaries may be violated at any time by the forces that inhabit the periphery." As Williams notes, however, the novel's "obsessive preoccupation with doubling," as a further manifestation of "the colonial characterization of space," finally locates the source of the terror within the Anglo-Irish Big House itself.[13]

At its most obvious level of psychological doubling, the novel splits into halves according to the houses, Austin's sheltering but unreliable Knowl and Silas's sinister Bartram-Haugh. Further, the two brothers form a related pattern as Maud's father and guardian, W. J. Mc Cormack arguing persuasively "that Silas in some way is the dead soul of Austin."[14] As Williams notices, however, Madame de la Rougierre, mistaken for Maud and ultimately killed in her stead, lends the novel its most revealing linkage.[15] When Madame first appears, suddenly and mysteriously, she startles both Maud as narrator and us as readers. Even as she jars one part of Maud's moonlight reverie, however, Madame fits seamlessly into a different part, one obscured by a lengthy interruption when Maud provides us with some background information that she would not have dwelt upon

---

13. Julia McElhattan Williams, "'The Nation Articulate': The Discourse of Colonialism and the Anglo-Irish Novel" (Ph.D. diss., Emory University, 1992), 156, 157, and 159.

14. Mc Cormack, *Sheridan Le Fanu*, 168. Mc Cormack's chapter in this study (148–94) provides an extensive discussion of patterns of symmetry within *Uncle Silas*. See also *Field Day*, 2:840–42, for Mc Cormack's analysis of patterns of repression in Le Fanu's *The House by the Church-yard*. In a further treatment of doubling in Le Fanu's work, see Achilles, *Sheridan Le Fanu*, 17, which demonstrates with systematic thoroughness the patterns of doubling and two-part structuring that inform nearly all of his narratives.

15. Williams, "The Nation Articulate," 165–67.

at the actual, experienced time of her reverie. If we bracket this interruption, we may see Madame as a manifestation, completely realistic within the dream logic of the gothic fantasy, of Maud's brooding thoughts upon her own dead mother. In our immediate reading experience, however, just as we accept the reality of Poe's Madeline Usher standing outside her brother's door, we accept Maud's literal account in which her father has hired Madame on as the new governess, ignoring the more potent symbolic connections by which psychological disturbances may call their own monsters forth from the tomb.

While Maud is incapable of recognizing it, then, Madame is thus a presence that Maud herself has invoked, a corporeal manifestation of Maud's own anxieties and dread. A kind of ghastly shadow self to Maud, she frequently acts out the gawky parodies of adolescent sexuality that we would more readily expect from the novel's main character, who is seventeen and—because of the loss of her mother—very inexperienced at the time of her encounter with villainy. Later in the novel, and again near a cemetery, Madame tries to lure the child-woman Maud into a grotesque dance among the tombstones: "Don't you love the dead, chaile? I will teach you to love them. You shall see me die here to-day, for half an hour, and be among them. That is what I love" (July 1864, 20). Maud's father frustrates his daughter with his rigid, aloof, and loveless manner; Maud's cousin Dudley courts her in boorish fashion and even attempts a clumsy abduction; and her Uncle Silas fascinates her, long before she encounters him in the flesh, with his refined, decadent sensuousness. And again, it is Madame who exhibits the sexual awareness that Maud must repress within these various relationships. In the case of Maud's father, Madame can bend him to her will in inexplicable ways; in the cases of Silas and Dudley, the novel hints that she has been a lover to both the father and the son. Even Maud's most trusted ally, her older cousin Monika, refuses ever to share with the girl the knowledge that she possesses of Madame's shameful past.

While *Uncle Silas* more properly observes the conventions of the sensationalist novel than the gothic fantasy, it partakes of both genres and thus thrives on secrecy. We also expect, however, for the secrets ultimately to be revealed, and since *Uncle Silas* passes over many of these in silence, restricted by Maud's ignorance of all the facts, we may feel pressed to look elsewhere for answers. In analyzing the "gothic mode" as a general feature within Irish literature, W. J. Mc Cormack observes that it "endured there in a fugitive and discontinuous manner throughout the nineteenth century." It is, Mc Cormack argues, a "distinctly protestant tradition," one associated with "the Irish middle classes."[16]

Once we begin to search through the (Protestant, middle-class, nineteenth-century) *DUM* for patterns of doubling, we run the risk of finding it everywhere, in the magazine's early penchant for dialogues, for instance, or in its insistence upon pseudonyms or anonymity. More obviously throughout the history of the magazine, stories and novels with a strain of gothic fantasy form one of the most enduring genres, and not just for ongoing contributors like Le Fanu. The attention to translation is yet another manifestation of the same phenomenon, especially in the work of such Poe-like writers as James Clarence Mangan. Even for the respectable Samuel Ferguson, however, within the struggle for control of the linguistic landscape, more is at stake than mere aesthetics, as revealed by Ferguson's interest in another type of translation, that of religious conversion. Through its more obvious political agenda, as well, translation comes to reveal its psychological overtones. If Irish society is to be explored, it requires a translation of the Celtic past, a recovery of a repressed cultural heritage. If the self is to be explored in any depth, then translating it becomes a first step that renders the exploration of the double manageable, the necessary repression and the desired revelation simultaneously intact. On the realistic surface, such tensions indicate their presence through uneasy shifts in the

---

16. *Field Day*, 2:831, 837, and 838.

linguistic landscape, Madame de la Rougierre's fractured English, for instance. In 1871 Le Fanu would publish his best tale ever, "Carmilla," whose complex and alluring vampirism draws its heroine within the spells of another foreign monster. The story inspired the work of a later Dubliner, Bram Stoker, and in *Dracula* (1897), as well, we find main characters such as Van Helsing and the Count struggling for mastery over each other and over their imperfect English.

In its capacity for plumbing complex psychological depths, then, doubling allows the gothic fantasy a range not accessible to the realism of standard nineteenth-century fiction. While we may describe various aspects of the technique, however, such analysis is always elusive. The double is, by definition, a sharer who must remain secret, loyal only to its own shadowy logic. Even more speculative, then, are any explanations for why the gothic fantasy might have held such an enduring place in the *DUM*, especially since the genre is hardly unique to Ireland. In nineteenth-century England, as with the American writer Poe, one could find many sources for the kind of anxieties and frustrations that might seek literary expression in a psychological double.

But again, *Uncle Silas* may be instructive. Near his death, Maud's father charges her with clearing the family name, then shrouded by hints of scandal. Like Poe's narrator in "The Fall of the House of Usher," charged with the task of cheering up his old childhood friend Roderick, Maud fails horribly in her quest. By the end of the novel, with her father and uncle both dead, with Dudley having moved to Australia and changed his name to conceal his own part in the new scandal, with Maud herself now married and known as Lady Ilbury, the once proud Ruthyn name has tumbled into fragments, its legitimacy and authority scattered. For Poe, too, the extinction of the Usher family name adds to the horror of his tale. Yet we may also detect a more specifically Irish element within *Uncle Silas*, with its patterns of doubling, or within the entire run of the *DUM*, with its recurring gothic tales. For the double, in Maud's narrative, is the cruel, brutal, sinister authority, incapable of bearing the children that will carry on its heritage and hence relying on raw force so that it might continue to hold the power that would otherwise be stripped away. Whether as Charles Archer, Silas Ruthyn, Madame de la Rougierre, or Carmilla, the vampire-like shadow-self reappeared often in Le Fanu's work, moving ever closer toward its strongest expression in Stoker's *Dracula*. At one level, the *DUM* sought to provide Protestant ascendancy with the legitimacy and respectability that it needed, sought to cast it in the role of innocent victim and to distinguish it from the uncivilized monsters who maimed cattle, held back tithes, and burned Protestant rectories, who staged periodic rebellions, who marched in mobs at the funerals of their dead chieftains. On another level, through fiction such as Le Fanu's, the *DUM* glanced sidelong and surreptitiously at another aspect of Protestant ascendancy, itself the Irish monster that maintained its power through force alone, that lacked legitimacy, that lived on the shadowy margins, that had no future but death.

v

Le Fanu had sought initially to place *Uncle Silas* in the *Cornhill Magazine,* whose circulation of over 80,000 readers would assure greater sales for the planned three-decker version. He mentioned these hopes to Richard Bentley, adding: "At present the editing of the University Magazine without assistance . . . cuts up my time very much—but a success [with the *Cornhill*] would make it worthwhile to discontinue these taxes on my time."[17] When the *Cornhill* failed to oblige, *Uncle Silas* quickly began its run in the magazine that continued to tax its editor's time for the next five years. Le Fanu

---

17. Le Fanu to Richard Bentley, 17 June 1864 (Univ. of Illinois Library), in Walter Eugene Edens, "Joseph Sheridan LeFanu: A Minor Victorian and His Publisher" (Ph.D. diss., University of Illinois, 1963), 172. Appendix A of Edens's study contains transcripts of 115 letters from the Le Fanu correspondence, most of them in the holdings of the University of Illinois library, with several others held by the British Museum.

finally sold the *DUM* in 1869 to the London printer Charles F. Adams for 1500 pounds, twice what he had paid for the magazine. But despite this sizable return on his investment, his financial affairs during these years were constantly troubled. By 1868, debt forced him to place his Merrion Square house under heavy mortgage. As the financial demands of his journal kept dictating one hasty novel after the next during this decade, Le Fanu's writing became progressively weaker, the plots looser, the characters thinner, even the language finally lapsing into cliche. In the latter half of *The Wyvern Mystery,* for instance, the last of the *DUM* group, the characters repeatedly fall back on one folk saying after another, becoming almost self-conscious parodies of human speakers, actors in a drama too tired to reach its own futile and apathetic conclusion.

At the very end of the 1860s, Le Fanu's work was to take another distinctive turn, toward a much greater emphasis on the short story. Having divested himself of the burdens of editing the *DUM,* he returned, with remarkable energy, to the literary form with which he had first begun his writing career over thirty years earlier. "Green Tea," appearing in 1869, charted significant new ground for the horror story, with "Carmilla" to follow in 1871. In their exploration of psychological horror, these later works established Le Fanu as one of the masters and originators of the modern ghost story. As editor of the *DUM,* he felt himself in the role of spokesman for many of Ireland's Protestants, and during his editorship, he restored much of the Irish character that had faded from the magazine during the 1850s. Yet the responsibilities of that role drained off a good deal of his time and energy while failing to relieve him of the market demands that drained still more and gave little in return.

In 1863 the narrator of *Wylder's Hand* says: ". . . I behold in myself an abyss, I gaze down and listen, and discover neither light nor harmony, but thunderings and lightnings, and voices and laughter, and a medley that dismays me. . . . How helpless and appalled we shut our eyes over that awful chasm" (Oct. 1863, 393). It is tempting to find in such a passage evidence that careful observers in the 1860s could foresee the eventual doom of Protestant ascendancy, its church disestablished and its estates broken up. But if this passage looks toward the future, it also echoes the past, as in this from Le Fanu's *DUM* short story "Spalatro": "My mind is full of doubts and fears. I have no more certainty, no more *knowledge,* mystery and illusion are above, and below, and around me. May God sustain me else my mind will be lost, irrevocably lost in the abyss of horror" (March 1843, 339). We can dismiss this as conventional sensationalist rhetoric, yet the phrases hung in Le Fanu's mind for fully twenty years. In its earlier form, the abyss was framed in devious ways. While an Italian robber awaits execution, he confesses to a priest, who feels unsettled by what he hears and whose troubled thoughts appear above. A "translator" then provides the English version for editor "Harry Lorrequer," who obligingly publishes it in the *DUM*. By 1863, Le Fanu has stripped away some of the narrative veils shrouding the abyss that he beholds "in myself." But the horror has lurked there all along. More than any other writer for the *DUM,* and throughout his extensive role in the history of the magazine, Le Fanu felt repeatedly driven down into the metaphors that reveal a part of his own nature just as they reveal a part of his whole Anglo-Irish class.

8

# THE PATTERNS EXHAUSTED

I

Once Le Fanu gave over the editorship in June 1869 to Charles Frederick Adams, the *DUM* entered into a generally depressing period, closing out its existence with what Michael Sadleir terms "years of melancholy ineffectiveness."[1] A London printer, Adams once again moved the proprietorship of the magazine out of Ireland, and beginning in November 1870, a number of issues opened with a standard directive that "all communications for the Editor . . . be addressed to the London Publishing Office." Adams edited the magazine for four years, then sold it to former editor Durham Dunlop in June 1873.[2] While Dunlop restored some of the *DUM*'s old political energy and Irish flavor, its literary offerings remained unremarkable. When Keningale Cook became proprietor in early 1877, then, assuming editorial control as of the July issue, the magazine lasted only six more months. Following the issue for December 1877, Cook changed its name and nature, and the forty-five-year run of the *DUM* had ended.

1. Sadleir, *"Dublin University Magazine,"* 79.
2. For a discussion of these editorial transactions, see the *Wellesley Index*, 4:205 and 208.

As had been the case in 1856, the London headquarters and the relatively rapid succession of editors during these final years indicate deeper problems with the magazine, besides contributing to them through an absence of editorial vision, conviction, and continuity. Nowhere in the entire history of the magazine is this absence more apparent than in the dismal period of Adams's editorship. Without acknowledgment, for instance, Adams's *DUM* ran fourteen chapters from the 1804 edition of Edward Ledwich's *Antiquities of Ireland*. While this had been an important archeological and antiquarian study in its time, it had long since been shown, by scholars such as George Petrie, to be riddled with factual errors and theoretical misconceptions. In addition, for much of the rest of his material, Adams simply plundered the last ten years of American and British magazines such as *St. James's, Putnam's,* and the *Atlantic Monthly,* reprinting numerous articles without acknowledgment. For the period April 1870 to April 1873, nearly fifty such pieces appear.

One of the reprints, "An American Opinion of Fenianism" (Nov. 1871), restated the politically conservative and Unionist sympathies of the *DUM*. In nearly every other case, however, the reprints reflect the magazine's whole tendency under Adams to avoid commenting on anything political and instead to build its issues around the cliched, the safe, the innocuous. The titles of the reprinted articles for December 1871 serve as examples: "Fables of Bidpai," "Heraldic Reform," "Heroes of Central Africa," and "The Custom of Burial with the Head Towards the East." To the extent that a political agenda underlies the choice of reprints, it can perhaps be found as a strategy of indirection, Ledwich's work, for instance, supporting the legitimacy of the Church of Ireland through historical analyses such as "St. Paul: First Attack on Paganism" (Dec. 1870).

Adams's own writing, somewhat over a dozen articles during his editorship, also preferred to circle around miscellaneous subjects at the level of cliche and vague generality. In a piece entitled "Pleasure and Pleasure-Taking," he lamented the "devouring mammon worship amongst the higher and middle classes" (July 1870, 14). In the same vein, but somewhat more ambitious and specific, are the contributions of Horace Pearce, about two dozen under Adams's editorship. Pearce's meditative essays, filled with details from his personal life, are usually inspired by a particular scene or object and reflect his interests in geology, the human condition, or nature in general. James Picciotto frequently surveyed current political and social conditions in Europe, occasionally swerving into history or drama although never into controversy. More specifically Irish was a series by Oliver J. Burke, "Lives of the Lord Chancellors of Ireland" (June 1870–Jan. 1873, thirty-two installments). And Patrick Kennedy, as he had under Le Fanu's editorship, continued his prolific output. For the period December 1865 to May 1873, well over half of the *DUM*'s monthly issues contained pieces by Kennedy as their lead articles. In one review, Kennedy was able proudly to announce Samuel Ferguson's newest and perhaps most significant poem, *Congal*: ". . . Ireland has at last been presented with a noble national epic by one of her sons" (Oct. 1872, 400).

The *DUM*'s own literary publications during the Adams years, although undistinguished, still retained a tinge of national flavor, with a number of short stories set in Ireland. Thomas Gaspey, a novelist who had not published a major work in decades, contributed "Shelah, the Fenian's Daughter" (Jan. 1871), a predictable conflict between an idealized woman and the usual gang of shameless, priest-led, agrarian terrorists. Gaspey's story builds its happy ending on a marriage and a promise of better relations between England and Ireland, as does another short work, "Myles O'Loughlin" (May–Aug. 1872, four installments). This latter story, by an unidentified writer, complicates the union, however. The series begins with the position that Irish Catholics themselves must decide to cast off the ultra-ecclesiasticalism and Ultramontanism that had lately come to characterize their religion. Until that time, "we shall continue to see them as backward and as far from civilisation" as in other "priest-ridden" countries (May 1872, 526). The story stops short of calling for conversions, however, ending with a marriage between the

Catholic title character and a Protestant woman who will now attempt to establish some religious middle ground as a basis for harmony. Further contrasting with Gaspey, another story, "Christmas Eve; or, The Sale of Cloonmore" (Dec. 1870), offers a sympathetic portrayal of a Catholic priest.

The old-line political stereotypes of Gaspey's story thus stand as the exception within the generally uncommitted positions, whether in the political or literary offerings, that characterize Adams's editorship. In one of the few political pieces from this period, "Past and Present Irish Discontent" (March 1872), the *DUM* found that legislative reforms such as Disestablishment and the 1870 Land Act were having a salutary effect in further improving conditions and reducing violence in Ireland. In the same issue, and also without bitterness, another article solicited individual subscriptions for the support of the "Disendowed Church." Even in his last issue as editor, that of May 1873, Adams's *DUM* continued to prefer the vague and noncontroversial middle ground. "The History of the Past and the Ireland of the Future" considers the possibility of repeal but finally and simply urges that Ireland stay in the Union until it has become ready for independence.

Adams's editorship began in the year of William Carleton's death, and in the final issue of Adams's tenure, the *DUM* took note of the death of Patrick Kennedy as well, grim reminders of the magazine's age. In addition, Charles Lever had died in 1872, Le Fanu in 1873, finally Charles Stuart Stanford later that same year. The growing number of obituaries included some of the most significant figures in the *DUM*'s history. As the century wore on, simple finances provide another measure of the *DUM*'s decline. Several months after relinquishing the editorship, Le Fanu sold the magazine to Adams in March 1870 for 1500 pounds. In June 1873, just three years later, when Adams sold the magazine in turn to former editor Durham Dunlop, he received only 490 pounds. The *DUM* was but a few years from the point when contributors would begin to wonder when they might get paid for their work.

11

Dunlop had spent the 1860s developing his career as a Belfast journalist, during which time he had edited the liberal *Daily Mercury*. He now lost no time in changing the face of his new enterprise, and political issues once more became a central feature of the *DUM* for the next several years, many of these articles attributed by the *Wellesley Index* to Dunlop himself. The issue for July 1873 opened with "The Irish Education Question," the first lead article on Irish politics in over eight years. While it continued to stress the *DUM*'s longstanding interests in education, this article, like many others during Dunlop's editorship, put particular emphasis on Ultramontanism, which now characterized Irish Catholicism through a heightened reverence for church forms and doctrines, hierarchical discipline, and the papacy in Rome. Especially associated with Paul Cullen, Archbishop of Dublin since 1852, Ultramontanism seemed to the *DUM* to be further synonymous with intellectual narrowness, intolerance, a lack of progress, and an absence of civilization.

The *DUM* continued to expand its attack on Cullen as the representative of a "narrow, illiberal, and superstitious" dogma (July 1874, 117). In "Papal Pretensions and Civil Allegiance" (Jan. 1875), the magazine reviewed those recent events that seemed to demonstrate Ultramontane influences. In 1873, Gladstone had proposed a University Bill, eagerly anticipated by the Catholic hierarchy as a way to create a denominational university. The following year, a Church directive declared that Irish Catholics had to accept such doctrines as the immaculate conception and papal infallibility. Fortunately—at least in the *DUM*'s view—Gladstone's bill had failed and Irish Catholics were themselves becoming increasingly distanced from Ultramontane positions. Still, the papacy was clearly impeding educational efforts and "the civilizing developments of modern progress" in Ireland (Jan. 1875, 4). In February 1875, the *DUM* began a nine-part series, "A Papal Retrospect," that surveyed the papacy historically. The implicit assumption here was one that informed many a retrospective series in the magazine: if the historical truth or origin of a subject could be established and examined, such facts could guide policy and belief in the present day. As it always had, the *DUM* continued to assert an underlying faith in education and in human progress. Ultramontanism might drive a temporary wedge between Protestant and Catholic, but, as the *DUM* asserted hopefully in April 1874, "the Protestants and Roman Catholics of Ireland, in their industry and property, intelligence and independence, are essentially loyal, and desirous of complete Union with Great Britain" (501).

In the wake of disestablishment, a measure to which Dunlop "had always given unwavering support,"[3] the position of the Anglican Church had become particularly complicated within the *DUM*'s vision of Ireland's future. The Church still needed to continue defining the cultural identity of the Protestant minority, a particularly important function in the face of growing attempts by Catholic nationalist forces to erase Protestant contributions to Ireland from its history. Having lost its status as a national religious establishment, however, the Church had first to define its own identity. In "The Church of Ireland" (Oct. 1873), the *DUM* reviewed those factors that had led to disestablishment, many of them longstanding abuses within the Church itself. Despite the past problems and present setbacks, the magazine foresaw a crucial role for the Church in shaping Ireland's future, especially "for the promotion of intellectual and moral culture" (506). The Church must remain "devoted to educational and moral progress," and especially now that it had been freed from "State servitude," it might be able to exercise these virtues in even greater measure (506).

On the secular front, and as firmly as ever in the magazine, Dunlop's *DUM* supported the Union. In 1870, however, a new political concept stepped forth to challenge the magazine's interests: Home

---

3. For Francis Joseph Bigger's account of Dunlop, see the *Irish Book Lover* 10 (1919): 102–4.

Rule, a phrase quickly linked to Rome Rule. The lead article for September 1873 denounced it as "an exploded delusion—an old sham ostentatiously paraded under the disguise of a new name—a stale artifice of political jugglery—in simple fact, nothing more or less than the unblushing revival of the Repeal-of-the-Union knavery" (258). Since Irish prosperity was on the rise, the *DUM*'s remedy for any remaining problems was "not to repeal the Union, but simply *to perfect it*" (272) into an even closer connection with England. Some reforms were clearly needed, to the administrative offices in Dublin, for instance. A later article suggested that problems had arisen because only a "partial union" had ever taken place: "The mockery of royalty was retained. Dublin Castle, with its corrupting influences, its partial administration of justice, its demoralizing associations, and notorious jobbery was, unfortunately, preserved, and the whole policy of successive British Cabinets from that time to the present has been *to conduct the Government of Ireland on the basis of an incomplete Union . . .*" (April 1874, 478). If the *DUM* chafed against England continuing to treat Ireland like "a mere colonial dependency," it foresaw similar problems in the political advance of Home Rule, which would "degrade Ireland to the pitiful condition of a province" (April 1874, 470). The general election for 1874 had returned sixty Irish members committed to Home Rule. Nonetheless, the *DUM* detected new opportunities to shape the future, in this case to "thoroughly incorporate Ireland with Great Britain, and establish a great constitutional party on the broad national basis of enlightened Progress" (March 1874, 360).

Other pieces from this period sounded the same ongoing note from the *DUM*'s past: "We want to emerge from a petty, miserable provincialism, and share in the elevating consciousness of an enlightened Imperialism" (Sept. 1873, 274). Within the framework of Protestant ascendancy, Ireland had come frustratingly close to full participation in the Empire and to full awareness of itself as a unified, noble, and productive culture. Now Protestantism might lose all of the gains for which it had so tenaciously struggled and sacrificed over the past several centuries, all of the cultural benefits that it had so painstakingly assembled. In the early months of his new editorship, Dunlop's *DUM* could still put an optimistic face on events, finding that the "industrious classes" in Ireland were "daily becoming more intelligent and self-reliant, and consequently less disposed to be the dupes and victims of political hucksters" (Sept. 1873, 269). By the end of his tenure just four years later, and more keenly aware of the growing strength of "Agrarianism, Nationalism, Ultramontanism," the *DUM* no longer bothered to argue for maintaining Protestantism as an ascendancy; it was "bad," the magazine announced, and besides, "it no longer exists." But since the "yoke" of a Catholic ascendancy would prove just as oppressive, the time had come to settle for basic human rights, to negotiate compensation for inevitable future losses, to ensure simple survival: "The Union must be maintained as the only possible means of getting fair play for all" (July 1877, 106).

Surprisingly few notes of desperation creep into such commentary, the main exception that recalls earlier passages from the *DUM*'s collection of political hysteria being reserved for Isaac Butt. The magazine termed his position "rash, untruthful," and Butt himself "reckless," an "agitator" (Sept. 1873, 269 and 272). A later article remembered the highlights of his career, especially the 1843 debate in which Butt had opposed Daniel O'Connell on the issue of repeal. Now, however, he was "the head and front of an agitation as wicked and demoralizing as O'Connell's was . . ." (April 1874, 470). In July 1874, Butt's Home Rule proposal was soundly defeated in the Commons. Still, the *DUM* complained, the conduct of Irish M.P.s in this debate had embarrassed the whole country. In the case of Butt, in particular, his current positions revealed "the barrenness and baseness of his whole political career" (Aug. 1874, 245). The virulence here, the rhetorical echoes of *DUM* attacks on previous bogeymen such as Daniel O'Connell, derived from Butt's dual position as a powerful leader in the assault upon the Union and as a perceived defector from the ranks of conservative Protestantism. By the latter half of 1877, however, the forces of Irish nationalism had acquired a new player, Charles Stewart Parnell, and already at this early stage in his career, he seemed to the *DUM* to make even Isaac Butt look moderate by comparison.

### III

Even while greatly expanding the *DUM*'s political commentary, however, Dunlop was unable to effect major changes in its cultural material. The Irish barrister Oliver J. Burke continued his series on the history of Dublin University, begun in May 1873, and added two additional series on Irish historical topics. After a lengthy hiatus, the second series of "Our Portrait Gallery" began in February 1874, with excellent photographic portraits now, although not always on Irish celebrities. The Dublin journalist John Sproule covered Irish subjects, and Richard Robert Madden, author of a lengthy history of the United Irishmen in the 1840s, wrote on "A Forgotten Irish Poet," Bernard Simmons (Feb. 1874). In November 1874, Standish James O'Grady (as "Arthur Clive"), then on the verge of a career that would gain him recognition as the "father of the Irish Renaissance," published the first of seven pieces for Dunlop's magazine, largely on Irish archeological topics. Of the short stories from this period, many of them containing Irish settings, those of Ella Jane Curtis are of some interest, although her titles indicate their stereotyped, tragic-Irish nature, as in "Kathleen's Revenge" (April 1875) or "The Banshee of the MacShanes" (July 1875).

Education remained a persistent concern for the magazine; one article deplored the increasing emphasis in schools on that which is practical and marketable and the corresponding decrease in "higher culture" (Dec. 1876). Several articles (see especially May 1874) urged reforms in the educational opportunities for women. Walter Parke, as the "London Hermit," published a lengthy series entitled "Essays and Sketches" (July 1873–Dec. 1875, twenty installments) plus a number of poems. One of these, "The Civilization of Tongataboo: A Lay of Progress" (Oct. 1873), uses a doggerel style only partially to soften a powerful critique of "civilization" and of zealous missionaries, and its contrast with earlier *DUM* positions on proselytizing indicates Dunlop's more liberal views on religion. Robert Hannay, a frequent contributor of poetry during Adams's editorship, continued publishing under Dunlop, now joined by Robert Batson and Rebecca Scott, with T. C. Irwin also adding a lengthy poem (Jan. 1876) and J. F. Waller chiming in with another short story by "Slingsby" (June 1876). In July 1873 Dunlop began closing nearly every issue with a section entitled "Literary Notices," a collection of short reviews.

It was just not a significant period for Irish literary contributions. One measure of how low the *DUM*'s creative energy had sunk can be gained from its novels throughout the 1870s. Of the thirteen novels serialized then, only two—*Annie with the Madonna Face* by Sarah Jane Mayne (Nov. 1869–March 1870, five installments) and *The Belle of Belgravia* by George W. Garrett (Oct. 1872–May 1873, eight installments)—were ever republished in book form. In addition, for only five of the remaining eleven has the *Wellesley Index* even been able to establish an attribution, particularly remarkable because more and more items throughout the 1870s were signed by their authors, a tendency that increased as the decade wore on.

The one major exception to this dearth of creative talent is the work of "Oscar O'F. Wills Wilde," as the *DUM* identified him for his first published appearance ever, a translation of a chorus from Aristophanes' *The Clouds*. Several other poems followed over the next several years, in styles that evoke Swinburne and the Pre-Raphaelites, and Wilde's contributions ended in July 1877 with "The Grosvenor Gallery," a review of an art exhibit in which Wilde also celebrated the British aesthetic revival built around the work of Ruskin, Swinburne, Pater, Symons, and Morris.[4] Wilde's mother, Jane Francesca Wilde, also contributed poetry to the *DUM* in these

4. As the *Wellesley Index* does not include poems in its list of entries, I provide those for Wilde here: Translation of "Chorus of Cloud Maidens" (Nov. 1875, 622);

years, as well as "The Destiny of Humanity," a philosophical essay speculating on the possibility of life elsewhere in the universe (May 1877), and a two-part piece on "The Fairy Mythology of Ireland" (July–Aug. 1877).

IV

By this time, however, the *DUM* had been passed on to yet another editor, who would close it out in inglorious fashion. Keningale Cook, an 1866 graduate of Trinity College, had gone on to clerk for several years in a London post office. In 1871, he married Minna Mabel Collins, the only child to Mortimer Collins and an up-and-coming author in her own right, for she would publish some two dozen novels in her lifetime and, along with Madame Blavatsky, would also coedit the theosophical monthly *Lucifer*. When Cook took over the editorial duties for the July issue of the *DUM*, then, the magazine very quickly shifted its emphases, in the direction of the occult and the esoteric. A review entitled "The Supernatural; and 'Supernatural Religion'" opened Cook's inaugural issue and was followed by a poem by Mortimer Collins, a sketch by Mabel Collins Cook in which various spiritual characters interact in a drawing room, and Keningale Cook's own article on "The Ancient Faith of Egypt." Amid such family-generated mysticism, Irish issues seemed hopelessly prosaic. But the magazine no longer attempted even a pretense at Irishness, its lead article for September 1877, for instance, beginning with the statement: "We English are essentially an unsympathetic people" (257).

The new directions charted for the *DUM* might well reflect Cook's belief that the magazine's old patterns had finally exhausted their journalistic resources. In May 1877, shortly before assuming editorial control, he sent assurances to Oscar Wilde that financial

---

"From Spring Days to Winter" (Jan. 1876, 47); "Graffiti D'Italia" (March 1876, 297–298); "The Dole of the King's Daughter" (June 1876, 682–683); and "O well for him who lives at ease" (Sept. 1876, 291).

prospects were finally looking up: "I hope in twelve months' time the D.U.M. may be restored to its true position again, and able to pay its contributors. The reception the July number met with at the hands of the Press was unexpectedly favourable."[5] Within this economic assessment, however, the "true position" of the magazine bore no relationship to the type of subject matter or ideological stance that long-time readers might have associated with the *DUM*, for the next few months followed the lead of Cook's first issue. Mabel Collins Cook published short stories containing elements of spiritualism and high passion, a lengthy biographical review of her father, and essays on writers such as Henry David Thoreau and Elizabeth Carter. This last piece, subtitled "Poet, Philosopher, and Old Maid" (Sept. 1877), praised the intellectual independence and learned scholarship of an eighteenth-century British writer. Keningale Cook wrote a number of poems plus some essays that speculated on religious and philosophical issues, "Does God Grow?" (Sept. 1877), for instance, or "Did Jesus Know Greek?" (Oct. 1877). Oddly placed within this collection was Thomas Henry Huxley's article "On Elementary Instruction in Physiology" (Aug. 1877), which stressed mechanical processes rather than supernatural ones and which puzzled Cook, in the middle of his press run, when he found the piece already published in another magazine. With no time to contact either Huxley or the other editor, Cook could do little but add a plaintive note to claim that Huxley had promised him the article some two months ago (256), at a time before Cook had started taking the *DUM* in distinctly unphysiological directions.

The *DUM* kept slipping ever deeper into journalistic phantasmagoria. After December 1877, Cook changed its name to the *University Magazine: A Literary and Philosophic Review.* Its political nature now excised in name as well as in editorial practice, the magazine

5. Keningale Cook to Oscar Wilde, 21 May 1877, in *Irish Book Lover* 10 (1919): 78. The *Wellesley Index*, 4:208, cites Horace Wyndham, *Speranza: A Biography of Lady Wilde* (1951), 109, regarding this letter as having been written by Wilde to Dunlop.

continued on as a monthly through June 1880, turned into a quarterly for two more issues, and then expired for good following the issue for Christmas 1880. But what's in a name? To settle on 1877 as the year in which the magazine "ends" is somewhat arbitrary, since one could also designate 1880; or 1869, with disestablishment and the transfer of editorships from Le Fanu to Adams; or perhaps 1865, with the death of Lord Palmerston and—looking towards the next stage in Irish literature—the birth of W. B. Yeats; or perhaps even 1851, the year of Samuel O'Sullivan's death.

The various dates here provide many of the explanations that one could give for why a magazine such as the *DUM* finally ended. Individual editors come and go for individual reasons, or death claims a major contributor or a key political figure, thus changing the identities of essential human actors. New political currents sweep across the stage, forcing those actors to maneuver now—or be unable to maneuver—within a completely different setting. In September 1877, one of the articles in Cook's *DUM* complained that "Men can only become great upon a wide stage, and Ireland is narrow . . ." (373). Here was the same old fear that had long concerned the *DUM*'s Protestant intelligentsia: that Ireland might remain provincial, a colonial dependency, mere summer-stock theatre where more and more of the best parts kept going to the Catholics.

The metaphor reminds us, though, that Ireland would have its own national theater before the end of the century. In 1885, literature and politics would again join forces via Yeats's meeting with John O'Leary, one that helped advance the movement towards a twentieth-century explosion of literary talent. In the 1870s, of course, the *DUM*'s disheartened contributors could not have foreseen such coming greatness. Yet the times themselves, in the decades following the Great Famine, were not as barren as the decline of the *DUM* might indicate. As R. V. Comerford notes, the number of newspapers, and their total sales, increased dramatically in Ireland during the 1850s and 1860s, keeping pace with such related phenomena as increases in education and public literacy and in the expansion of the railway system.[6] Longstanding contributors to the magazine such as Samuel Ferguson, Sheridan Le Fanu, and Charles Lever continued to produce powerful work, and Patrick Kennedy greatly enriched the *DUM* from 1850 to 1873. William Carleton lived until 1869, and Charles Kickham appeared in print that same year, joining the ranks of such recently published writers as William Allingham, Frances Browne, Dion Boucicault, Aubrey de Vere, John Mitchel, and Eugene O'Curry. Oscar Wilde had begun his published work with the *DUM*. There was more than enough richness here, in both journalistic opportunities and literary talent, to keep an Irish monthly flourishing.

Yet Wilde's contributions were originating out of Magdalen College, Oxford; his career already pointing toward London and not Dublin. Of the other figures listed here, only Kennedy and Le Fanu helped to sustain the *DUM*. More and more in the wake of the Famine, Irish politics became identified with Irish Catholicism and democratic processes, and more and more, the Protestant minority chose to look toward London rather than to reconstruct their disestablished Church. In "A Dialogue Between the Head and Heart of an Irish Protestant," Samuel Ferguson had rehearsed many of the same humiliations that were still being visited upon Ireland's religious minority. In 1833, however, against the charge that they were "but a peddling colony" (Nov. 1833, 591), the intellectuals of the *DUM* could still muster a formidable combination of evangelistic zeal, political vision, and literary talent. Forty-five years later, with the zeal and vision gone, the talent looked elsewhere for its expression.

The *DUM*'s founders occasionally complained about their magazine's name, whether because it associated them too closely with Dublin University or because "[t]he name of Dublin on a title-page

---

6. For a wide-ranging review of Ireland's social progress and advances during the whole period 1850 to 1870, see R. V. Comerford, "Ireland 1850–70: Post-Famine and Mid-Victorian," *A New History of Ireland, V: Ireland Under the Union, I (1801–70)*, ed. W. E. Vaughan (Oxford: Clarendon, 1989), 372–95.

was a sufficient reason for neglect, and, in the case of periodical literature, it was too truly the indication of youthful incompetence . . ." (March 1837, 374). But they never discarded that name, which did after all link their magazine to Ireland; nor did ever they complain about their subtitle: "A Literary and Political Journal." After December 1877, Keningale Cook stripped away both the "Dublin" and the "political," and the *Dublin University Magazine* had truly ended.

# CONCLUSION

I

In a poem from his collection *North* (1975), Seamus Heaney writes:

> On all sides "little platoons" are mustering—
> The phrase is Cruise O'Brien's via that great
> Backlash, Burke—[1]

We will find this phrase in Edmund Burke's *Reflections on the Revolution in France* (1790) and, with many editions to choose from, might select the one edited, with an introduction, by Conor Cruise O'Brien himself. Burke had written: "To be attached to the subdivision, to love the little platoon we belong to in society, is the first principle (the germ as it were) of public affections. It is the first link in the series by which we proceed towards a love to our country and to mankind."[2] O'Brien's *States of Ireland*, barely three years after this introduction, would recall Burke again for us: "It is to the Irish Catholic community that I belong. That is my 'little platoon'.... I

---

1. Seamus Heaney, "Whatever You Say, Say Nothing," *North* (London: Faber and Faber, 1975): 58–59. In this edition, Heaney actually uses the term "Blacklash," changed (and presumably corrected) to "Backlash" in *Poems 1965–1975* (New York: Farrar, Straus, and Giroux, 1980): 213–14.

2. Edmund Burke, *Reflections on the Revolution in France, and On the Proceedings in Certain Societies in London Relative to That Event*, ed. Conor Cruise O'Brien (Harmondsworth: Penguin, 1969), 135.

am motivated by affection for that platoon, identification with it, and fear that it may destroy itself, including me, through infatuation with its own mythology."[3]

By this point, the associations that O'Brien attaches to the phrase have departed somewhat from Burke's. One measure of these differences is Heaney's verb "mustering," in which a platoon might prepare to destroy rather than to proceed toward love of mankind. Heaney's usage relies much more on the violent, military associations that O'Brien found in the phrase than on the comforting, domestic ones placed there by Burke. To grasp the phrase as Heaney intends, then, we must travel through Burke to O'Brien and, in that journey, survey two centuries of bitter struggle and dashed ideals, the platoons still not quite finished with their infatuated musterings.

Along the way, as well, we would find the little platoon that gathered around the *DUM*, and Burke is again a useful guide. The *Reflections*, O'Brien tells us, "aroused and rallied the first modern counter-revolutionary movement,"[4] a process especially relevant to the *DUM* insofar as Burke's insights took into account political events in Ireland as well as in France and England. For a magazine that needed definition, then, that sought to identify its own little platoon with past authorities, Burke helped give the *DUM* a rich intellectual heritage, and the magazine would, in its turn, help to sustain and advance the conservative, counter-revolutionary ideology of a kindred spirit like Burke for the next forty-five years.

II

If there is much to admire in this ideology, however, as it manifested itself within a nineteenth-century, conservative-Protestant-Tory magazine, there is also much to deplore: its authoritarianism, its hostility to democracy, its resistance to change, its toleration of poverty, its contempt for opposing ideologies, its deliberate myth-

---

3. O'Brien, *States of Ireland*, 315–16.
4. Conor Cruise O'Brien, introduction to Edmund Burke, *Reflections*, 70.

making as a strategy for perpetuating imperialism, its willingness to use raw power when necessary, its occasional lapses into pettiness and meanness. Oliver MacDonagh argues that much of the contemporary criticism against Daniel O'Connell arose from the perception that he was vulgar, that he lacked gentility, that he simply refused to behave—or was incapable of behaving—like a gentleman. The "spearhead of the attack was social," MacDonagh concludes,[5] and a reading of the DUM does not vindicate the magazine from this general assessment, its attacks on O'Connell frequently smacking of a country-club snobbishness.

In a similar fashion, the DUM's language often betrays a more general materialist impulse to expand Protestant ascendancy in Ireland. Assessing the cultural resources inventoried for the nation by the Ordnance Survey, for instance, the DUM noted: "The rich mine of Irish antiquities has been made to yield up its hidden treasures to an extent hitherto unequalled, and which cannot fail of being duly appreciated by all who derive the slightest pleasure from such pursuits" (March 1838, 353). The DUM sought to employ ideal, spiritual weapons as one means of legitimizing the real, material position of Protestant ascendancy, threatened with exclusion from Ireland's future as that position came to seem. In developing its own brand of cultural nationalism, the magazine in many respects was out of touch with more popular expressions of nationalism, whose political goals and emerging political consciousness the DUM found inadequate and alien. Within the more broadly based human realities of nineteenth-century Ireland, then, we cannot disregard the magazine's narrow elitism, its class-conscious desire to sustain and enrich its own social privileges.

In one sense, these strategies ultimately failed. The DUM sought to solidify the status of Irish Protestantism by proposing a kind of cultural unity that was finally too elusive in Ireland, a nation frag-

---

5. Oliver MacDonagh, *The Emancipist: Daniel O'Connell, 1830–47* (New York: St. Martin's, 1989), 125.

mented by too many factions separated by too wide a set of differences. Even within the much narrower circle of Irish Protestantism itself, the internal contradictions and ambivalences resisted such attempts at unity. One of Samuel Ferguson's complaints, in his 1833 "Dialogue between the Head and Heart," was that his Irish Protestants kept being told they were neither "fish nor flesh." The metaphor implies, however, that they might well be something else, if only that creature could be identified and described. In a more revealing application of Ferguson's metaphor, we might consider Irish Protestantism as both fish and flesh simultaneously, an impossible contradiction bound to cause identity problems somewhere.

Increasingly marginalized within Ireland, Protestant ascendancy could have begun counting its days from the very outset of the nineteenth century. And still it hung on, at least as late as the Wyndham Land Act of 1903. Strategies such as those employed by the *DUM* thus enjoyed a surprising measure of success. Throughout the lifetime of the magazine, conservative forces retained a strong representation among Irish members of Parliament. The terms upon which Disestablishment was settled, like those of the various land acts from 1870 to 1903, were quite favorable for Ireland's Protestants. For this durability and these considerable political achievements, the *DUM* must be granted some of the credit.

One key element in this political process was literature as a guarantor of respectability, at least if that literature appeared in a handsome monthly format virtually identical in appearance to an established magazine such as *Blackwood's*. Within the expanding power of the periodical press, literature could now exploit the contractual and manageable quality of print rather than the fragmentary and unpredictable quality of broadside ballads or tales told in rural cabins. Moreover, the absence in 1833 of anything that England would recognize as a national literature could be used by the *DUM* as linguistic evidence to show just how badly nineteenth-century Ireland needed development and unity—needed, in other words, a respectable level of civilization.

We aspire to be "the monthly advocate and representative of the Protestantism, the intelligence, and the respectability of Ireland," the magazine claimed (Dec. 1835, 710). The journal would build its authority on a combination "at once elegant and solid, ornamental and yet chaste" (Jan. 1833, 89). Literature improves a society, argued the magazine, by offering "the blessing of civilization" (March 1837, 365). To a great extent, and partly by fostering standards of literary respectability, the *DUM* succeeded in its attempt to equate "Protestantism" with "civilization." In one measure of this success, we can turn to an 1852 essay by William Carleton:

> [The *DUM*] has been, and is, a neutral spot in a country where party feeling runs so high, on which the Roman Catholic Priest and the Protestant parson, the Whig, the Tory, and the Radical, divested of their respective prejudices, can meet in an amicable spirit. . . . It is surely a gratification to know that literature, in a country which has been so much distracted as Ireland, is progressing in a spirit of noble candour and generosity, which is ere long likely to produce a most salutary effect among the educated classes of all parties, and consequently among those whom they influence. . . . Ireland in a few years will be able to sustain a native literature as lofty and generous, and beneficial to herself, as any other country in the world can boast of.[6]

We may admire the noble sweep and optimism of Carleton's vision here, even as we observe that he left many blank spaces in his portrayal of the *DUM*: that its literary energies were badly dissipated by the end of the Great Famine, that the second half of its existence would fail to sustain the level of excellence from its first half, that it would continue to emphasize proselytizing and to foster religious differences.

By 1852, though, Carleton's own career was practically over, his vision of Irish experience flawed and wavering. He demonstrates to us the *DUM*'s success, not for his words themselves, but for the truth value subsequently attached to them, for they have been chosen by the *Wellesley Index*, in its introductory overview of the *DUM*, to pro-

---

6. This selection from William Carleton's "General Introduction" to his *Traits and Stories of the Irish Peasantry* (1:vi–vii) is cited in the *Wellesley Index*, 4:210.

vide the "last word of evaluation" for the magazine. Such choices reflect our own nostalgic longings for an Ireland in which religious differences do not matter, for a world in which prejudices give way to an amicable spirit and in which literature indeed produces candor and generosity. Wishing for life to be lofty and generous, we discover in Carleton that it can be so, that a single journalistic voice can sustain such high ideals for nearly half a century. Yet we do the *DUM* a disservice in casting such an overly idealized mantle over its achievements. If Carleton's words apply to the literary goals of the magazine, they still, in dismissing its political goals, tell barely half the story.

### III

In serving as a rallying point and collective voice for its Protestant readership, and as a forum capable of influencing wider public opinion in Ireland and England, the *DUM* pursued a two-pronged strategy, in the areas of both literature and politics. We find the most comprehensive analysis of this strategy, and a better means of evaluating the magazine's achievements, in the *DUM* essay "Past and Present State of Literature in Ireland," a work that Mc Cormack has termed "the first attempt to examine the theoretical base for a distinctive Anglo-Irish literature . . ."[7] The essay opens with the recognition that "the literature of a nation, and of this nation in particular, is affected by its political state and influential upon it"

---

7. W. J. Mc Cormack, "Isaac Butt (1813–79) and the Inner Failure of Protestant Home Rule," in *Worsted in the Game: Losers in Irish History*, ed. Ciaran Brady (Dublin: Lilliput, 1989), 126. The essay "Past and Present State of Literature in Ireland" is reprinted in *Field Day*, ed. Deane, 1:1200–1212, where Mc Cormack describes it as "the first attempt at a theory of Anglo-Irish literature" (1200). See also Mc Cormack's summary of the essay in his "J. Sheridan Le Fanu's 'Richard Marston' (1848): The History of an Anglo-Irish Text," *1848: The Sociology of Literature. Proceedings of the Essex Conference on the Sociology of Literature, July 1977*, ed. Francis Barker, et al. (Essex: University of Essex Press, 1978), 109–10. In all three of these sources, Mc Cormack attributes the essay, on the basis of internal evidence, to Isaac Butt; the *Wellesley Index*, less persuasively, attributes it to Samuel O'Sullivan, finding that the style "rules out Butt" (4:231).

(March 1837, 365). Such a relationship has become particularly complicated in Ireland because so much of its literature "has been recently engrafted" (366), with largely unfavorable results, from England, or because its literary capabilities are "concealed by the overpowering demand of the English marts" (371). Moreover, the English literary atmosphere itself now stagnates under a "spirit of utilities" (369), interested only in the public writing of political pamphlets or the trivial writing of ornamental books.

Conditioned by the better-known positions of Young Ireland and the Gaelic Revival, we may anticipate the next stage in the argument: to foster the development of a literature native to Ireland, Irish writers should de-Anglicize Irish culture, cast off British manners, shun British influences, boycott the British marts. Yet the *DUM*, rejecting separatism as a stultifying provincialism, instead proposes a cosmopolitan strategy based upon "the settled principles of commerce" (375): compete on the world market with a specifically Irish product that will succeed through its intellectual excellence. Its list of "public advantages" for such a strategy looks both inward and outward:

To retain at home, a large portion of our native genius and learning . . . to give encouragement and hope to more; to awaken that literary tone which humanizes, polishes and adorns private life; to shed a civilized grace over the name of Ireland in foreign countries; to give a home direction to the sympathies of the better mind of our countrymen who spend fortune and talent abroad; to attract capital and enterprize to our shore; and, by shewing the way, awaken that life in the Irish publishing trade, which alone is wanting to raise us to the level of our neighbours. (374–75)

This last point, in particular, would "well supply the place which a native legislature once held—a focus of talent, and a nursery for the production of eminent men" (375). It is a program of great literary ambitions balanced delicately across Ireland's many political constituencies and interests.

In developing these ambitions, the *DUM* set itself openly to strike "a decided and uncompromising political tone" (374). It would oppose the "dominant superstition" of Catholicism, a dogma "conspired to foster ignorance and retard civilization" (370). It would declare to all comers: "We are conservative" (376). And it would claim that "we humanize the land" (376). Seeking "the more profound and elevated realms of truth, excellence and beauty" (371), the magazine would not hesitate to pass through the rag-and-bone shop of politics as a necessary stage in its search.

In religious terms, the *DUM*'s brand of Irish Protestantism retained many elements of an eighteenth-century tradition, with its rationalism and spirit of inquiry, its opposition to narrow dogma and superstition. To this tradition, it joined the nineteenth-century sources of emotional, enthusiastic evangelicalism. Those Protestants who entered into such a union could draw sustenance from it throughout the turmoils of the century, its strength and cohesion growing in the face of opposition. As the century wore on, as Catholic gains and Protestant losses mounted, many Protestants found it simpler just to retreat into an isolated, defensive posture. The *DUM* conducted a more active level of resistance, restating its ideology, proposing new strategies, maintaining its hopes.

It based its vision on solid moral beliefs and idealistic principles, on a faith in the spirit of free inquiry and critical thinking, on a conviction that the human mind has the capacity to discover truth and to gain certitude in matters of ethics, religion, values. At the level of action, such a vision led the magazine to emphasize education, national unity, the best interests of the whole society. Like missionaries plunging into the jungle, the *DUM*'s writers combined a moral earnestness, serious and fixed, with an enthusiastic zeal, confident in the belief that they possessed both "right knowledge and sincere intent" (March 1837, 370). Reviewing Stopford Brooke's *Theology in the English Poets* (1874), the *DUM* wrote: "To the true poet—he who is really a *maker*, and not a self-crowned laureate of negation and destruction—the whole world is part of what may be called, in a large sense of the word, a sacramental system; in which material phenomena are both the types and the instruments of real things unseen. Every phenomenon is to him the accidental incorporation of a divine idea" (July 1874, 94). If we consider the *DUM*'s vision strictly as sociology or history, we will find it wanting. The magazine sought to emphasize Ireland, not as it was, but as it might become. It might portray the material and the accidental, but its more important role would be to help reveal the divine system that lay beneath the surface and that offered such transformative possibilities. In its evangelistic consciousness, it saw a fallen world and imagined ways in which that world might better conform to its ideal. Aware of its own mythmaking as a deliberate strategy, the magazine had little reason to mistrust its metaphors and dialogues, for these were but means to an end. As the voice for a small minority clinging precariously to the margins of its society, the *DUM* met the threats against Protestant ascendancy with the means that were at hand, to a remarkable extent creating many of those means out of desperately limited resources.

In a number of ways, the *DUM* achieved its ends, for it is difficult to imagine twentieth-century Irish literature, the successful careers of James Joyce or W. B. Yeats, without Carleton, Ferguson, Le Fanu, Lever, Mangan, just as it is difficult to imagine the careers of these five without the *DUM* as a nurturing and respectable forum. We are Ireland's "first successful attempt at native literature" (March 1837, 374), the magazine claimed, having already defined such concepts as "successful" and "literature" in terms of "respectability." Like Gabriel Conroy, smarting under his mother's dismissive phrase for his wife Gretta, the *DUM*'s writers dreaded the prospect of being considered "country cute." Yet they did not require the shock of Gabriel's epiphany in order to direct their vision toward Ireland as a subject that would inspire the magazine for forty-five years. Had the *DUM* folded after its first few issues, had the Gaelic tradition instead come to be more widely accepted as the "first successful attempt at native literature" in Ireland, we would doubtless still have had the little platoons we call Yeats or Joyce, maybe better or worse, but certainly much different.

# SELECTED BIBLIOGRAPHY

Achilles, Jochen. *Sheridan Le Fanu und die schauerromantische Tradition: Zur psychologischen Funktion der Motivik von Sensationsroman und Geistergeschichte.* Tübingen: Gunter Narr, 1991.

Akenson, Donald Harmon. *The Church of Ireland: Ecclesiastical Reform and Revolution, 1800–1885.* New Haven: Yale University Press, 1971.

———. *Small Differences: Irish Catholics and Irish Protestants, 1815–1922: An International Perspective.* McGill: Queen's University Press, 1988.

Altick, Richard D. *The Presence of the Present: Topics of the Day in the Victorian Novel.* Columbus: Ohio State University Press, 1991.

Anderson, Benedict. *Imagined Communities: Reflections on the Origin and Spread of Nationalism.* London: Verso, 1983.

Bareham, Tony, ed. *Charles Lever: New Evaluations.* Savage, Md.: Barnes and Noble, 1991.

Beckett, J. C. *The Anglo-Irish Tradition.* Ithaca: Cornell University Press, 1976.

Black, R. D. C. *Economic Thought and the Irish Question, 1817–1870.* Cambridge: Cambridge University Press, 1960.

Bowen, Desmond. *The Protestant Crusade in Ireland, 1800–70: A Study of Protestant–Catholic Relations between the Act of Union and Disestablishment.* Dublin: Gill and Macmillan, 1978.

Bowen, Elizabeth. Introduction to *Uncle Silas: A Tale of Bartram-Haugh,* by Joseph Sheridan Le Fanu, 7–23. London: Cresset, 1947.

Boyce, D. George. *Nineteenth-Century Ireland: The Search for Stability.* Savage, MD: Barnes and Noble, 1991.

Brown, Malcolm. *The Politics of Irish Literature: From Thomas Davis to W. B. Yeats.* Seattle: University of Washington Press, 1972.

———. *Sir Samuel Ferguson.* Lewisburg: Bucknell University Press, 1973.

Brown, Terence, and Barbara Hayley, eds. *Samuel Ferguson: A Centenary Tribute.* Dublin: Royal Irish Academy, 1987.

Browne, Nelson. *Sheridan Le Fanu.* New York: Roy, 1951.

Brynn, Edward. *The Church of Ireland in the Age of Catholic Emancipation.* New York: Garland, 1982.

Burke, Edmund. *Reflections on the Revolution in France, and On the Proceedings in Certain Societies in London Relative to That Event.* Edited by Conor Cruise O'Brien. Harmondsworth: Penguin, 1969.

Cahalan, James M. *Great Hatred, Little Room: The Irish Historical Novel.* Syracuse: Syracuse University Press, 1983.

———. *The Irish Novel: A Critical History.* Boston: Twayne, 1988.

Cairns, David, and Shaun Richards. *Writing Ireland: Colonialism, Nationalism, and Culture.* Manchester: Manchester University Press, 1988.

Clark, Samuel. *Social Origins of the Irish Land War.* Princeton: Princeton University Press, 1979.

Coughlan, Patricia. "Doubles, Shadows, Sedan-Chairs and the Past: The 'Ghost Stories' of J. S. Le Fanu." In *Critical Approaches to Anglo-Irish Literature,* edited by Michael Allen and Angela Wilcox, 17–39. Totowa, N.J.: Barnes and Noble, 1989.

Curwen, Henry. *A History of Booksellers, the Old and the New.* London: Chatto and Windus, [1873?].

Deane, Seamus. *Celtic Revivals: Essays in Modern Irish Literature 1880–1980.* London: Faber and Faber, 1985.

———. *A Short History of Irish Literature.* Notre Dame: University of Notre Dame Press, 1986.

———. *Strange Country: Modernity and Nationhood in Irish Writing since 1790.* Oxford: Clarendon, 1997.

Deane, Seamus, ed. *The Field Day Anthology of Irish Writing.* 3 vols. Derry: Field Day, 1991.

Denman, Peter. *Samuel Ferguson: The Literary Achievement.* Savage, Md.: Barnes and Noble, 1990.

Downey, Edmund. *Charles Lever: His Life in His Letters.* 2 vols. Edinburgh: Blackwood, 1906.

Duffy, Sir Charles Gavan. *Thomas Davis: The Memoirs of an Irish Patriot, 1840–1846.* London: Kegan Paul, 1890.

———. *Young Ireland: A Fragment of Irish History, 1840–1850.* New York: Appleton, 1881.

Dunne, Tom. "Haunted by History: Irish Romantic Writing, 1800–50." In *Romanticism in National Context,* edited by Roy Porter and Mikulas Teich, 68–91. Cambridge: Cambridge University Press, 1988.

Eagleton, Terry. *Heathcliff and the Great Hunger: Studies in Irish Culture.* London: Verso, 1995.

Eagleton, Terry, et al. *Nationalism, Colonialism, and Literature.* Minneapolis, University of Minnesota Press, 1990.

Edens, Walter Eugene. "Joseph Sheridan LeFanu: A Minor Victorian and His Publisher." Ph.D. diss., University of Illinois, 1963.

Ellis, S. M. *Wilkie Collins, Le Fanu, and Others.* London: Constable, 1931.

## Selected Bibliography 243

Flanagan, Thomas. *The Irish Novelists 1800–1850*. New York: Columbia University Press, 1959.

Foster, Roy. *Modern Ireland, 1600–1972*. New York: Viking, 1988.

Gash, Norman. *Politics in the Age of Peel: A Study in the Technique of Parliamentary Representation, 1830–1850*. London: Longmans, 1953.

Gettmann, Royal. *A Victorian Publisher: A Study of the Bentley Papers*. Cambridge: Cambridge University Press, 1960.

Hachey, Thomas E., and Lawrence J. McCaffrey, eds. *Perspectives on Irish Nationalism*. Lexington: University of Kentucky Press, 1989.

Harris, Wendell V. *British Short Fiction in the Nineteenth Century: A Literary and Bibliographic Guide*. Detroit: Wayne State University Press, 1979.

Hayley, Barbara. *Carleton's* Traits and Stories *and the 19th Century Anglo-Irish Tradition*. Gerrards Cross: Colin Smythe, 1983.

———. "Irish Periodicals from the Union to the *Nation*." In *Anglo-Irish Studies* II, edited by P. J. Drudy, 83–108. Atlantic Highlands: Humanities, 1976.

———. "A Reading and Thinking Nation: Periodicals as the Voice of Nineteenth-Century Ireland." In *Three Hundred Years of Irish Periodicals*, edited by Barbara Hayley and Enda McKay, 29–48. Dublin: Association of Irish Learned Journals, 1987.

Heaney, Seamus. *Poems 1965–1975*. New York: Farrar, Straus, and Giroux, 1980.

———. "Whatever You Say, Say Nothing." *North*. London: Faber and Faber, 1975).

Hilton, Boyd. *The Age of Atonement: The Influence of Evangelicalism on Social and Economic Thought, 1795–1865*. Oxford: Clarendon, 1988.

Hoppen, K. Theodore. *Elections, Politics, and Society in Ireland 1832–1885*. Oxford: Clarendon Press, 1984.

Houghton, Walter E., ed. *The Wellesley Index to Victorian Periodicals 1824–1900*. Vol. 4. Toronto: University of Toronto Press, 1987.

Hughes, Patrick Michael. "The Literature of National Identity: A Case Study of Revitalization in 19th Century Colonial Ireland." Ph.D. diss., City University of New York, 1983.

Hughes, Winifred. *The Maniac in the Cellar: Sensation Novels of the 1860s*. Princeton: Princeton University Press, 1980.

Hutchinson, John. *The Dynamics of Cultural Nationalism: The Gaelic Revival and the Creation of the Irish Nation State*. London: Allen and Unwin, 1987.

Kerr, Donal A. *Peel, Priests and Politics: Sir Robert Peel's Administration and the Roman Catholic Church in Ireland, 1841–1846*. Oxford: Clarendon, 1982.

Kiberd, Declan. *Inventing Ireland: The Literature of the Modern Nation*. London: Jonathan Cape, 1995.

Kiely, Benedict. *Poor Scholar: A Study of the Works and Days of William Carleton (1794–1869)*. New York: Sheed and Ward, 1948.

Kinealy, Christine. *This Great Calamity; The Irish Famine 1845–52*. Dublin: Gill and Macmillan, 1994.

Le Fanu, William R. *Seventy Years of Irish Life: Being Anecdotes and Reminiscences*. London: Macmillan, 1893.

Lewis, Gifford. *Somerville and Ross: The World of the Irish R. M.* New York: Viking, 1985.
Lloyd, David. *Anomalous States: Irish Writing and the Post-Colonial Moment.* Dublin: Lilliput, 1993.
———. *Nationalism and Minor Literature: James Clarence Mangan and the Emergence of Irish Cultural Nationalism.* Berkeley: University of California Press, 1987.
Longford, Christine. "Joseph Sheridan Le Fanu." *The Bell* (Sept. 1942): 434–38.
Lonoff, Sue. *Wilkie Collins and His Victorian Readers: A Study in the Rhetoric of Authorship.* New York: AMS, 1982.
Lubbers, Klaus. *Geschichte der irischen Erzählprosa. Vol. I: Von den Anfängen bis zum ausgehenden 19. Jahrhundert.* Munich: Wilhelm Fink, 1985.
Lyons, F. S. L. *Ireland since the Famine.* Rev. ed. Glasgow: Fontana/Collins, 1973.
Lyons, F. S. L., and R. A. J. Hawkins, eds. *Ireland under the Union: Varieties of Tension. Essays in Honour of T. W. Moody.* Oxford: Clarendon, 1980.
MacDonagh, Oliver. *The Emancipist: Daniel O'Connell, 1830–47.* New York: St. Martin's, 1989.
———. *The Hereditary Bondsman: Daniel O'Connell, 1775–1829.* New York: St. Martin's, 1988.
———. *The Nineteenth Century Novel and Irish Social History: Some Aspects.* Dublin: National University of Ireland, 1971.
———. *States of Mind: A Study of Anglo-Irish Conflict 1780–1980.* London: George Allen and Unwin, 1983.
Mansergh, Nicholas. *The Irish Question, 1840–1921: A Commentary on Anglo-Irish Relations and on Social and Political Forces in Ireland in the Age of Reform and Revolution.* 3rd ed. Toronto: University of Toronto Press, 1975.
Marcus, Phillip L. *Yeats and the Beginning of the Irish Renaissance.* 2d ed. Syracuse: Syracuse University Press, 1987.
McBride, John P. "The *Dublin University Magazine:* Cultural Nationality and Tory Ideology in an Irish Literary and Political Journal, 1833–1852." 2 vols. Ph.D. diss., Trinity College, Dublin, 1987.
Mc Cormack, W. J. *Dissolute Characters: Irish Literary History through Balzac, Sheridan Le Fanu, Yeats and Bowen.* Manchester: Manchester University Press, 1993.
———. *From Burke to Beckett: Ascendancy, Tradition and Betrayal in Literary History.* Cork: Cork University Press, 1994.
———. "Isaac Butt (1813–79) and the Inner Failure of Protestant Home Rule." In *Worsted in the Game: Losers in Irish History,* edited by Ciaran Brady, 121–31. Dublin: Lilliput, 1989.
———. "J. Sheridan Le Fanu's 'Richard Marston' (1848): The History of an Anglo-Irish Text." In *1848: The Sociology of Literature. Proceedings of the Essex Conference on the Sociology of Literature, July 1977,* edited by Francis Barker, et al., 107–25. Essex: University of Essex Press, 1978.
———. *Sheridan Le Fanu and Victorian Ireland.* Oxford: Clarendon, 1980.
McDowell, R. B. *Public Opinion and Government Policy in Ireland, 1801–1846.* London: Faber and Faber, 1952.

Mercier, Vivian. *Modern Irish Literature: Sources and Founders.* Edited by Eilis Dillon. Oxford: Clarendon, 1994.

Mokyr, Joel. *Why Ireland Starved: A Quantitative and Analytical History of the Irish Economy, 1800–1850.* London: George Allen and Unwin, 1983.

Morash, Christopher. *Writing the Irish Famine.* Oxford: Clarendon, 1995.

Moynahan, Julian. *Anglo-Irish: The Literary Imagination in a Hyphenated Culture.* Princeton: Princeton University Press, 1995.

Nowlan, Kevin B. *The Politics of Repeal: A Study in the Relations between Great Britain and Ireland, 1841–50.* London: Routledge and Kegan Paul, 1965.

O'Brien, Conor Cruise. *States of Ireland.* New York: Pantheon, 1972.

O'Donoghue, David. *The Life of William Carleton: Being His Autobiography and Letters; and an Account of His Life and Writings, from the Point at which the Autobiography Breaks Off.* 2 vols. London: Downey, 1896.

O'Driscoll, Robert. *An Ascendancy of the Heart: Ferguson and the Beginnings of Modern Irish Literature in English.* Dublin: Dolman, 1976.

O'Ferrall, Fergus. *Catholic Emancipation: Daniel O'Connell and the Birth of Irish Democracy, 1820–30.* Dublin: Gill and Macmillan, 1985.

———. *Daniel O'Connell.* Dublin: Gill and Macmillan, 1981.

O Grada, Cormac. *Ireland Before and After the Famine: Explorations in Economic History, 1800–1925.* Manchester: Manchester University Press, 1988.

O'Neill, Patrick. "German Literature and the *Dublin University Magazine*, 1833–50: A Checklist and Commentary." *Long Room* 14–15 (Autumn 1976–Spring/Summer 1977): 20–31.

———. *Ireland and Germany: A Study in Literary Relations.* New York: Peter Lang, 1985.

Rashid, S. "Political Economy in the *Dublin University Magazine*, 1833–40." *Long Room* 14–15 (Autumn 1976–Spring/Summer 1977): 16–19.

Ray, Gordon N. "The Bentley Papers." *The Library*, 5th ser., 7 (Sept. 1952): 178–200.

Richards, B. "Pre-Raphaelite Standards in the *Dublin University Magazine*'s Art Criticism." *Long Room* 14–15 (Autumn 1976–Spring/Summer 1977): 9–15.

Sadlier, Michael. "*Dublin University Magazine,* Its History, Contents and Bibliography." *Bibliographical Society of Ireland Publications* 5, no. 4 (1938): 59–85.

———. *Things Past.* London: Constable, 1944.

Shannon-Mangan, Ellen. *James Clarence Mangan: A Biography.* Dublin: Irish Academic Press, 1996.

Shattock, Joanne, and Michael Wolff, eds. *The Victorian Periodical Press: Samplings and Soundings.* Toronto: University of Toronto Press, 1982.

Spence, Joe. "Nationality and Irish Toryism: The Case of the *Dublin University Magazine,* 1833–52." *Journal of Newspaper and Periodical History* 4, no. 3 (Autumn 1988): 2–17.

Stevenson, Lionel. *Dr. Quicksilver: The Life of Charles Lever.* London: Chapman and Hall, 1939.

Sullivan, Jack. *Elegant Nightmares: The English Ghost Story from Le Fanu to Blackwood.* Athens: Ohio University Press, 1978.

Sullivan, Kevin. "*The House by the Churchyard:* James Joyce and Sheridan Le Fanu." In *Modern Irish Literature: Essays in Honor of William York Tindall,* edited by Raymond J. Porter and James D. Brophy. New York: Iona College Press, 1972.

Thornley, David. *Isaac Butt and Home Rule.* London: MacGibbon and Kee, 1964.

Vance, Norman. *Irish Literature: A Social History. Tradition, Identity and Difference.* Oxford: Basil Blackwell, 1990.

Vaughan, W. E., ed. *A New History of Ireland, V: Ireland Under the Union, I (1801–70).* Oxford: Clarendon, 1989.

Welch, Robert. *A History of Verse Translation from the Irish, 1789–1897.* Totowa: Barnes and Noble, 1988.

———. *Irish Poetry from Moore to Yeats.* Totowa: Barnes and Noble, 1980.

White, Terence de Vere. *The Anglo-Irish.* London: Gollancz, 1972.

———. *The Road of Excess.* Dublin: Browne and Nolan, 1946.

Williams, Julia McElhattan. "'The Nation Articulate': The Discourse of Colonialism and the Anglo-Irish Novel." Ph.D. diss., Emory University, 1992.

Wolff, Robert Lee. *William Carleton, Irish Peasant Novelist: A Preface to His Fiction.* New York: Garland, 1980.

Young, Robert J. C. *Colonial Desire: Hybridity in Theory, Culture and Race.* New York: Routledge, 1995.

# INDEX

Act of Union (1800), 16, 22, 26, 59, 170
Adams, Charles Frederick, 215, 217–20, 226, 229
Addison, Henry Robert, 105–6
Ainsworth, W. H., 108
Akenson, D. H., 31
Alexander, Cecil Frances, 189
Alexander, Rev. William, 184, 189
Alison, Archibald, 166
Allingham, William, 3, 166, 189, 230; *Laurence Bloomfield in Ireland*, 166, 189
Ansted, David, 193
Anster, John, 3–4, 36, 38, 64, 113, 122, 175
Anti-Maynooth Committee, 127
Aristophanes, 226
Arnold, Matthew, 88; *On the Study of Celtic Literature*, 48
*Athenaeum*, 187
*Atlantic Monthly*, 218

Ball, John Thomas, 166, 175
Banim, John and Michael, 3, 21, 172–73; *Clough Fionn*, 172–74; *Tales of the O'Hara Family*, 22
Bareham, Tony, 109, 134
Barrett, Elizabeth, *see* Browning
Barry, Michael Joseph, 42, 116, 166
Batson, Robert, 226
Beckett, J. C., 6, 7, 29
Bentley, George, 197–98
Bentley, Richard, 96, 214; *Bentley's Miscellany*, 108

Berkeley, Grantley, 133
Black, R. D. C., 147
Blacker, William, 60
*Blackwood's*, 17, 36, 38–39, 43, 45–46, 52, 66, 78, 80, 133, 193, 235
Blackwood's publishing house, 85
Blavatsky, Madame, 227
Boucicault, Dion, 230
Bowen, Desmond, 24, 32, 68, 159
Bowen, Elizabeth, 201, 203
Boyd, Percy, 141
Brady, Cheyne, 175, 177, 179, 183, 191, 193
Brittaine, George, 66, 77
Brooke, Charlotte, *Reliques of Irish Poetry*, 21
Brooke, Richard Sinclair, 166, 181–82, 186–87
Brooke, Stopford, 166, 187–88, 239
Brooks, Charles William Shirley, 191
Broughton, Rhoda, 3, 197; *Cometh Up As A Flower*, 198; *Not Wisely, But Too Well*, 197
Brown, Desmond, 38
Browne, Frances, 230
Browne, Mary Anne (Mrs. James Gray), 86–88, 117–18, 166
Browning, Elizabeth Barrett, 113, 117, 188–89, 196; *Aurora Leigh*, 188–89
Brunswick Clubs, 34
Brynn, Edward, 32
Bulwer-Lytton, Edward, 191
Bunting, Edward, 94, 175; *Ancient Music of Ireland*, 94

247

Burke, Edmund, 5–7; *Reflections on the Revolution in France*, 5–6, 232–33
Burke, Oliver J., 219, 225
Burns, Robert, 113
Butler, William Archer, 3, 37, 42, 65, 113, 117, 164, 175, 177
Butt, Isaac, 3, 36, 43, 46, 53–54, 56, 59–60, 62, 64, 66–67, 69–72, 75, 81–86, 91, 108, 113, 121, 143–49, 169, 207, 224–25; *Chapters of College Romance*, 80–84; "The Famine in the Land," 143; "Measures for Ireland," 143
Byron, George Gordon, Lord, 117, 164, 189; *Don Juan*, 116

Cairns, David, 7, 49
Calderon, P., 166
Calvin, John, 6
Campbell, Thomas, 133
Carleton, William, 3, 21, 34, 42, 45, 53, 66, 75–80, 86, 96, 131–32, 149–53, 155–56, 169, 172, 180–82, 190, 193, 195, 220, 230, 236–37, 240; *The Black Prophet*, 132, 149–55, 161, 169, 172; *Christian Examiner*, 78; *Fardorougha the Miser; or, the Convicts of Lisnamona*, 78–80, 96; *Traits and Stories of the Irish Peasantry*, 21, 44, 78
Carlyle, Thomas, 189
Carter, Elizabeth, 228
Catholic Association, 26
Catholic Emancipation, 56, 199
Chermside, Richard Seymour Conway, 191
*Christian Examiner and Church of Ireland Magazine*, 34
Church Education Society, 94
Church Missionary Society, 67
Civil War (U.S.), 185
Colburn, Henry, 178
Cole, John William, 3, 166, 195
Cole, Nina, 197
Coleridge, Samuel Taylor, 3, 4; *Biographia Literaria*, 4
Collins, Minna Mabel, 227
Collins, Mortimer, 165–66, 180, 189, 195–96, 227
Comerford, R. V., 229
*Comet*, 102

Committee of Public Instruction in Bengal, 57
Cook, Keningale, 217, 227–29, 231
Cook, Mabel Collins, 228
Corkran, John Frazer, 180
Corn Laws, 91–92, 157–58
*Cornhill Magazine*, 193, 214
Corrigan, D. J., 151
Costello, Louisa Stuart, 114
Cotton, Samuel George, 141
Craik, Dinah Maria Mulock, *see* Mulock
Craik, Georgina Marion, 190
Crimean War, 165, 174–5, 180–81, 184–85, 188
Croker, Crofton: *Fairy Legends and Traditions of the South of Ireland*, 22
Cromwell, Oliver, 119–21
Crowe, Eyre Evans, *Today in Ireland*, 22
Cullen, Archbishop Paul, 192, 206, 221
Curran, J. P., 6
Curry, William, 52, 85–86, 109, 133, 137, 162
Curtis, Ella Jane, 225
Curtis, Robert, 191

*Daily Express*, 39
*Daily Mercury*, 221
Darwin, Charles, 193; *On the Origin of Species*, 192
Davis, Francis, 180, 189
Davis, Thomas, 122, 132
de Valera, Eamon, 49
de Vere White, Terence, 83, 85
de Vere, Aubrey, 3, 166, 230
Devon Commission, 126
Deane, Seamus, 3–5, 7–8, 21, 100, 104
Denman, Peter, 46, 63
Dickens, Charles, 108, 132, 164
Dickson, Maria Frances, 89, 114
Dillon, John Blake, 132
Dobbin, Orlando Thomas, 192, 195
Doyle, James, 30
*Dublin Review*, 131, 161
Dublin University, *see* Trinity College
*Dublin University Review*, 36
Duffy, Sir Charles Gavan, 37, 63, 77, 98, 132, 172; *The Ballad Poetry of Ireland*, 63
Dunlop, Durham, 175, 177, 179–81, 188, 193, 217, 220–22, 224–25
Dwyer, Francis Doyne, 175, 180

Eagleton, Terry, 149, 150
Edgeworth, Maria, 164; *Castle Rackrent*, 21
Elgee, Jane Francesca, 163
Emancipation Act (1829), 2, 28–29, 124, 156
Encumbered Estates Act (1849), 159–60
Encumbered Estates Court, 183
Engels, F., 147
*Evening Mail*, 83

Famine, 92, 142–50, 155–58, 161–62, 168–69, 173, 176, 181, 230, 236
Fenianism, 205–7, 218
Fenians (Irish Republican Brotherhood), 71, 186
Ferguson, Samuel, 3, 13, 19, 21, 23, 37, 45–51, 53, 62, 63–64, 88, 103–5, 117, 122, 131, 145, 161–62, 166, 175, 193, 212, 219, 230, 240; "Dialogue Between the Head and Heart of an Irish Protestant," 6, 12, 18, 47, 50, 83, 230, 235; *Hibernian Nights' Entertainments*, 53, 62–63; *Lays of the Western Gael*, 51
Ferris, Henry, 105, 114
Fitzgerald, George Robert, 97
Fitzgerald, Percy, 3, 196
Flanagan, Thomas, 99–100
Franchise Act (1850), 148
*Fraser's*, 17, 36, 39, 52, 66, 133
*Freeman's Journal*, 83

Garrett, George W., 226
Garrick, David, 196
Gaskell, Elizabeth, 3, 188, 190
Gaspey, Thomas, 219–20
Gilfillan, Robert, 42, 65
Gladstone, William Ewart, 7, 206, 108, 221
Goethe, J. W. v., 64; *Faust*, 38, 66
Goldsmith, Oliver, 66
Goldsmith, William, 6
Gordon, Robert, 113, 115
Gore, Catherine, 3, 118–19
Grant, James, 175
Grattan, Henry, 6
Gray, James, 117
Great Industrial Exhibition (Dublin), 176
Gregg, Rev. Tresham Dames, 91

Gregory, Lady Augusta, 10, 146
Gregory, William, 146; Gregory Clause, 146
Griffin, Gerald, 21; *Tales of the Munster Festival*, 22

Hall, Anna Maria, 3, 65, 89, 161; *Sketches in Ireland*, 22
Hall, Samuel Carter, 111, 132
Hamilton, Sir William Rowan, 3, 115, 166
Hannay, Robert, 226
Hardiman, James, 47–48, 50, 62–63, 88, 103, 105, 162; *Irish Minstrelsy*, 21, 46–47, 105
Hayley, Barbara, 34, 132
Hayman, Samuel, 115, 131, 163, 166
Heaney, Seamus, 232–33
Heard, J. B., 184–85, 192, 195
Hemans, Felicia, 3, 42, 65
Hemphill, Barbara, 3, 65
Herder, Johann Gottfried von, 20
Hervey, Charles, 116
Hill, O'Dell Travers, 195
Hodges, Smith and Co., 178
Hogg, James, 3, 66, 117
Home Rule, 35, 60, 70–72, 148, 222–24
Hoppen, K. Theodore, 148, 182
Hurst and Blackett, 178–79
Hurton, William, 190
Hutchinson, John, 7
Hutton, Margaret, 89
Huxley, Thomas Henry, 3, 228

Inglis, Henry David, 60–61, 73, 98; *Scenes from the Life of Edward Lascelles, Gent.*, 60
Irish Brigade, 176
Irish Church Missions, 207
Irish Church Temporalities Act (1833), 31, 40
Irish Metropolitan Conservative Society, 67–68
Irish National Exhibition (Cork), 176
Irish Parliamentary Elections Act (1829), 28
Irish Poor Law Extension Bill (1847), 146
Irish Protestant Association, 67
Irish Republican Brotherhood, see Fenians

Irish Tenant League, 160
Irwin, Thomas Caulfield, 3, 189, 195, 226

James, G. P. R., 3, 101, 109, 119–21, 166; *Arrah Neil; or, Times of Old*, 119–20
Jerrold, William Blanchard, 184
Jewsbury, Geraldine, 197
Johnson, Zachariah, 115
Johnston, William, 42, 66, 113
Joyce, James, 10, 240; *Ulysses*, 12; *A Portrait of the Artist as a Young Man*, 22

Keegan, John, 105
Kenealy, Edward Vaughan Hyde, 132–33, 166
Kennedy, Patrick, 3, 175, 186, 195, 207, 219–20, 230
Kickham, Charles, 230

Labour Rate Act (1846), 146
Lalor, James Fintan, 159
Larrey, Baron, 188
Lawson, James, 184
Le Fanu, Eleanor Frances, 196
Le Fanu, Joseph Sheridan, 3, 53, 66, 71, 80–82, 86, 89, 110, 113, 132, 163, 169–72, 179–80, 187, 192–93, chapter 7 *passim*, 207, 217, 219–20, 229–30, 240; *The House by the Church-yard*, 172, 194, 196, 198–201, 208–9; *The Purcell Papers*, 80, 203; *Uncle Silas*, 171–72, 194, 200–3, 208–14
Ledwich, Edward, 218; *Antiquities of Ireland*, 21
Lever, Charles, 3, 37, 53, 66, 72–73, 75, 79, 85–86, 88, 90, 97–101, 108–16, 118–21, 124–25, 128, 130–38, 149, 167–68, 172, 177–78, 180, 189, 193, 194–95, 220, 230, 240; *Charles O'Malley, the Irish Dragoon*, 97–101, 120; *Confessions of Harry Lorrequer*, 72–75, 79, 97, 108; *Loiterings of Arthur O'Leary*, 111; *Maurice Tiernay, the Soldier of Fortune*, 167–68; *Our Mess; Jack Hinton, the Guardsman*, 98, 109–11, 134; *Tom Burke of "Ours,"* 134
Lever, John, 110
Lever, Katherine, 110
Lichfield House Compact (1835), 67

Lloyd, David, 9, 102–3
London Exhibition (1851), 176
Longfield, Mountifort, 42, 67, 92, 124–25, 184
Lover, Samuel, 3, 43–45, 62, 97, 101–2, 163; *Rory O'More, a National Romance*, 62
Luther, Martin, 6

MacDonagh, Oliver, 16, 27, 30, 33, 234
MacManus, Terence Bellew, 206
*Macmillan's*, 187
Macpherson, "Ossian" poems, 20
Madden, Richard Robert, 225
Magee, William, 25, 58
Maginn, William, 133
Manchester School, 157
Mangan, James Clarence, 3, 23, 42, 47, 53, 60, 64, 102, 104–5, 113, 115–16, 132, 162–63, 193, 212, 240; "Dark Rosaleen," 47
Martin, James, *Ireland's Dirge*, 21
Martin, Marian E., 141
Martin, Violet, 141 (*see also* Somerville, Edith)
Martineau, Harriet, 3, 114, 188; *Illustrations of Political Economy*, 114
Marx, Karl: *Manifesto of the Communist Party*, 147
Maturin, Charles Robert, 65
Maxwell, Reverend William Hamilton, 3, 42–43, 66, 72, 98–99, 101, 172
Mayne, Sarah Jane, 226
Maynooth College, 127–28
M'Carthy, Denis Florence, 3, 140–41, 166
McBride, John, 139
Mc Cormack, W. J., 4–5, 7, 62, 67, 134, 201, 203, 210, 212, 237
McGhee, Robert J., 39
Meagher, Thomas Francis, 203–4
Melbourne, Lord William, 67
Melville, Herman, 164; *Moby-Dick*, 164
Mercier, Vivian, 149
M'Glashan, James, 52, 85–88, 90, 93, 95, 98, 102, 105–6, 108–9, 121, 124, 138, 162, 177–79, 187, 193
Mitchel, John, 203–4, 230
Mokyr, Joel, 23, 146
Montgomery, Henry R., 162

Moore, George, 10
Moore, Thomas, 130, 164; *Memoirs of Captain Rock,* 38; *Travels of an Irish Gentleman in Search of a Religion,* 38
Morash, Christopher, 150
Morgan, Lady Sydney, 21
Morris, William, 226
Mulock, Dinah Maria, 3, 141–42, 188
Municipal Corporations Act (1840), 91
Murray, John Fisher, 114, 166

Napier, W. F. P., 60
Napoleonic Wars, 23–24, 100
*Nation,* 75, 98, 103, 131–32, 140, 159, 162–63, 195, 203
National Association of Ireland, 206
National Board [System] of Education (1831), 30, 58–59, 114, 128
National Clubs, 158
Nightingale, Florence, 188

O'Brien, Conor Cruise, 232–33
O'Brien, Henry, 65
O'Brien, James Thomas, 161
O'Brien, William Smith, 122, 147, 207
O'Casey, Sean, 10
O'Connell, Daniel, 26–27, 35, 41, 53, 67, 90, 95, 97, 100, 106–8, 121–22, 124, 126, 145, 159, 224, 234
O'Curry, Eugene, 23, 230
O'Donoghue, David, 149
O'Donovan, John, 23
O'Driscoll, Robert, 49–50
O'Ferrall, Fergus, 26–27, 29
O'Flanagan, J. R., 164
O'Grady, Standish James, 3, 225
O'Leary, John, 229
O'Neill, Charles Henry, 186
O'Neill, Patrick, 102
Orange Order, 91
Ordnance Survey (1824), 23, 234
O'Sullivan, Mortimer, 3, 38–39, 58, 66, 107–8, 118, 122–25, 128, 130; *Nevilles of Garretstown—A Tale of 1760,* 128–30
O'Sullivan, Samuel, 1, 3, 6, 10–11, 18, 37–39, 43, 56, 58, 66–67, 71, 77–78, 108, 115, 118, 123–25, 128, 177, 229
Otway, Caesar, 3, 34, 37, 58; *Christian Examiner,* 17, 77; *Sketches in Ireland,* 22

Palmerston, Lord, 92, 204–5, 229
Parke, Walter, 225
Parker, Sarah, 166
Parnell, Charles Stewart, 225
Pater, Walter, 226
Patmore, Coventry, 140, 188; *The Angel in the House,* 140, 188
Pearce, Horace, 219
Peel, Sir Robert, 28, 66–68, 89, 93, 106–7, 122, 126–28, 144, 157–58, 177
Petrie, George, 3, 23, 175, 218
Picciotto, James, 219
Poe, Edgar Allan, 112, 163, 211–13
Poor Law (1838), 69, 147–48
Pre-Raphaelitism, 187, 189, 226
Protestant Conservative Society of Ireland, 67
Protestant Operatives' Associations, 91
Protestant Repeal Association, 145
*Punch,* 119, 191
*Putnam's,* 218

Reform Act (1832), 2, 29, 34, 40
Relief Act (1793), 58
Religious Tract and Book Society, 24
Rent-Charge Act (1838), 68, 90
Repeal of the Union, 2, 27, 53–54, 59, 70, 90, 140, 145–46, 157–59, 223
Repeal Association, 90, 122
Richards, Shaun, 7, 49
Robertson, Annie, 196
Roden, Earl of, 145
Rowsley, Harry, 42
Royal Hibernian Military School in Dublin, 199
Royal Irish Academy, 20
Ruskin, John, 164, 189, 226
Russell, Lord John, 127, 144, 149, 155, 158

Sadleir, Michael, 198
*Satirist,* 102
Savage, Marmion, 175, 180
Schiller, J. C. F. v., 64
Scott, James Anderson, 195, 204–5
Scott, Rebecca, 226
Scouler, John, 66, 124
Shannon-Mangan, Ellen, 115
Shelley, P. B., 164

Sheridan, William, 6
Simmons, Bernard, 225
Singer, J. H., 34
Sirr, Henry Charles, 175
Smith, Barbara Leigh, 188
Society for the Relief of Distressed Protestants, 67
Somerville, Edith, and Martin Ross, 10
Southey, Robert, 117, 164
Spence, Joe, 36
Spencer, Alexander, 177–78
Spenser, Edmund, 2; *View of the Present State of Ireland*, 2
*Spirit of the Nation*, 103
Sproule, John, 225
*St. James's*, 218
St. Patrick, 21
Stanford, Charles Stuart, 35, 37–38, 45, 52–53, 86, 187, 220
Stanley, Lord, 30
Starkey, Digby Pilot, 42, 64, 113, 115, 117, 179, 190
Stephens, Frederick George, 186–87
Stephens, James, 186, 206
Sterne, Laurence, 196
Stevenson, Lionel, 109
Stoker, Bram, 213–14; *Dracula*, 213–14
Stokes, William, 183
Stott, Thomas: *The Songs of Deardra*, 21
*Sun* [London], 54
Swedenborg, Emanuel, 208
Swinburne, A. C., 226
Symons, Arthur, 226
Synge, John Millington, 10

Taylor, William Cooke, 114
Tenant League, 176
Tennyson, Alfred, Lord, 164
Thackeray, William, 119, 131; *Irish Sketch Book*, 131
Theatre Royal (Dublin), 166
Thoreau, Henry David, 228
Thornbury, George Walter, 189
Thornley, David, 121
Tithe Campaign, 30, 35
Tithe-Rent Charge Act (1838), 126

Tithe War, 44, 68–69
Trench, Power le Poer, 25
Trinity College, 16, 34–38, 42, 53, 56, 81–82, 91, 99, 108, 115, 122, 132, 186, 225, 227, 230
Trinity College Historical Society, 132, 163
Trollope, Anthony, 3, 175, 191
Trotter, L. J., 195–96
Tupper, Martin Farquhar, 191

United Irishmen, 99
*University Magazine*, 83

Victoria, Queen, 89–90

Wakeman, W. F., 23
Waller, John Francis, 3, 37, 43, 65, 113, 116, 135, 137–42, 157, 161–66, 169, 174–75, 177, 180, 189, 195, 226
Walmesley, Bishop Charles: *The General History of the Christian Church*, 25; "Signore Pastorini," 25
Walsh, John Edward, 114
Walsh, Rev. Robert, 90
Warburton, Eliot, 114; *The Crescent and the Cross*, 114
Welch, Robert, 103–4
*Wellesley Index to Victorian Periodicals*, 10, 11 130, 179–80, 183, 193, 221, 226, 236
Wellington, Duke of, 28, 177
Wilde, Lady Jane Francesca, 3, 180, 186, 189, 226
Wilde, Oscar, 3, 226–27, 230
Wilde, William, 163
William IV, 69
Williams, Julia, 209–10
Wills, James, 42, 65; *Lives of Illustrious and Distinguished Irishmen*, 65
Wolff, Robert Lee, 149
Wordsworth, William, 4, 66, 117, 164
Wyndham Land Act (1903), 235

Yeats, William Butler, 7–8, 10, 13, 51, 63–64, 98, 149, 229, 240
Young Ireland, 114, 132, 147, 168, 203, 238

*Dialogues in the Margin: A Study of the* Dublin University Magazine was designed and composed in Monotype Dante by Kachergis Book Design, Pittsboro, North Carolina; and printed on 60-pound Glatfelter and bound by Cushing-Malloy, Inc., Ann Arbor, Michigan.